D0507177

ON TO JAVA

Patrick Henry Winston

Massachusetts Institute of Technology

Sundar Narasimhan

Ascent Technology, Incorporated

ADDISON-WESLEY

An imprint of Addison Wesley Longman, Inc.

Reading, Massachusetts • Menlo Park, California • New York
Harlow, England • Don Mills, Ontario • Amsterdam • Bonn
Sydney • Singapore • Tokyo • Mexico City • Madrid

Library of Congress Cataloging-in-Publication Data

Winston, Patrick Henry
   On to Java / Patrick Henry Winston. Sundar Narasimhan.
      p.   cm.
   ISBN 0-201-49826-X
   1. Java (Computer program language).   I. Narasimhan, Sundar.
QA76.73.J38W56   1996
005.13'3–dc20

96-19447
CIP

Reprinted with corrections, February 1997.

Reproduced by Addison-Wesley from film supplied by the author.

3 4 5 6 7 8 9 10-CRW-00999897

CONTENTS

ACKNOWLEDGMENTS

The cover photograph, the cover design, and the interior design are by Chiai Takahashi, with counsel from Karen A. Prendergast. Access to the projector in the photograph, which has been used to entertain many generations of MIT students, was kindly provided by the MIT Audio-Visual Service.

Lyn Dupré was the developmental editor. She has a special gift for rooting out problems and suggesting improvements. The errors in this book were introduced—by authors who never stop writing—after Ms. Dupré finished her work.

If you write technical material, you should read *BUGS in Writing*, Ms. Dupré's book (Addison-Wesley, 1995).

In addition, Nancy Benjamin, Julie Champagne, Lisa B. Freedman, Chris Mlsna, Lynn A. Stein, and Chiai Takahashi found grammatical and typographical errors that were introduced during final editing.

And finally, Philippe Brou, Jean Dollimore, Dick Lyon, and Eric Zocher found several difficult-to-find technical errors in the first printing.

1 HOW THIS BOOK TEACHES YOU THE LANGUAGE

1   The purpose of this book is to help you learn the essentials of Java™ programming. In this section, you will learn about Java's history, Java's special features, and how this book is organized.

2   Java was designed for writing programs for small computers embedded in consumer electronics appliances, such as microwave ovens and television sets. Accordingly, the design choices made by the developers of Java reflect the expectation that the language would be used to implement small, distributed, and necessarily robust programs.

3   Java has captured the interest and attention of programmers because certain features—conceived in the expectation that Java would be used to build programs for consumer electronics—happen to make Java the ideal language for building programs for use on the Internet:

- Java programs run on a wide variety of hardware platforms.

- Java programs can be loaded dynamically via a network.

- Java provides features that facilitate robust behavior.

In addition, Java has features that make it an excellent language even for applications that have nothing to do with networks:

- Java is a completely object-oriented language.

- Java programs can work on multiple tasks simultaneously.

- Java programs automatically recycle memory.

4   To make Java programs **portable**, so that they will run on a variety of hardware platforms, they are translated into **byte code** by the Java **compiler**. Such translated programs are said to have been **compiled** into byte code.

Programs translated into byte code seem to be written in the instruction set of a typical computer, but byte code is neutral in that it does not employ the instruction set of any particular computer. Instead, byte code is executed by a program that pretends it is a computer based on the byte-code instruction set. Such a program is called a **byte code interpreter**. A byte code interpreter intended to execute the byte code produced by the Java compiler is called a Java **virtual machine**.

Once a Java virtual machine has been implemented for a particular computer, that computer will run any compiled Java program. Or, said the other way around, any Java application will run on every machine for which a Java virtual machine has been implemented.

Java is a trademark of Sun Microsystems Computer Corporation.

5   You might think that byte-code interpretation must mean slow execution, relative to, say, C or C++ programs that are compiled directly into the native instruction set of a particular machine.

Fortunately, however, a full-capability Java virtual machine can translate byte code into the native instruction set of the computer through a process called **just-in-time compilation**. Accordingly, Java programs can run nearly as fast as programs written in older, less portable programming languages.

6   The Java virtual machine helps to find errors, because the Java virtual machine performs **run-time checks** that complement the **compile-time checks** performed by all compilers. For example, the Java virtual machine displays an informative message and halts when programs are about to access array elements that do not exist, thus catching a common programming error before a hard-to-debug crash occurs.

7   Because Java is **object oriented**, programs consist of **class definitions**.

In Java, some **class definitions** establish the characteristics of arrays and other generic program elements. Other class definitions, the ones you define yourself, establish the characteristics of application-specific categories, such as railroad cars, stocks, foods, movies, or whatever else happens to come up naturally in your application. Once a class is defined, you can create **class instances** that describe the particular properties of the individuals that belong to a category.

When you design a program around classes and class instances, you are said to practice **object-oriented programming**. In contrast, when you design programs around procedures, you are said to practice **procedure-oriented programming**.

8   In this book, you learn more about what *object oriented* means and why many programmers prefer object-oriented languages. For now, it suffices to know that Java is a completely object-oriented programming language, whereas most programming languages, such as C, are *procedure-oriented* programming languages and other programming languages, such as C++, are half-procedure-oriented–half-object-oriented hybrids.

9   When you run a Java program, each class definition is fetched by your program only when it is needed. Thus, Java is said to **load classes dynamically** or **on demand**.

10   Certain Java programs are intended to be used in cooperation with a **network browser** such as Netscape Navigator™, which contains a Java virtual machine capable of loading Java classes dynamically via a local area network or via the Internet.

Java applications loaded by web browsers are often called **applets**, a word meant to be a diminutive of the word *application*.

11   Distributing software via web browsers is wonderfully effective: No disks need to be packaged for sale and no update or bug-fix disks need to be mailed.

12   Another distinguishing feature of Java is that Java allows you to create **multiple threads**. Each thread is like a separate program in that a thread seems to run at the same time as

---

Netscape Navigator is a trademark of Netscape Communications Corporation.

other threads, but unlike separate programs, all of a program's threads share the same memory.

By exploiting the thread feature, you can write programs in which one thread is working through complex statistical formulas, another thread is fetching data from a file, still another thread is transmitting data over a network, and yet another thread is updating a display, with each sharing your computer's time. Because no thread ever has to wait for another thread to finish a task, threads enable you to write programs that exhibit an extraordinarily responsive look and feel.

13 Java increases your productivity by providing for automatic memory recycling. When you use a language such as C++, you have to remember to free the memory allocated to program elements, such as class instances, once you are finished with them. Failing to free memory produces a **memory leak** that may exhaust all the memory available to your program, leading either to erratic behavior or a total program crash.

Java frees memory automatically, by performing **automatic garbage collection**, so you never need worry about memory leaks, nor must you waste time looking for one. Thus, you are more productive, and less likely to be driven crazy via tedious, mind-numbing debugging.

Most programming languages do not offer garbage collection, even though languages such as Lisp and Smalltalk established the great value of garbage collection decades ago.

14 In addition to automatic garbage collection, the Java virtual machine provides a variety of other features that facilitate **secure, robust behavior**. For example, no Java program, run via a web browser, can open, read, or write files on your computer, thus making it difficult for someone to corrupt or hobble your software, either deliberately or inadvertently.

15 For many programmers, Java is easy to learn because Java's syntax is largely based on that of the popular C and C++ programming languages.

16 Although Java programs resemble C and C++ programs when viewed at a distance, the Java programming language excludes many of the characteristics of C and C++ believed by Java's designers to harm program readability and robustness. For example, Java programmers do not think in terms of pointers and they do not overload operators.

17 To get you up and running in Java quickly, the sections in this book generally supply you with the most useful approach to each programming need, be it to display characters on your screen, to define a new method, or to read information from a file.

18 To answer your basic questions explicitly, this book is divided into parts that generally focus on one issue, which is plainly announced in the title of the section. Accordingly, you see titles such as the following:

- How to Compile and Run a Simple Program
- How to Define Constructor Instance Methods
- How to Benefit from Data Abstraction

3

- How to Define Abstract Classes and Abstract Methods

- How to Design Classes and Class Hierarchies

- How to Modularize Programs Using Compilation Units and Packages

- How to Catch Exceptions

- How to Use Interfaces to Impose Requirements

- How to Use the Model-View Approach to Interface Design

- How to Access Applets from Web Browsers

- How to Use Threads to Implement Dynamic Applets

- How to Design Applets Using Layout Managers

19   So that you are encouraged to develop a personal library of solutions to standard programming problems, this book introduces many useful, productivity-increasing, general-
purpose, templatelike patterns—sometimes called **cliches** by experienced programmers—
that you can fill in to achieve particular-purpose goals.

Cliches are introduced because learning to program involves more than learning to use
rules of program composition, just as learning to speak a human language involves more
than learning to use vocabulary words.

20   So that you can deepen your understanding of the art of **good programming practice**, this
book emphasizes the value of such ideas as procedure abstraction and data abstraction, and
explains important principles, such as the explicit-representation principle, the modularity
principle, no-duplication principle, the look-up principle, and the need-to-know principle.

21   In this book, single-idea segments, analogous to slides, are arranged in sections that are
analogous to slide shows. There are several segment varieties: **basic segments** explain
essential ideas; **sidetrip segments** introduce interesting, but skippable, ideas; **practice segments** provide opportunities to experiment with new ideas; and **highlights segments** sum-
marize important points.

22   The book develops a simple, yet realistic Java program, which you see in many versions
as your understanding of the language increases. In its ultimate version, the program
reads from a file that contains information about movies, computes an overall rating for
a selected movie, displays the rating on a meter, and shows an advertising poster, if one is
available. The program runs either as a standalone application or as an applet meant to
be used via a network viewer. The applet version presents the following appearance:

4

In the following display, click on a movie to see its rating.

Apocalypse Now	
The Sting	
The Wizard of Oz	
Bedtime for Bonzo	
The Last House on the Left	
Gone with the Wind	
Casablanca	
The King of Hearts	
My Fair Lady	
The Sound of Music	

The Sting

Applet MovieApplet running

- Java features make it ideally suited for writing network-oriented programs.

- Java is an object-oriented programming language. When you use an object-oriented programming language, your programs consist of class definitions.

- Java class definitions and the programs associated with classes are compiled into byte code to facilitate program portability.

- Java class definitions and the programs associated with them can be loaded dynamically via a network.

- Java's compiler detects errors at compile time; the Java virtual machine detects errors at run time.

- Java programs can be multithreaded, thereby enabling them to perform many tasks simultaneously.

- Java programs collect garbage automatically, relieving you of tedious programming and frustrating debugging, thereby increasing your productivity.

- Java has syntactical similarities with the C and C++ languages.

2 HOW TO COMPILE AND RUN A SIMPLE PROGRAM

24 In this section, you learn how to compile and run a simple program that computes the overall rating of a movie from ratings provided for the movie's script, acting, and directing. You also review standard terminology used throughout the rest of this book.

25 When you work with Java, you work either within a vendor-specific **development environment** or with an **editor**, with which you write your program, and a **compiler**, with which you translate your program into a form with which your Java virtual machine can work.

   If you try to learn Java using a vendor-specific development environment, you learn a great deal about the vendor-specific development, but not enough about Java itself. Accordingly, this book introduces Java in the expectation that you will use a traditional editor and compiler.

26 In its original form, your program is **text** or **source code**. Once translated, the source code becomes **byte code**. You use the Java virtual machine to **run** your byte code, or, said another way, you **execute** your program.

27 As usual, you generally go around two key loops many times as you search for bugs:

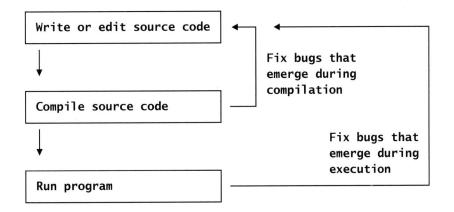

28 All Java programs contain one or more **class definitions**, each of which may contain various **method definitions**.

   In particular, every standalone Java program must contain a class definition that defines a method named `main`. When you start a Java program, the Java virtual machine performs the computations specified in the `main` method.

29 Java applets do not contain a `main` method; instead, applets are started via an `init` method,
SIDE TRIP as explained in Section 38.

30 Java's methods take the place of the **functions** or **procedures** talked about in conjunction
SIDE TRIP with other languages. Methods are much like functions and procedures, except that each
method definition must be embedded in a class definition.

31 Suppose, for example, that you want to compute the overall rating of a movie, given
integers that specify individual ratings for the script, acting, and directing. In Java, your
program will contain a simple arithmetic expression:

```
6 + 9 + 8
```

32 To arrange for your arithmetic expression to be evaluated, you define `main`, inside a class
definition, such that the arithmetic expression appears in that method:

```
public static void main (String argv[]) {
  6 + 9 + 8;
}
```

To understand the definition of `main`, you need to zoom in to look at the definition piece
by piece. Then, in Segment 36, you learn how to embed the `main` definition in a class
definition.

33 You need to know that **keywords** are words to which Java attributes special meanings.
Three such keywords appear in the example:

```
       ┌─ Keywords
       │
       ▼
  ──────────────
public static void main (String argv[]) {
  6 + 9 + 8;
}
```

- The keyword `public` indicates how accessible the `main` method is to be. You learn
  more about the `public` keyword in Section 34.

- The keyword `static` indicates that the `main` method is a **class method**, rather than an
  instance method. You learn about the distinction in Section 10.

- The keyword `void` indicates that the `main` method returns no value. You learn more
  about the `void` keyword in Section 5.

You should accept the use of the three keywords as ritual for now. You will come to
understand the ritual as you study the language.

34 Following the method name, `main`, you see a **parameter specification** surrounded by parentheses:

8

```
public static void main (String argv[]) {
   6 + 9 + 8;
}
```

Again, you can think of the parameter specification as a matter to be understood later: You learn about parameter specifications in general in Section 5, and about the parameter specification for main methods in Section 28.

For now, just accept the parameter specification as ritual that you will understand later in your learning process.

35   Finally, you come to matched braces that delimit the method's **body**. In general, a method's body contains a sequence of one or more **statements**, which tell the Java compiler about the computations to be performed. In the example, the body consists of a single statement:

```
public static void main (String argv[]) {
   6 + 9 + 8;                              ⟵ Body
}
```

The statement, like most Java statements, consists of an **expression**, 6 + 9 + 8, and the **statement terminator**, a semicolon, ;.

36   At this point, you are ready to embed the main method in a class definition. Because you are defining a demonstration program, you name the class Demonstrate.

You must store the definition of the Demonstrate class in a **source file** identified by Demonstrate.java. Thus, the **file name**, Demonstrate, is the name of the class contained in the file, and the **extension** is java.

37   Most Java programmers, by convention, start each class name with an uppercase letter.

38   The definition of the Demonstrate class begins with two keywords, public and class:

     Keywords

```
public class Demonstrate {
   ...
}
```

- The keyword public indicates how accessible the Demonstrate class is to be.

- The keyword class indicates that a class is about to be defined.

39   Following the name of the class, Demonstrate, you come to the **body** of the class definition, found between the matched braces. In the example, the body consists of a single method

definition—the one for the `main` method—which computes the rating of a movie, given ratings for the movie's script, acting, and directing:

```
public class Demonstrate {
 public static void main (String argv[]) {
  6 + 9 + 8;
 }
}
```

40 The semicolon, ;, the parentheses, (), and the braces, {}, act as punctuation. Occasionally, such markers, in such contexts, are called **punctuators**.

41 Note that the sample program is catatonic: It accepts no input data and produces no output result. And, because the program does nothing with the arithmetic it performs, discriminating Java compilers refuse to compile it.

42 To relieve the sample program of its catatonia, you provide **display statements** that tell the Java compiler that you want information to be displayed, as in the following revised program:

```
public class Demonstrate {
 public static void main (String argv[]) {
  System.out.print("The rating of the movie is ");
  System.out.println(6 + 9 + 8);
 }
}
```
———————————————— Result ————————————————
```
The rating of the movie is 23
```
————————————————————————————————

The revised program introduces several new concepts. Accordingly, you need to zoom in, and to look at the revised program piece by piece.

43 The **display methods**, `print` and `println`, display the information delimited by parentheses. Whenever you use `println` instead of `print`, Java not only displays information, but also terminates the line on which the information is displayed.

44 In the sample program, there are two display statements. In the first, the display method displays a **string**; in Java, a string is denoted by a sequence of characters delimited on both ends by double quotation marks:

```
System.out.print("The rating of the movie is ");
```

45 In the second instance, the display method displays the result produced by an arithmetic expression:

10

```
                    ┌── Arithmetic expression

                    ▼
                    ─────────
System.out.println(6 + 9 + 8);
```

46 The `System.out` part of the display statement stipulates that the information is to be shown on your display:

```
        ┌── Stipulates where information is to be sent

        ▼
        ─────────
System.out.print("The rating of the movie is ");
```

47
SIDE TRIP Said with more precision, `print` and `println` are display methods that are defined to work on instances of the `PrintStream` class. `System.out` is an expression that produces the particular instance of the `PrintStream` class associated with your display. You learn about the syntax involved in Section 9, and you learn about the `PrintStream` class in Section 32.

48 A value that appears explicitly in a program is said to be a **literal**. Explicit numbers, such as 6, are integer literals. Explicit strings, such as `"The rating of the movie is "`, are string literals.

49 Spaces, tabs, line feeds, and carriage returns are said to be **whitespace characters**. Java is **blank insensitive**: it treats all sequences of whitespace characters—other than those in strings—as though there were just a single space. Thus, the following are equivalent:

```
public class Demonstrate {
 public static void main (String argv[]) {
  System.out.print("The rating of the movie is ");
  System.out.println(6 + 9 + 8);
 }
}

public class Demonstrate
{
public static void main (String argv[])

{

        System.out.print("The rating of the movie is ");
        System.out.println(6 + 9 + 8);

}

}
```

Neither of these layout options is "better" or "official." In fact, many experienced Java programmers argue heatedly about how to arrange methods to maximize transparency and to please the eye. In this book, the methods are written in a style that both uses paper efficiently and lies within the envelope of common practice.

50 Java is **case sensitive**; if you write `Main` or `MAIN` when you mean `main`, Java cannot understand your intent.

51 At this point, you have seen sample uses of just one Java operator: the addition operator. In general, an **operator** is a built-in method that works on inputs supplied to it according to the conventions of arithmetic; such methods are interspersed among their inputs, and those inputs are called **operands.**

52 To initiate compilation on a UNIX system running X windows, you open the `xterm` window. On Windows systems, you open a DOS window.

Next, you type the following line, assuming that your class definition is in a source file named `Demonstrate.java`:

javac Demonstrate.java

Such a line is called a **command line.** The example command line has two parts:

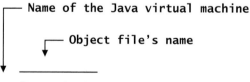

```
javac Demonstrate.java
```

The Java compiler places the resulting byte code in a file named `Demonstrate.class` in the current directory.

53 Once the Java compiler has placed the resulting byte code in `Demonstrate.class`, you can run the `main` program defined inside the class definition by typing another command line:

> ── Name of the Java virtual machine
>
>   ── Object file's name

java Demonstrate

54 Although the sample program communicates with you by way of output data displayed on your screen, it does not receive any input data after it has been compiled. Instead, it works with data that were supplied as the program was written. Such data are said to be **wired in** or **hard coded.** You learn to work with data in a data file in Section 26.

55 In this book, you see many templatelike, general-purpose program patterns that you can fill in to suit your own specific purpose. In these patterns, each place to be filled in is identified by a box that contains a description of the item to be inserted, `such as this`.

When you fill in a pattern, replacing descriptions with specific instances of the general categories described, you are said to **instantiate** the pattern.

56
PRACTICE
Write a program that computes and displays the volume of the earth.

57
HIGHLIGHTS

- When you work with Java, you write source code, the Java compiler translates source code into byte code, and the Java virtual machine runs that byte code.

- Java programs consist of class definitions, one of which must contain a definition for a method named `main` if the program is to be a standalone program. When you run a standalone Java program, you initiate the computations specified in that `main` method.

- Java methods contain sequences of computation-specifying statements.

- Many statements involve built-in operators, such as the addition operator, +. Operators do their work on operands.

- To test simple programs, you often use data that you supply when you write the program. Such data are said to be wired in.

- **If** you wish to display data, **then** use a display statement:

  `System.out.print( expression whose value is to be displayed );`

- **If** you want not only to display data, but also to terminate a line, **then** use `println` instead of `print`.

3 HOW TO DECLARE VARIABLES

58 In this section, you learn how to declare variables in Java. You also learn more of the terminology used throughout the rest of this book.

59 A Java **identifier** is a name consisting of letters and digits, the first of which must be a letter. The underscore, _, and the dollar sign, $, count as letters.

Most Java programmers do not use the underscore when they run words together to produce long identifiers. Instead, they initiate each interior word with an uppercase character, as in `movieRating`.

60 A **variable** is a chunk of computer memory that contains a **value**. The **name** of a variable is an identifier that refers to the variable.

A variable's **data type** determines the size of the chunk and the way that the bits in the chunk are interpreted. If the data type of a variable is `int`, the variable holds a 32-bit signed **integer**. If the data type of a variable is `double`, the variable holds a 64-bit signed floating-point number.

As a program runs, a variable's value may change, but a variable's data type never changes. Thus, the value of a variable named `script`, with type `int`, could be 8 at one time and 9 at another, but `script`'s value could never be a number with type `double`, such as `8.5`.

61 Because every variable is typed, the Java compiler can **allocate** a memory chunk of the right size for each variable, once and for all, taking advantage of the fact that the value of the variable always will fit within the allocated memory chunk.

62 When you tell the Java compiler the type of a variable, you are said to **declare** the variable. Thus, the following program fragment exhibits three variable declarations. All three variables are declared to be integer variables, because each is preceded by the data-type–declaring `int` keyword.

```
public class Demonstrate {
 public static void main (String argv[]) {
   int script;
   int acting;
   int directing;
   ...
 }
}
```

63 You can combine several separate variable declarations into one, more concise variable declaration if each variable has the same data type. In the following program fragment, for example, all three variables are declared to be integer variables in a single declaration:

```
public class Demonstrate {
 public static void main (String argv[]) {
   int script, acting, directing;
   ...
 }
}
```

Note the obligatory, variable-separating commas.

64 Storing a value in the memory chunk allocated for a variable is called doing **variable assignment**. Accordingly, whenever Java places a value in such a memory chunk, the variable is said to be **assigned a value**, and the value is said to be **assigned to the variable**.

65 You can **initialize** a variable in the same statement in which the variable is declared:

```
public class Demonstrate {
 public static void main (String argv[]) {
   int script = 6;
   int acting = 9;
   int directing = 8;
   ...
 }
}
```

You can combine several declarations, with initializations, into one concise statement, as in the following example:

```
public class Demonstrate {
 public static void main (String argv[]) {
   int script = 6, acting = 9, directing = 8;
   ...
 }
}
```

Again, note the obligatory commas.

66 All Java variables have a **standard default value** until they are initialized or assigned. Thus, no Java variable is ever without a value. The standard default value of a number is 0.

Java expects you to assign a value to every variable, even though Java supplies default values. If Java can determine that you do not assign a value to a variable before you use that variable's value, Java will refuse to compile your program.

67 For the moment, the sample programs use test data that are wired in by way of initialized variables. Later on, in Section 26, you learn how to use test data that you provide via a file. Still later, in Segment 44, you learn how to provide data via a text field in a graphical user interface.

68 To change the value of a variable, you use the **assignment operator**, =. Three assignment statements appear in the following program:

```
public class Demonstrate {
 public static void main (String argv[]) {
  int result, script = 6, acting = 9, directing = 8;
  result = script;
  result = result + acting;
  result = result + directing;
  System.out.print("The rating of the movie is ");
  System.out.println(result);
 }
}
```

———————————————— Result ————————————————

```
The rating of the movie is 23
```

Of course, this program is a bit awkward—the only reason to split the computation into three separate statements is to demonstrate that a variable can be assigned and then reassigned.

69 Your variable-declaration statements do not need to lie before all other statements. Accordingly, most programmers prefer to declare a variable close to its first use, as in the following example:

```
public class Demonstrate {
 public static void main (String argv[]) {
  int result, script = 6;
  result = script;
  int acting = 9;
  result = result + acting;
  int directing = 8;
  result = result + directing;
  System.out.print("The rating of the movie is ");
  System.out.println(result);
}}
```

———————————————— Result ————————————————

```
The rating of the movie is 23
```

70 For storing integers, Java provides a range of data-type possibilities, including byte, short, int, and long. Java compiler implementers are required to use a standard number of bytes for each:

Type	Bytes	Stores
byte	1	integer
short	2	integer
int	4	integer
long	8	integer

71   The char data type ordinarily is used for storing characters; however, because character codes can be viewed as integers, char also is viewed as one of the **integral data types**, as are byte, short, int, and long. Java uses 2 bytes for the char data type, so as to accommodate the characters in not only English, but also many of the world's other languages, such as Bengali, Kannada, and Telugu.

72   The byte, short, int, and long data types carry a sign, so as to accommodate negative numbers. The char data type has no sign.

73   For storing floating-point numbers, Java provides two types, float and double. Again, Java compiler writers are required to use a standard number of bytes for each:

Type	Bytes	Stores
float	4	floating-point number
double	8	floating-point number

74   Implementers of compilers for C and C++ are allowed to use as many bytes as they like
SIDE TRIP   for the integral and floating-point types, as long as they honor certain relative-length constraints. Flexibility interferes with portability, however, so Java requires compiler implementers to use the standard number of bytes for each data type.

75   For most integers, the byte and short integer types are a little small, and long is unnecessarily large, so the int data type, lying between, is popular. For most floating-point numbers, the float floating-point type is a little small, so the double data type, being twice as big, is popular. Accordingly, all the programs in the rest of this book use int for all integers and double for all floating-point numbers.

76   Experienced programmers occasionally use byte, short, or float when either maximizing execution speed or minimizing program size are of prime importance.

77   All the integer and floating-point types are said to be **primitive types**, along with boolean type, which you learn about in Section 20, and the character type, which you learn more about in Section 30. All other types, which you begin to learn about in Section 9, are called reference types.

78   You can include **comments** in Java programs in two ways. First, whenever the Java compiler encounters two adjacent forward slashes, //, anywhere in a line, the Java compiler ignores both the slashes and the remainder of the line on which the slashes appear:

```
// Short comment
```

Second, whenever Java encounters a slash followed immediately by an asterisk, /*, Java ignores both the /* characters and all other characters up to and including the next asterisk followed immediately by a slash, */.

```
/*
Long comment
that just goes on
and on
*/
```

If you wish to test how a program works without certain lines of source code, you can hide those lines in a comment, instead of deleting them.

79   Many programmers develop a personal style for writing comments, to make their comments attractive and easy to find.

80   In Java documentation, you often see comments that begin with a slash and two asterisks,
SIDE TRIP   and continue with a column of asterisks down the left side:

```
/**
 * A documentation comment
 * with a left column filled
 * with asterisks
 */
```

Such comments are designed to be noted and processed by an automatic documentation generator.

81   Note that you cannot place a /* · · · */ comment inside another /* · · · */ comment. If you try to do so, you find that the inner comment's terminator, */, terminates the outer comment, and your Java compiler cannot compile your program:

```
/*  ◄─────────────────────────────────┐

First part of outer comment           │

/*  ◄── Commented out                  │     Delimiter, */, of inner
                                       │     comment terminates delimiter,
Inner comment                          │     /*, of outer comment

*/ ────────────────────────────────────┘

Second part of outer comment

*/  ◄── Dangles
```

82   Write a program that computes the volume of the earth. Wire in the radius of the earth
PRACTICE   using a variable, r.

83

HIGHLIGHTS   • A variable is an identifier that names a chunk of memory.

- If you wish to introduce a variable, **then** you must declare the data type of that variable in a variable declaration:

  `data type` `variable name` ;

- If you wish to provide an initial value for a variable, **then** you can include that initial value in the declaration statement:

  `data type` `variable name` = `initial-value expression` ;

- If you wish to reassign a variable, **then** use an assignment statement:

  `variable name` = `new-value expression` ;

- The integral data types are `char`, `byte`, `short`, `int`, and `long`.

- The floating-point data types are `float` and `double`.

4 HOW TO WRITE ARITHMETIC EXPRESSIONS

84 So far, you have seen sample expressions involving the addition operator, +. In this section, you learn about other arithmetic operators, and about the way that Java handles operator precedence and associativity.

85 You arrange for basic arithmetic calculations using the +, -, *, and / operators for **addition, subtraction, multiplication,** and **division:**

```
6 + 3          // Add, evaluating to 9
6 - 3          // Subtract, evaluating to 3
6 * 3          // Multiply, evaluating to 18
6 / 3          // Divide, evaluating to 2
6 + y          // Add, evaluating to 6 plus y's value
x - 3          // Subtract, evaluating to x's value minus 3
x * y          // Multiply, evaluating to x's value times y's value
x / y          // Divide, evaluating to x's value divided by y's value
```

86 When an integer denominator does not divide evenly into an integer numerator, the division operator rounds the result toward zero, producing another integer. The **modulus operator,** %, produces the integer remainder:

```
5 / 3          // Divide, evaluating to 1
-5 / 3         // Divide, evaluating to -1
5 % 3          // Divide, evaluating to the remainder, 2
-5 % 3         // Divide, evaluating to the remainder, -2
```

Of course, when it divides floating-point numbers, Java produces a floating-point result:

```
5.0 / 3.0      // Divide, evaluating to 1.66667
```

87 Arithmetic expressions can contain one operator, but they can also contain no operators or more than one operator:

```
6              // Constant expression
x              // Variable expression
6 + 3 + 2      // Produces 11
6 - 3 - 2      // Produces 1
6 * 3 * 2      // Produces 36
6 / 3 / 2      // Produces 1
```

88 Java follows standard practice with respect to the syntax rules that dictate how the Java compiler crystallizes operands around operators. In the following, for example, the Java compiler takes 6 + 3 * 2 to be equivalent to 6 + (3 * 2), rather than to (6 + 3) * 2, because multiplication has **precedence** higher than addition:

```
6 + 3 * 2      // Equivalent to 12, rather than to 18
```

89   When an expression contains two operators of equal precedence, such as multiplication and division, the Java compiler handles the expression as in the following examples:

```
6 / 3 * 2        // Equivalent to (6 / 3) * 2 = 4,
                 // rather than to 6 / (3 * 2) = 1
6 * 3 / 2        // Equivalent to (6 * 3) / 2 = 9,
                 // rather than to 6 * (3 / 2) = 6
```

Thus, in Java, the multiplication and division operators are said to **associate** from left to right. Most operators associate from left to right, but certain operators do not, as shown in Segment 96 and in the table provided in Appendix A.

90   Of course, you can always deploy parentheses around subexpressions whenever the Java compiler's interpretation of the entire expression is not the interpretation you want:

```
6 + 3 * 2        // Value is 12, rather than 18
(6 + 3) * 2      // Value is 18, rather than 12
```

You can also use parentheses to make your intentions clear. In the following, for example, the parentheses are not required, but many programmers insert them anyway, just to make the meaning of the expression absolutely clear:

```
6 + 3 * 2        // Value is clearly 12
6 + (3 * 2)      // Value is even more clearly 12
```

Inserting such parentheses is a good idea, especially when you are working with large expressions.

91   Most operators are **binary operators**; that is, they have two operands. In Java, those two operands are found on the immediate left and immediate right of the operator. Some operators, such as the **negation operator**, -, and **unary plus operator**, +, have just one operand, found on the immediate right of the operator. Such operators are **unary operators**.

You can always determine whether the - and + denote unary or binary operators by looking to see whether there is any constant, variable, or subexpression to the immediate left. If there is, then - denotes subtraction and + denotes addition; otherwise, - denotes negation and + is handled as though it were not there at all.

92   The precedence of the negation operator, -, is higher than that of +, -, *, or /:

```
- 6 * 3 / 2      // Equivalent to ((- 6) * 3) / 2 = -9
```

93   When an arithmetic expression contains values that have a mixture of data types, it is called a **mixed expression**. When Java evaluates a mixed expression, it first uses the given values to produce a set of values that have identical types. Then, Java performs the prescribed arithmetic.

Thus, when given a mixed expression that multiplies a floating-point number by an integer, Java first produces a floating-point number from the integer, and then multiplies.

94 If you want to tell Java explicitly to convert a value from one type to another, rather than relying on automatic conversion, you **cast** the expression. To cast, you prefix the expression with the name of the desired type in parentheses.

If, for example, i is an `int` and d is a `double`, you can cast i to a `double` and d to an `int` as follows:

```
(double) i        // A double expression
(int) d           // An int expression
```

Note that the original types of the i and d variables remain undisturbed: i remains an `int` variable, and d remains a `double` variable.

95 The assignment operator, =, like all operators in Java, produces a value. By convention, the value produced is the same as the value assigned. Thus, the value of the expression y = 5 is 5.

Because assignment expressions produce values, assignment expressions can appear as subexpressions nested inside larger expressions.

In the following assignment expression, for example, the assignment expression, y = 5, which assigns a value to y, appears inside a larger assignment expression, which assigns a value to x:

```
x = (y = 5)
```

96 The assignment operator, =, in contrast to all the other operators that you have seen so far, associates from right to left. Accordingly, the expression x = y = 5 is equivalent to the expression x = (y = 5).

Fortunately, x = y = 5 *does not* mean (x = y) = 5, because the value of an assignment statement, such as x = y, is *not* a variable name. Thus, (x = y) = 5 makes no sense, and, if the assignment operator were to associate left to right, x = y = 5 would make no sense either.

97 The precedences and associativity of the operators that you have learned about so far are given in the following table. A complete table is provided in Appendix A.

Operators	Associativity
+ (unary) - (negation)	right to left
* / %	left to right
+ -	left to right
=	right to left

- Java offers negation, addition, subtraction, multiplication, division, and assignment operators.

- Java follows standard precedence and associativity rules.

- The assignment operator, =, has precedence lower than that of the arithmetic operators.

- **If** the standard precedence and associativity rules do not produce the result you want, **then** use parentheses to create subexpressions.

5 HOW TO DEFINE SIMPLE METHODS

99   In this section, you learn how to define Java methods other than the required `main` method. In the process, you learn how to work with arguments, parameters, and returned values.

100   If you propose to compute the ratings of many movies, you certainly should define a rating-computing method, perhaps named `movieRating`, to do the work. Once you have defined it, you can **call** the `movieRating` method as in the following example:

```
public class Demonstrate {
  // ... Definition of movieRating method goes here ...
  public static void main (String argv[]) {
    System.out.print("The rating of the movie is ");
    System.out.println(movieRating(6, 9, 8));
  }
}
```

In the example, the `movieRating` method has three **arguments**: 6, 9, and 8. As illustrated, Java requires method arguments to be separated by commas.

The arguments shown are all constant expressions, but, of course, arguments can be variable expressions or expressions containing operators.

101   Whenever a call to the `movieRating` method appears, the Java compiler must arrange for the following to be done:

- Determine which `movieRating` method you have in mind.

- Reserve chunks of memory for the values of the argument expressions.

- Write the values of those argument expressions into those memory chunks.

- Identify the memory chunks with special variables, the **parameters** of the method—say, s, a, and d.

- Evaluate the expression s + a + d.

- Return the value of s + a + d for use in other computations.

102   You define the `movieRating` method as follows:

```
public class Demonstrate {
  // ... Definition of main ...
  public static int movieRating (int s, int a, int d) {
    return s + a + d;
  }
}
```

103   Here is what each part of a method definition does:

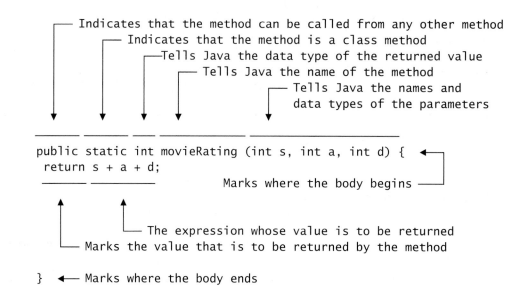

Indicates that the method can be called from any other method
Indicates that the method is a class method
Tells Java the data type of the returned value
Tells Java the name of the method
Tells Java the names and data types of the parameters

```
public static int movieRating (int s, int a, int d) {
  return s + a + d;
```

Marks where the body begins

The expression whose value is to be returned
Marks the value that is to be returned by the method

```
}
```
Marks where the body ends

104 A method's **parameters** are just variables that are initialized with argument values each time that the method is called. You can assign parameters to new values, just as you can other variables, but many programmers consider such assignment to be bad programming practice.

105 Note also that you must specify data types for parameters and returned values when you define a Java method:

- You specify the data type of each parameter in each method at the place where you introduce the parameter.

- You specify the data type of the value returned by each method in every Java program at the place where you name the method to be defined.

106 Finally, you use keywords to indicate what sort of method you are defining.

- The `static` keyword indicates that the `movieRating` method is a class method. If you were to leave out the `static` keyword, you would define an instance method, as described in Section 10.

- The `public` keyword indicates that any method, defined in any class, can call the `movieRating` method. If you were to use the `protected` or `private` keywords instead, you would indicate that access to the `movieRating` method is restricted, as described in Section 34.

107 In the following example, the definition of the `movieRating` method appears in a complete program:

```
public class Demonstrate {
 public static void main (String argv[]) {
   int script = 6, acting = 9, directing = 8;
   System.out.print("The rating of the movie is ");
   System.out.println(movieRating(script, acting, directing));
 }
 public static int movieRating (int s, int a, int d) {
   return s + a + d;
 }
}
```
——————————————————— Result ———————————————
```
The rating of the movie is 23
```

108 Most Java programmers, by convention, start each method name with a lowercase letter.

109 You must specify the data type of each parameter individually, because data types in parameter declarations, unlike data types in variable declarations, do not propagate across commas. Thus, the following is wrong:

┌— BUG: Data type does not propagate

```
public static int movieRating (int s, a, d) {
  ...
}
```

110 The Java compiler does not require Java programs to be ordered such that each method's
SIDE TRIP definition appears before calls to that method appear. Thus, movieRating does not need to be defined before main is defined, just because main contains a call to movieRating.

In this respect, Java is much easier to work with than is C or C++, both of which require that you define functions—their analogs of methods—before you use those functions.

111 You never can leave out the specification of a method's return value data type. In this
SIDE TRIP respect, Java differs from C and C++, which allow you to leave out the return-value data type if that type happens to be int.

112 When movieRating is called with three integer variables as arguments, a copy of the value of the first argument becomes the value of the first parameter, s; a copy of the value of the second argument becomes the value of the second parameter, a; and a copy of the value of the third argument becomes the value of the third parameter, d.

113 Some methods *do not* return values used in other computations. Instead, they are executed for some other purpose, such as for displaying a value.

Accordingly, Java allows you to use the void keyword as though void were a data type for return values. When Java sees void used as though void were a return value data type, Java knows that nothing is to be returned.

114 For example, in the following variation on the program in Segment 107, display is handled in the displayMovieRating method, so there is no value to be returned. Accordingly, void appears instead of a data-type name in the definition of displayMovieRating, and displayMovieRating contains no return statement:

```
public class Demonstrate {
 public static void main (String argv[]) {
  int script = 6, acting = 9, directing = 8;
  displayMovieRating(script, acting, directing);
 }
 public static void displayMovieRating (int s, int a, int d) {
  System.out.print("The rating of the movie is ");
  System.out.println(s + a + d);
 }
}
```

115 Because displayMovieRating has no return statement, it is said to **fall off its end**, returning nothing; that behavior is allowed for only those methods that have a void return type.

Picky programmers think that defining a method that can fall off its end is inelegant. Those programmers write empty return statements, as in the following slightly amended version of displayMovieRating:

```
public class Demonstrate {
 public static void main (String argv[]) {
  int script = 6, acting = 9, directing = 8;
  displayMovieRating(script, acting, directing);
 }
 public static void displayMovieRating (int s, int a, int d) {
  System.out.print("The rating of the movie is ");
  System.out.println(s + a + d);
  return;
 }
}
```

116 You do not need to define a method called in the main method in the same class in which you define that main method. For example, you can define movieRating in the Movie class in the Movie.java file:

```
// Movie class defined in Movie.java
public class Movie {
 public static int movieRating (int s, int a, int d) {
  return s + a + d;
 }
}
```

Then, you can define main in the Demonstrate class in the Demonstrate.java file:

```
// Demonstrate class defined in Demonstrate.java
public class Demonstrate {
 public static void main (String argv[]) {
  int script = 6, acting = 9, directing = 8;
  System.out.print("The rating of the movie is ");
  System.out.println(Movie.movieRating(script, acting, directing));
 }
}
```

117 As shown in Segment 116, if you define movieRating in a class that is different from the one in which movieRating is called, you must preface the name of the method, movieRating, by the name of the class in which that method is defined, and you must join the two names by a dot.

Java programmers think in terms of selecting the method from a **field** in the appropriate class. Accordingly, the dot is called the **field-selection operator**.

118 The reason for the appearance of the class name and the field-selection operator is that Java allows you to define movieRating methods in more than one class. Thus, you must always specify which particular movieRating method you have in mind.

119 You might, for example, define not only the Movie class, but also the JamesBondMovie class, in which the movieRating method reflects, say, a belief that 10 should be used instead of the value of the script parameter, s, when rating James Bond movies:

```
public class JamesBondMovie {
 public static int movieRating (int s, int a, int d) {
  return 10 + a + d;
 }
}
```

120 Once you have defined and compiled both the Movie class and the JamesBondMovie class, you can use both:

```
public class Demonstrate {
 public static void main (String argv[]) {
  int script = 6, acting = 9, directing = 8;
  System.out.print("The ordinary rating of the movie is ");
  System.out.println(Movie.movieRating(script, acting, directing));
  System.out.print("The James Bond movie rating of the movie is ");
  System.out.println(
    JamesBondMovie.movieRating(script, acting, directing)
  );
 }
}
───────────────────────── Result ──────────────────────
The ordinary rating of the movie is 23
The James Bond movie rating of the movie is 27
```

121 Whenever there is more than one definition for a method, the method name is said to be **overloaded**. The use of the word *overloaded* is unfortunate, because *overloaded* usually suggests imminent breakdown, as in *the overloaded circuit blew a fuse*. In Java, no suggestion of imminent breakdown is intended, however. Rather, the ability to handle method overloading is a powerful feature of the language.

122 Java also allows you to define multiple methods with the same name in the same class, as long as each version has a different arrangement of parameter data types.

You can, for example, define one `displayMovieRating` method that handles integers, and another `displayMovieRating` method that handles floating-point numbers. Then, you can put both methods to work in the same program:

```
public class Demonstrate {
 public static void main (String argv[]) {
  int intScript = 6, intActing = 9, intDirecting = 8;
  double doubleScript = 6.0, doubleActing = 9.0, doubleDirecting = 8.0;
  displayMovieRating(intScript, intActing, intDirecting);
  displayMovieRating(doubleScript, doubleActing, doubleDirecting);
 }
 // First, define displayMovieRating with integers:
 public static void displayMovieRating (int s, int a, int d) {
  System.out.print("The integer rating of the movie is ");
  System.out.println(s + a + d);
  return;
 }

 // Next, define displayMovieRating with floating-point numbers:
 public static void displayMovieRating (double s, double a, double d) {
  System.out.print("The floating-point rating of the movie is ");
  System.out.println(s + a + d);
  return;
 }
}
```

————————————————— Result —————————————————
```
The integer rating of the movie is 23
The floating-point rating of the movie is 23
```

123 Because Java allows method overloading, Java is said to be a **polymorphic** language.

124 The + operator, which normally means *add*, has an entirely different meaning when one of the operands is a string. In such situations, the + operator converts the other operand into a string, if that operand is not already a string, and **concatenates** the two strings, producing a third string.

Because + has two fundamentally different meanings, + is said to be an **overloaded operator**.

30

125   You frequently see the + operator, viewed as the **concatenation operator**, in print statements. Such use of the + operator often enables compact display statements.

For example, you can certainly write an expression such as the following:

```
System.out.print("The rating of the movie is ");
System.out.println(s + a + d);
```

Alternatively, you can combine the two statements into one, using concatenation to bring the information together:

```
System.out.print("The rating of the movie is " + (s + a + d));
```

Note that the parentheses around the summed variables are essential. Otherwise, Java assumes that you want to concatenate the first string with the value of s, transformed into a string, then a, then d; Java does concatenation, but does no addition.

126   Although Java allows you to overload methods, you cannot overload operators. In this
SIDE TRIP   respect, Java differs from C++, which allows you to overload both method and operators.

Java itself comes with overloaded operators, however. The use of the + operator for concatenation is a conspicuous example. The use of the + operator for adding together all sorts of arithmetic types is a less conspicuous example.

127   Java offers a variety of powerful built-in class methods for the Math class. The following
SIDE TRIP   illustrates:

```
public class Demonstrate {
 public static void main (String argv[]) {
   System.out.println("Natural logarithm of 10:     " + Math.log(10));
   System.out.println("Absolute value of -10:       " + Math.abs(-10));
   System.out.println("Maximum of 2 and 3:          " + Math.max(2, 3));
   System.out.println("5th power of 6:              " + Math.pow(6, 5));
   System.out.println("Square root of 7:            " + Math.sqrt(7));
   System.out.println("Sin of 8 radians:            " + Math.sin(8));
   System.out.println("Random number (0.0 to 1.0): " + Math.random());
 }
}
```

——————————————————— Result ———————————————————

```
Natural logarithm of 10:      2.30259
Absolute value of -10:        10
Maximum of 2 and 3:           3
5th power of 6:               7776
Square root of 7:             2.64575
Sin of 8 radians:             0.989358
Random number (0.0 to 1.0):  0.566339
```

128   You can define more than one class in the same file, as you learn in Section 33. For now,
SIDE TRIP   however, you are to assume that each class is defined in a file dedicated to that class.

129
PRACTICE
Write a program that computes the volume of any planet in cubic meters. Have the volume computation performed by a method named sphereVolume. Arrange to provide the radius by wiring a value into the main method.

130
PRACTICE
The energy of a moving mass is given by the formula $\frac{1}{2}mv^2$. Write a program that determines the ratio of energies of a car moving at two specified velocities. Write and use a method named square in your solution. Use your program to determine the ratio of enerties for one car moving at 80 miles per hour and another moving at 55 miles per hour. Use numbers of type double throughout.

131
HIGHLIGHTS

- Whenever a method is called, that method's arguments are evaluated, and copies of the resulting values are assigned to the method's parameters. Then, the statements in the method's body are evaluated. When a return statement is evaluated, the argument of the return expression is evaluated, and that value becomes the value of the method call.

- Every method in Java is defined inside a class definition.

- If you want to define a public class method, in a public class, **then** instantiate the following pattern:

```
public class  class name  {
  public static  return type   method name
    ( data type 1  parameter 1 ,
     ...,
     data type 1  parameter 1 ) {
    declaration 1
    ...
    declaration m
    statement 1
    ...
    statement n
}
```

- If you want to call a class method from another class, **then** specify both the class and the method name, joining them by the field-selection operator:

```
class name . method name
```

- If you want to define a method that does not return a value, **then** supply void in place of an ordinary data-type declaration.

- You can define many identically named methods, as long as each of them appears in a different class.

- You can define many identically named methods, as long as each of them has a unique pattern of parameter data types.

6 HOW TO UNDERSTAND VARIABLE SCOPE AND EXTENT

132   In this section, you learn where a parameter or variable can be evaluated or assigned.

133   It is important to know that the parameter values established when a method is entered are available only inside the method. It is as though Java builds an isolating fence to protect any other uses of the same parameter name outside of the method.

Consider movieRating, for example:

```
public class Movie {
 // Define movieRating:
 public static int movieRating (int s, int a, int d) {
  return s + a + d;
 }
}
```

When movieRating is used, any existing values for other variables that happen to be named s, a, and d are protected:

movieRating fence————
 The value of s, a, and d inside
 this fence are isolated from
 the values outside

 movieRating method computes the
 value of s + a + d using their
 values inside this fence

The values of s, a, and d
outside the fence, if any,
are not affected by the
values inside

134   The reason Java acts as though it builds an isolating fence around each method's parameters is that Java reserves a chunk of memory for each parameter every time that the method is called. Java copies argument values into those reserved chunks.

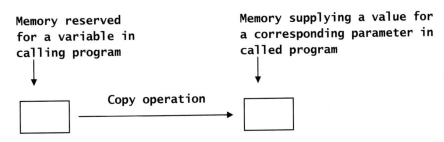

Memory reserved
for a variable in
calling program

Memory supplying a value for
a corresponding parameter in
called program

Copy operation

In the movieRating example, a new chunk of memory is reserved for each of the integer parameters, s, a, and d. Argument values are copied into those chunks.

135 Because Java generally reserves new chunks of memory for parameters of primitive type, into which values are copied, Java's parameters are said to be **call-by-value parameters,** and Java is said to be a **call-by-value language.**

136 One alternative to call-by-value parameters, allowed by some languages, is provided by **call-by-reference parameters.** If a parameter is a call-by-reference parameter and the corresponding argument is a variable, then the parameter shares the same chunk of memory with the argument variable:

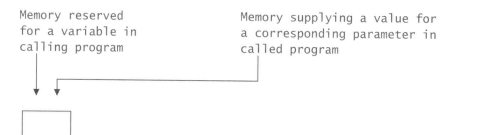

Memory reserved
for a variable in
calling program

Memory supplying a value for
a corresponding parameter in
called program

If a parameter is a call-by-reference parameter and the corresponding argument is a variable, a parameter reassignment inside the called program propagates outside to the calling program.

137 The following program defines movieRating, albeit awkwardly, to illustrate the limited availability of parameter values:

```java
public class Demonstrate {
  // First, define adder:
  public static int adder () {
    return s + a + d;                              // BUG!
  }
  // Next, define movieRating:
  public static int movieRating (int s, int a, int d) {
    return adder();                                // BUG!
  }
  // Then, define main:
  public static void main (String argv[]) {
    int script = 6, acting = 9, directing = 8, result;
    result = movieRating(script, acting, directing);
    System.out.print("The rating of the movie is ");
    System.out.println(s + a + d);                 // BUG!
  }
}
```

In this program, movieRating asks adder—a method with no parameters—to perform the computation of s + a + d. However, the Java compiler cannot compile adder, because no values for the s, a, or d parameters of movieRating are available to adder.

Moreover, Java cannot compile the second print statement in the `main` method. The reason is that s, a, and d exist only during the execution of the method in which they appear as parameters; s, a, and d no longer exist once that method has returned.

138 By way of summary, the following are the important consequences of parameter isolation:

- A method's parameter values are not available after the execution of that method.

- When one method calls another, the values of the parameters in the calling method are not available during the execution of the called method.

139 A **block** is a group of statements surrounded by braces. Accordingly, the body of a method is a block, as is any other group of statements surrounded by braces.

You see examples of blocks that are not method bodies in Section 21, because blocks are used liberally inside Java's `if` and `if-else` statements.

140 Variables that are declared inside blocks are said to be **local variables**.

A **parameter** is treated as though it were a local variable declared inside a method body. Accordingly, a parameter is really a local variable that happens to be initialized with an argument value.

141 Because parameters are just local variables that are initialized by argument values, what you have learned about parameters also applies to the local variables that appear in any block, including method bodies:

- A block's local variables are not available after the execution of that block.

- When one method calls another, the values of the local variables in the calling method are not available during the execution of the called method.

142 Because parameters and local variables can be evaluated and assigned only in the method or block in which they are declared, parameters and local variables are said to have **local scope**.

Because the memory allocated for parameters and local variables is reallocated as soon as the corresponding method has finished executing, parameters and local variables are said to have **dynamic extent**.

143

HIGHLIGHTS

- A local variable is a variable that is declared inside a block, such as a block that constitutes a method body.

- Java isolates parameters and local variables, enabling you to reuse their names. The values of a method's parameters and local variables are not available after that method has returned. Also, when one method calls another, the values of the parameters and of the local variables in the calling method are not available during the execution of the called method.

7 HOW TO BENEFIT FROM PROCEDURE ABSTRACTION

144 In this section, you review the procedure-abstraction idea, by which you increase your efficiency and make your programs easier to maintain.

145 When you move computational detail into a method, you are said to be doing **procedure abstraction**, and you are said to be hiding the details of how a computation is done behind a **procedure-abstraction barrier**.

The key virtue of procedure abstraction is that *you make it easy to reuse your programs*. Instead of copying particular lines of program, you—or another programmer—arrange to call a previously defined method.

146 A second virtue of procedure abstraction is that *you push details out of sight and out of mind*, making your programs easier to read and enabling you to concentrate on high-level steps.

147 A third virtue of procedure abstraction is that *you can debug your programs easily*. By dividing a program into small, independently debuggable pieces, you exploit the powerful **divide-and-conquer** problem-solving heuristic.

148 A fourth virtue of procedure abstraction is that *you can augment repetitive computations easily*. For example, in Segment 116, you have seen the movieRating method defined as follows:

```
public class Movie {
 // Define movieRating:
 public static int movieRating (int s, int a, int d) {
  return s + a + d;
 }
}
```

You can easily add a line that displays the rating every time that the rating is computed:

```
public class Movie {
 // Define movieRating:
 public static int movieRating (int s, int a, int d) {
  System.out.print("The rating of the movie is ");
  System.out.println(s + a + d);
  return s + a + d;
 }
}
```

Thus, you do not need to bother to find all the places where a rating is computed, because you need only to change the movieRating method's definition.

149 A fifth virtue of procedure abstraction is that *you easily can improve how a computation is done*. You might decide, for example, that it is wasteful for your movieRating method

to multiply out the ratings for the script, acting, and directing twice. Accordingly, you decide to do the computation just once, using a variable to hold on to the value:

```
public class Movie {
 // Define movieRating:
 public static int movieRating (int s, int a, int d) {
  int result = s + a + d;
  System.out.print("The rating of the movie is ");
  System.out.println(result);
  return result;
 }
}
```

Again, you do not need to bother to find all the places where the rating is computed via the movieRating method; you need only to change the movieRating method's definition.

150 A sixth virtue of procedure abstraction is that *you can easily change the way that a computation is done*. If you decide to combine ratings by multiplying, rather than by adding, you can redefine movieRating easily.

151 **PRACTICE** Write a method named convert, for converting Celsius temperature to Fahrenheit, that transforms an integer argument into twice that integer plus 30.

Next, arrange for your method to display the result every time that the method is called.

Next, amend your method such that it performs temperature conversion only once.

Finally, improve your method by having it add 40 to the argument, multiply by 9/5, and subtract 40.

For each change, comment on the corresponding benefit provided by method abstraction.

152 **HIGHLIGHTS**

- Procedure abstraction hides the details of computations inside methods, thus moving those details behind an abstraction barrier.

- You should practice procedure abstraction to take advantage of the following benefits:

  - Your programs become easier to reuse.

  - Your programs become easier to read.

  - Your programs become easier to debug.

  - Your programs become easier to augment.

  - Your programs become easier to improve.

  - Your programs become easier to adapt.

8 HOW TO DECLARE CLASS VARIABLES

153   In this section, you learn about class variables. Such variables are particularly useful when you need a variable with values that are broadly accessible.

154   Suppose that you want to adjust your way of calculating movie ratings by introducing weights. You could insert those weights into the movie-rating method directly:

```
public class Movie {
 // Define movieRating:
 public static int movieRating (int s, int a, int d) {
   return 6 * s + 13 * a + 11 * d;
 }
}
```

Such direct insertion is not a good idea, however. Sprinkling numbers throughout a program creates problems, as a program grows, because you easily can forget where such numbers are located.

A safer approach is to use variables. You cannot use local variables, however, because they exist only during the execution of the corresponding block.

155   You have learned that classes act as repositories for class methods. They also act as repositories for **class variables**:

A class definition

```
Class methods

Class variables

.
.
.
```

In contrast to local variables, class variables continue to exist as long as the class exists; their life is not limited to the execution of a block.

156   You tell Java about class variables in much the same way that you tell Java about local variables, but there are two important differences. First, you declare the class variables inside the body of the class definition, but not inside the body of any method definition. Second, you mark class-variable declarations with the `static` keyword, to distinguish them from instance variables, which you learn about in Section 9.

The following, for example, declares wScript, a public class variable meant to capture a weight:

```
public class Movie {
 public static int wScript;
```

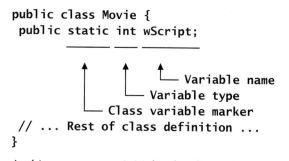

```
 // ... Rest of class definition ...
}
```

And just as you can initialize local variables, you also can initialize class variables:

```
public class Movie {
 // Define class variables:
 public static int wScript = 6;
 ...
}
```
            └── Initial value

157 You can combine several class-variable declarations, as is done in the following example. There, several class variables are declared and initialized for use instead of literal numbers in the movieRating method:

```
public class Movie {
 // Define class variables:
 public static int wScript = 6, wActing = 13, wDirecting = 11;
 // Define movieRating:
 public static int movieRating (int s, int a, int d) {
  return wScript * s + wActing * a + wDirecting * d;
 }
}
```

In the example, variable names provide access to the class-variable values, because the variables and the method in which they appear are defined in the same class.

158 To access a public class variable that is defined in a class different from that of the method that uses that variable, you must use the class name, the field-selection operator, and the variable name, just as you would to access a class method in a different class. For example, to access the value of the wScript variable in the Demonstrate class, you write the following expression:

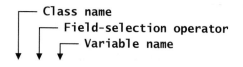

```
Movie.wScript
```

159 With the `Movie` class and `movieRating` method defined as in Segment 157, you produce the following result with the `Demonstrate` program:

```
public class Demonstrate {
 public static void main (String argv[]) {
   int script = 6, acting = 9, directing = 8;
   System.out.print("The rating of the movie is ");
   System.out.println(Movie.movieRating(script, acting, directing));
 }
}
```
——————————— Result ———————————
```
The rating of the movie is 241
```

160 The values of public class variables defined in public classes are available everywhere, except in places in which there is a parameter or local variable that happens to have the same name. Such parameters or local variables are said to **shadow**, or to **override**, the corresponding class variables.

In places where a public class variable value is not shadowed, you can change its value using an assignment statement. For example, if you want to change the value of the class variable that serves as a weight for script ratings, you can write the following assignment statement:

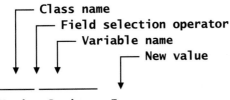

```
Movie.wScript = 7
```

The change affects all subsequent evaluations of the class variable.

161 If you intend never to change a class variable, such as `wScript`, you should inform Java that no change will be made by including the keyword `final` in the variable declaration. The `final` keyword indicates that the variable is not variable at all; once that variable is initialized, the value never changes, so such a variable is really a **constant**:

```
      ┌── The variables are all constants
      ↓
public static final int wScript = 6, wActing = 13, wDirecting = 11;
```

Constants also are called **final variables**. Note that they must be initialized, because no value can be assigned later.

162 In general, a **declaration** is a program element that provides a compiler with essential information or useful advice. For example, when you introduce a local variable or parameter, you are said to *declare* it, because you tell the compiler its type. On the other hand, no

memory is set aside for local variables or parameters at compile time, because neither local variables nor parameters exist until the method is called.

In contrast, a **definition** causes a compiler to set aside memory at compile time. For example, when you introduce a class variable, you both *declare* and *define* the variable, because you inform the compiler about the variable's type and you cause the compiler to set aside memory for the variable at compile time.

Generally, when a variable is both declared and defined, you say, as a sort of shorthand, that it is defined; otherwise, it is declared.

163 Public class variables defined in public classes can be evaluated and assigned at any point in a program, so public class variables are said to have **universal scope**.

The memory set aside for a class variable is never reallocated, so class variables are said to have **static extent**; that explains why `static` is the keyword used to mark class variables.

164 Class variables provide you with a way to collect together the values, such as weights, that determine a program's behavior. Such collection makes those elements easy to find, and thus makes your program easy to understand.

165
SIDE TRIP Java's class variables take the place of the **global variables** used in other languages. Class variables are much like global variables, except that each class variable is associated with a class.

166
SIDE TRIP Java offers two useful built-in final class variables for the `Math` class. The following illustrates:

```
public class Demonstrate {
 // First, define displayMovieRating with integers:
 public static void main (String argv[]) {
  System.out.println("Value of pi: " + Math.PI);
  System.out.println("Value of e:  " + Math.E);
 }
}
```
———————————————————— Result ————————————————————
```
Value of pi: 3.14159
Value of e:  2.71828
```

167
PRACTICE Amend the temperature-conversion method that you were asked to write in Segment 151 such that, each time that it is called, it reports the number of times that it has been called.

168
HIGHLIGHTS
- If you need a variable with a value that is accessible everywhere, **then** define a public class variable by instantiating the following pattern:

  `public static int variable name ;`

- **If** you want a variable to be a constant, **then** add the keyword `final` to the variable declaration, **and** be sure to initialize the variable in the declaration statement.

9 HOW TO CREATE CLASS INSTANCES

169   To remember the characteristics of a particular movie, you think naturally in terms of the quality of the script, the acting, and the directing. To describe the characteristics of a particular symphony, you think naturally in terms of the quality of the music, the performers, and the conductor.

If you express quality in terms of numbers, then the numbers that describe a particular movie or symphony constitute a natural bundle—a bundle of three numbers for each individual that belongs to the movie category, or of three for each that belongs to the symphony category.

In this section, you learn that one of Java's great virtues is that Java offers you the means to describe, construct, and manipulate bundles of descriptive data items that mirror real-world individuals and categories. These special mechanisms help to distinguish object-oriented programming from traditional programming.

170   Once you have defined a class, you can create any number of **class instances** that belong to that class, each of which corresponds to an individual that belongs to the corresponding category.

When you define the Movie class, for example, you indicate that all movies are associated with numbers that express the quality of the script, the acting, and the directing. Then, you can construct movie instances with particular numbers for the script, the acting, and the directing. Thus, the employment of classes enables you to create information bundles in your programs that describe naturally occurring individuals.

171   The variables that appear in particular class instances are called **instance variables**, as distinguished from **class variables**. There are as many sets of instance variables as there are class instances belonging to a class; there is just one set of class variables for an entire class.

Thus, in the following diagram, the Movie class definition contains descriptions of instance variables, whereas the descriptions of particular Movie instances contain instance-variable values.

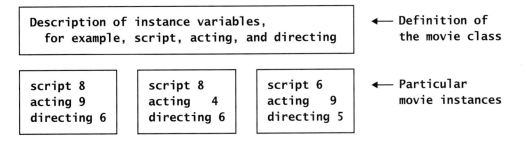

172   With the introduction of instance variables, you now know of three elements that can appear in class definitions:

A class definition

```
┌─────────────────────────┐
│                         │
│  Class methods          │
│                         │
│  Class variables        │
│                         │
│  Instance variables     │
│                         │
│       .                 │
│       .                 │
│       .                 │
│                         │
└─────────────────────────┘
```

173   In this book, you often see a `Movie` instance referred to as a movie. In general, you may refer to a class instance by the name of the class, set in all lowercase letters, as long as the context makes the meaning clear.

174   The following is a Java definition of the `Movie` class in which instance variables are declared; evidently, the chunks of memory that describe movies hold values for three integers: script, acting, and directing:

```
public class Movie {
  // First, define instance variables:
  public int script, acting, directing;
  // ... Remainder of class definition goes here ...
}
```

This definition indicates, via the absence of the `static` keyword, that the variables are instance variables, rather than class variables.

Furthermore, the definition of the `Movie` class indicates, via the `public` keyword, that all the instance variables describing a `Movie` instance will be available, and changeable, from anywhere in your program. You learn about other kinds of instance variables in Section 34.

175   In Segment 162, you learned that a **declaration** is a program element that provides a compiler with information or advice, whereas a definition causes the compiler to allocate storage. Class definitions in which only instance variables appear may not cause storage to be allocated. Accordingly, purists prefer to use the phrase **class declaration** unless storage actually is allocated. Nevertheless, the declaration–definition distinction tends to be blurred when programmers talk about classes, and the phrase **class definition** tends to be used whether or not storage is allocated.

176   In other programming languages, instance variables are called **member variables, fields,** or **slots.** The virtue of terms such as *slot* is that they encourage you to think of class definitions as patterns and of class instances as filled-in patterns. Bowing to convention, however, this book uses the term *instance variable* throughout.

177   Once the `Movie` class is defined, you can introduce a variable with `Movie` as the variable's data type:

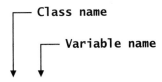

```
Movie m;
```

The syntax is the same as that that you use when you introduce a variable with, say, `int` or `double` as the data type.

178   To create a `Movie` instance, you deploy the `new` keyword, with the class name and a pair of parentheses, as shown in the following expression:

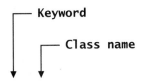

```
new Movie()
```

You will learn why you need the parentheses in Segment 217; for now, just accept the parentheses as ritual to be understood later.

179   Just as you can combine variable declaration and initialization for a variable that has integral or floating-point type, you also can combine declaration of and initialization for a variable with a class as its type:

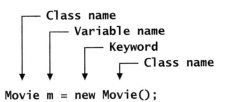

```
Movie m = new Movie();
```

180   Once you have created a variable and have assigned an instance of the `Movie` class to it, you can refer to the instance's `script`, `acting`, and `directing` instance variables. To refer to an instance variable, you join the name of the `Movie` variable, via the field-selection operator, to the name of the instance variable in which you are interested. Thus, `m.script` produces the value of the `script` instance variable of the `Movie` instance assigned to the variable named `m`.

Once you know how to refer to a `Movie` instance's instance variables, you are free to assign values to those instance variables, as well as to retrieve previously assigned values:

```
m.script       ← Retrieve a value from the script instance variable
m.script = 3 ← Assign a new value to the script instance variable
```

181   In the following definition of the Movie class, three instance variables appear, along with the movieRating class method:

```
public class Movie {
 public int script, acting, directing;
 public static int movieRating (int s, int a, int d) {
  return s + a + d;
 }
}
```

182   In the following definition of the Demonstrate class, Movie instance is created, values are assigned to the instance variables, and the Movie instance's rating is computed by a class method named movieRating. The field-selection operator appears frequently:

```
public class Demonstrate {
 public static void main (String argv[]) {
  Movie m = new Movie();
  m.script = 8; m.acting = 9; m.directing = 6;
  System.out.print("The rating of the movie is ");
  System.out.println(
   Movie.movieRating(m.script, m.acting, m.directing)
  );
 }
}
```

183   Instead of handing three integer arguments to movieRating, you can write a rating method that takes just one argument, which you declare to be a Movie instance. Of course, you need to change the body: instead of s, a, and d parameters, the body must refer to the Movie instance's script, acting, and directing instance variables.

```
public class Movie {
 public int script, acting, directing;
 public static int rating (Movie m) {
  return m.script + m.acting + m.directing;
 }
}
```

Because the method defined in this segment works only on those arguments that are movies, there is no need to call the method movieRating—the method cannot be called on any argument that is not a movie.

184   With rating defined to operate on Movie instances—instead of on script, acting, and directing values—you can rewrite the program in Segment 182 as follows:

```
public class Demonstrate {
 public static void main (String argv[]) {
   Movie m = new Movie();
   m.script = 8; m.acting = 9; m.directing = 6;
   System.out.print("The rating of the movie is ");
   System.out.println(Movie.rating(m));
 }
}
```

185   The **arithmetic** types are like atoms in ordinary chemistry: you cannot take apart particular integral and floating-point values. Accordingly, those data types are said to be **primitive types**. The primitive types also include the boolean type, which you learn about in Section 20, and the character type, which you learn about in Section 30.

In contrast to primitive types, **class** instances, which you learned about in this section, and **array** instances, which you learn about in Section 27, are like molecules in ordinary chemistry: you can take apart particular instances. Those data types are called **reference types**.

186   The **standard default value** of a reference variable is null—a value that indicates that there is no class instance assigned to the variable.

187   The Movie and Demonstrate classes are not the first classes that you have encountered in this book. You have, for example, encountered many strings. Each string is actually an instance of the String class. By the convention mentioned in Segment 173, a String instance is also known, simply, as a **string**.

188   If a variable or parameter is of primitive type, then you can think of it as a label for a chunk of memory that holds a value.

Memory allocated for primitive-type variable

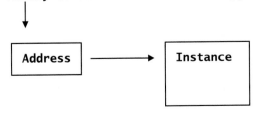

If, however, a variable or parameter is of reference type, then you can think of it as a label for a chunk of memory that holds the memory address for a chunk of memory that holds an instance.

Memory allocated for reference-type variable

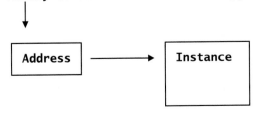

You do not need to know that Java handles reference-type arguments differently from primitive-type arguments, except to understand a nuance of the argument–parameter relationship described in the following segments.

189   In Section 8, you learned that Java is a **call-by-value** language: memory is allocated for each parameter when a method is called, so parameter reassignments inside a method are prevented from propagating outside the method.

When the argument is a reference type, rather than a primitive type, the memory allocated for the parameter holds a copy of the address of the argument, rather than a copy of the argument itself:

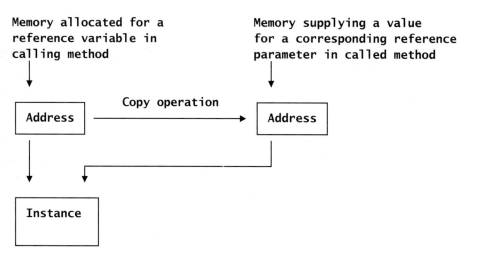

Because the address is copied, a parameter reassignment inside a method cannot propagate outside the method.

190   Now, suppose that you hand an instance to a method as an argument, and then, inside that method, you use the corresponding parameter to reassign an instance variable. Then, because the argument and the parameter share the same chunk of memory for the instance, and hence the instance variables, the change survives the method call.

191   You might wonder what happens to the memory that is allocated for an instance when that instance is no longer accessible. Such no-longer-accessible instances are created, for example, when variables are reassigned:

```
...
movie m;              ⟵ Declaration
...
m = new movie();      ⟵ Assignment
...
m = new movie();      ⟵ Reassignment; first instance abandoned
...
```

The answer is that Java has built-in mechanisms that find the memory allocated for abandoned instances. Inasmuch as those instances cannot enter into any further computations, Java returns the memory to the **free-storage list**, making that memory available to create new, useful instances.

The process of returning abandoned memory to the free-storage list is called **garbage collection**.

192
SIDE TRIP

192 Because Java has automatic garbage collection, there are no mechanisms for manual memory reclamation. Automatic garbage collection banishes the tedium of manual memory reclamation and eliminates the memory leaks that plague C++ programmers.

193 Devise a class, `boxCar`, for railroad box cars. Include instance variables for the height, width, and length of individual box cars.
PRACTICE

194 Devise a `volume` class method for the `boxCar` class.
PRACTICE

195

HIGHLIGHTS

- Java classes correspond to categories; Java instances correspond to individuals.

- Class definitions generally include instance variables, also known as member variables, slots, or fields.

- If you want to define a class with public instance variables, **then** instantiate the following pattern:

```
public class class name {
 public instance-variable type  instance-variable name ;
```

- If you want to declare a variable such that the value of the variable can be an instance, **then** instantiate the following pattern:

```
class name  variable name ;
```

- If you want to create a new instance, **and** you want to assign that new instance to a variable, **then** instantiate the following pattern:

```
variable name = new class name ();
```

- If you want to define a reference variable, initialized with an instance, **then** instantiate the following pattern:

```
class name  variable name = new class name ();
```

- If you wish to assign an instance-variable value, **then** instantiate the following pattern:

```
variable name . instance-variable name = expression ;
```

53

10 HOW TO DEFINE INSTANCE METHODS

196 In this section, you learn how you can define methods that are called to work on class instances in a special way: through the field-selection operator, rather than via the usual argument–parameter mechanism.

197 In the program in Segment 183, you saw the `rating` method defined as follows for `Movie` instances:

```
public static int rating (Movie m) {
  return m.script + m.acting + m.directing;
}
```

You can transform `rating` from a **class method** into an **instance method**. Each instance method has one special argument, called the **target**:

- The special argument's value is a class instance that belongs to the same class as does the instance method.

- The special argument does not appear in parentheses with other, ordinary arguments. Instead, the special argument is joined, via the field-selection operator, the dot, to the name of the member method, in a manner reminiscent of member-variable references.

For example, to call the `rating` instance method—the one that is a member of the `Movie` class—to work on a `Movie` instance named by a variable, `m`, you write the following:

```
m.rating()
```

Note that the `rating` member method, as defined in this segment, happens to have no ordinary arguments.

198 In instance methods, all references to instance variables refer to the particular instance variables that belong to the target instance.

Thus, you define `rating` as an instance method as follows:

```
public class Movie {
  public int script, acting, directing;
  public int rating () {
    return script + acting + directing;
  }
}
```

When this `rating` instance method is called on a particular `Movie` target, the `script`, `acting`, and `directing` variables that appear in the definition of `rating` automatically refer to the `script`, `acting`, and `directing` instance variables that are associated with that target:

```
public class Demonstrate {
 public static void main (String argv[]) {
  Movie m = new Movie();
  m.script = 8; m.acting = 9; m.directing = 6;
  System.out.println("The rating of the movie is " + m.rating());
 }
}
```
——————————————— Result ———————————————
The rating of the movie is 23

199 Note the contrast between the definition of a rating instance method and a rating class
method:

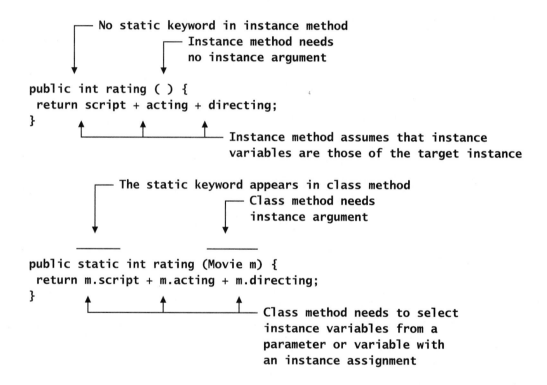

200 Also, note the difference in the way that instance methods and class methods are called:

┌─ Instance method has an instance target
│   ┌─ No need for an instance argument
│   │
↓   ↓

m.rating( )

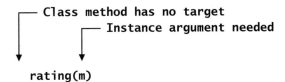

```
rating(m)
```

201 Now you can write the program with one version of rating defined as an instance method of the Movie class, as in Segment 198, and another version defined as an instance method of the Symphony class:

```
public class Symphony {
 public int music, playing, conducting;
 public int rating () {
   return music + playing + conducting;
 }
}
```

Java picks the right method on the basis of the target instance, as shown in the following example:

```
public class Demonstrate {
 public static void main (String argv[]) {
   Movie m = new Movie();
   m.script = 8; m.acting = 9; m.directing = 6;
   Symphony s = new Symphony();
   s.music = 7; s.playing = 8; s.conducting = 5;
   System.out.println("The rating of the movie is " + m.rating());
   System.out.println("The rating of the symphony is " + s.rating());
 }
}
```
——————————————— Result ———————————————
```
The rating of the movie is 23
The rating of the symphony is 20
```

202 Java does not copy the target instance when an instance method is called. Consequently, when you reassign an instance variable inside an instance method, you change the value of the instance variable in the target instance.

203 Instance methods can have ordinary arguments, in addition to the target instance. You might, for example, have an instance method named scaledRating that multiplies the rating of its target instance by a scale factor supplied as an ordinary argument:

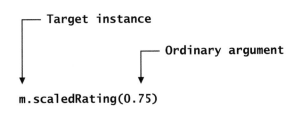

```
m.scaledRating(0.75)
```

The definition of a `scaledRating` instance method is similar to that of a `rating` instance method. The only difference is the addition of an ordinary parameter, `scaleFactor`:

```
public class Movie {
 // First, define instance variables:
 public int script, acting, directing;
 // Define rating:
 public int rating (double scaleFactor) {
   return (int)(scaleFactor * (script + acting + directing));
 }
}
```

The following shows the new version in action:

```
public class Demonstrate {
 // Define main:
 public static void main (String argv[]) {
  Movie m = new Movie();
  m.script = 8; m.acting = 9; m.directing = 6;
  System.out.println("The rating of the movie is " + m.rating(0.75));
 }
}
```
————————————————— Result —————————————————
```
The rating of the movie is 17
```

204 With the introduction of instance methods, you now know of all of the four elements that can appear in class definitions:

A class definition

```
Class methods

Class variables

Instance variables

Instance methods
```

205 Convert into an instance method the `volume` method for `boxCar` instances, which you
PRACTICE were asked to define in Segment 194.

- If you want to convert a class method with a class-instance parameter into an instance method, **then** delete the `static` keyword, **and then** eliminate the class-instance parameter from the parameter list and from the instance variable references.

- If you want to call an instance method, **then** use the field-selection operator to identify the target instance on which the method is to work:

  `target instance . instance method ( arguments )`

11 HOW TO DEFINE CONSTRUCTOR INSTANCE METHODS

207   In this section, you learn about constructor methods, which are special methods that are called when you create class instances.

208   In Section 9, you saw how to create an instance in one statement and to initialize that instance's instance variables in others. The following illustrates instance creation and initialization for a `Movie` variable, `m`:

```
Movie m = new Movie();
m.script = 8; m.acting = 9; m.directing = 6;
```

As the new `Movie` instance is created, zeros are assigned to all the arithmetic instance variables. Then, three statements reassign those instance variables.

209   Java allows you to initialize instance variables in the same way that you initialize local variables and class variables. For example, you could, pessimistically, arrange for the instance variables in every `Movie` instance to have an initial value of 3.

```
public class Movie {
  public int script = 3, acting = 3, directing = 3;
  public int rating () {
    return script + acting + directing;
  }
}
```

If you have not initialized an instance variable, that variable will have the **standard default value** prescribed for its type. The standard default value of a variable with arithmetic type is 0.

210   Java also allows you to define special methods, called **constructors**, which are called automatically whenever a new class instance is created. You can use such constructors to assign values to the instance variables in class instances, instead of supplying initializing values in variable-declaration statements.

211   In class definitions, constructor methods stand apart from other instance methods in two ways:

- Constructor-method names are the same as the name of the class.

- Constructor methods never return values; accordingly, no return type is ever specified.

To define a zero-parameter constructor for the `Movie` class, you would write the following:

```
            ┌─── No return type specified
            │ ┌─── Constructor name is the same as class name
            │ │
            ▼ ▼
public Movie() {
...
}
```

212   In the following program, the Movie class definition includes a constructor method that
      assigns the value 5 to all the instance variables in Movie instances; 5 is intended to represent
      typical ratings for an average movie.

```
public class Movie {
 public int script, acting, directing;
 public Movie() {
   script = 5; acting = 5; directing = 5;
 }
 public int rating () {
   return script + acting + directing;
 }
}
```

Using the new definition of the Movie class, the following main method does not need to
assign values to the instance variables:

```
public class Demonstrate {
 // Define main:
 public static void main (String argv[]) {
   Movie m = new Movie();
   System.out.println("The rating of the movie is " + m.rating());
 }
}
```
──────────────────── Result ────────────────────
```
The rating of the movie is 15
```
──

213   Now, suppose that you want to provide values for the script, acting, and directing in-
      stance variables when you create certain Movie instances. You should define a constructor
      with three parameters:

```
public class Movie {
 public int script, acting, directing;
 public Movie() {
   script = 5; acting = 5; directing = 5;
 }
```

```
public Movie(int s, int a, int d) {
  script = s; acting = a; directing = d;
}
public int rating () {
  return script + acting + directing;
}
}
```

Note that the constructor for three parameters, like the one for zero parameters, is named for the class in which it appears.

214   To tell Java to use the three-parameter constructor, blocking the involvement of the zero-parameter constructor, you modify the Movie creation statement:

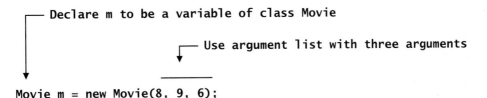

```
Movie m = new Movie(8, 9, 6);
```

The arguments dictate that initialization is to be done with the three-parameter constructor; it is *not* to be done with the zero-parameter constructor.

215   The following program uses both the zero-parameter constructor and the three-parameter constructor:

```
public class Demonstrate {
 // Define main:
 public static void main (String argv[]) {
  Movie m1 = new Movie();
  Movie m2 = new Movie(8, 9, 6);
   System.out.println("The first movie rating is " + m1.rating());
   System.out.println("The second movie rating is " + m2.rating());
 }
}
```
———————————————————— Result ————————————————————
```
The first movie rating is 15
The second movie rating is 23
```

216   If you do not define any constructors, Java defines a do-nothing **default constructor** for you. The default constructor is a **zero-parameter constructor**.

217   Now you can understand how the instance-creation expression shown in Segment 178 works, and why it has parentheses:

```
new Movie()
```

The parentheses, with no arguments, indicates that a zero-parameter constructor is to be called. In Segment 178, no constructors are defined, so the do-nothing default constructor, supplied by Java, is called.

218   All instance variables are initialized before any constructor is called. Thus, an initial value supplied by a constructor for an instance variable survives an initial value supplied in an instance-variable–definition statement.

219
SIDE TRIP   You must include a definition for your own zero-parameter constructor in a class definition under the following condition: you define a constructor with parameters *and* you create instances using a constructor with no arguments.

The rationale is as follows: if you have not defined a zero-parameter constructor, then the lack of arguments suggests that you have forgotten to include arguments for the parameter-bearing constructor that you have defined.

220
PRACTICE   Devise a zero-parameter constructor and a three-parameter constructor for the boxCar class that you were asked to design in Segment 193. The three-parameter constructor is to receive height, width, and length values. Assume reasonable default dimensions for the zero-parameter constructor.

221
HIGHLIGHTS

- Constructors perform computations, such as initial-instance variable assignment, that you want to occur when your program creates an instance.

- Each constructor is named for the class in which it is defined. No constructor returns a value.

- In the absence of any constructors defined by you, Java creates a default constructor, which has no parameters.

- If you want to define a zero-parameter constructor to displace the default constructor, **then** instantiate the following pattern:

```
public class name () {
  ...
}
```

- If you want to define a constructor with parameters, **then** instantiate the following pattern:

```
public class name (parameters) {
  ...
}
```

- When you create instances, the number of arguments that you supply, and their types, determine which constructor is called.

12 HOW TO DEFINE GETTER AND SETTER METHODS

222 In this section, you learn that getter and setter instance methods help you to work with instance-variable values.

223 You know that you can refer to an instance-variable value directly by using the field-selection operator. For example, suppose that you have defined the `Attraction` class with a `minutes` instance variable that records the length of an attraction in minutes. You can refer to the value of that instance variable in a particular attraction, x:

```
x.minutes
```

Alternatively, you can refer to an instance-variable value indirectly by defining an instance method that returns the instance-variable value. In the following `Attraction` class definition, for example, an instance method named `getMinutes` returns the value of the `minutes` instance variable:

```
public class Attraction {
  // First, define instance variable:
  public int minutes;
  // Define zero-parameter constructor:
  public Attraction () {minutes = 75;}
  // Define one-parameter constructor:
  public Attraction (int m) {minutes = m;}
  // Define getter:
  public int getMinutes () {
    return minutes;
  }
}
```

With `getMinutes` defined, you have another way to refer to the value of the `minutes` instance variable of a particular attraction, x:

```
x.getMinutes()
```

224 A **getter** is a method that extracts information from an instance. Getters are also called **readers**.

One reason that you may wish to use a getter, rather than referencing an instance variable directly, is that you can include additional computation in a getter. For example, if you are concerned about how often your program references the `minutes` instance variable, you can add a statement to the `getMinutes` getter that announces each reference:

```
public class Attraction {
  public int minutes;
  public Attraction () {minutes = 75;}
  public Attraction (int m) {minutes = m;}
  // Define getter:
  public int getMinutes () {
    System.out.println("Reading an attraction's minutes ...");
    return minutes;
  }
}
```

225 Analogously, you do not need to assign an instance-variable value directly. Instead, you can assign an instance-variable value indirectly by defining an instance method that does the actual value assigning. In the following Attraction class definition, for example, the addition of a definition for an instance method named setMinutes indicates that setMinutes assigns a value to the minutes instance variable:

```
public class Attraction {
  public int minutes;
  public Attraction () {minutes = 75;}
  public Attraction (int m) {minutes = m;}
  // Define getter:
  public int getMinutes () {
    return minutes;
  }
  // Define setter:
  public void setMinutes (int m) {
    minutes = m;
  }
}
```

With setMinutes defined, you have another way to assign a value to the minutes instance variable of a particular attraction, x:

```
x.setMinutes(4)
```

Because the only purpose of setMinutes is to assign a value to a instance variable, setMinutes is marked void, indicating that no value is to be returned. If you prefer, you can write setters that return the previous value or the new value.

226 A **setter** is a method that inserts information into an instance. Setters are also known as **writers** or **mutators**.

One reason that you may wish to use a setter, rather than writing into an instance variable directly, is that you can include additional computation in a setter. In Segment 224, you saw how to add a statement to the getMinutes getter that announces each reference. The following provides the same enhancement to the setMinutes setter:

```
public class Attraction {
 public int minutes;
 public Attraction () {minutes = 75;}
 public Attraction (int m) {minutes = m;}
 // Define getter:
 public int getMinutes () {
  return minutes;
 }
 // Define setter:
 public void setMinutes (int m) {
  System.out.println("Writing an attraction's minutes ...");
  minutes = m;
 }
}
```

227 Setters are especially valuable when you need to coordinate instance-variable changes with display changes. You learn about such coordination in Section 40.

228 You may also wish to use getters and setters to provide access to **imaginary instance variables** that exist only in the sense that their values can be computed from instance variables that do exist. For example, you can create getHours and setHours, which seem to refer to the contents of an imaginary hours instance variable, of type double, but which actually work with the contents of the minutes instance variable:

```
public class Attraction {
 public int minutes;
 public Attraction () {minutes = 75;}
 public Attraction (int m) {minutes = m;}
 // Define getters:
 public int getMinutes () {return minutes;}
 public double getHours () {
  return minutes / 60.0;
 }
 // Define setters:
 public void setMinutes (int m) {minutes = m;}
 public void setHours (double h) {
  minutes = (int)(h * 60);
 }
}
```

229 The names of the getMinutes, setMinutes, getHours, and setHours methods, with the get and set prefixes, makes it clear that the methods are getters and setters, but the use of get and set is a personal convention, rather than a Java convention.

230 Constructor methods are part of the Java language, whereas getter and setter methods are not. You should understand, however, that the use of getter and setter methods, as explained in this section, is recommended by many expert programmers, no matter what programming language you happen to use. You learn why in Section 13.

PRACTICE   Write getters and setters for the boxCar class that you were asked to design in Segment 193.

HIGHLIGHTS

- Getter and setter instance methods provide an indirect route to instance-variable reference and assignment.

- You can define getter and setter instance methods for imaginary instance variables.

- If you want to refer to an instance-variable value using a getter, **then** instantiate the following pattern:

  `instance . getter method ()`

- If you want to assign an instance-variable value using a setter, **then** instantiate the following pattern:

  `instance . setter method ( expression )`

13 HOW TO BENEFIT FROM DATA ABSTRACTION

233 You now know how to use constructor, getter, and setter methods. Moreover, you have seen how getters and setters make it easy to add computation at the point where information is read from or written into instances, and how getters and setters can be defined for imaginary instance variables. In this section, you learn how constructors, getters, and setters help you to practice data abstraction, thereby increasing your efficiency and making your programs easier to maintain.

234 Suppose that you develop a big program around an `Attraction` class definition that includes getters and setters for the `minutes` instance variable, as well as for an imaginary `hours` instance variable.

Next, suppose that you discover that your program refers to `hours` more often than to `minutes`. If speed is a great concern, you should arrange to store a number representing hours, rather than a number representing minutes, to reduce the number of multiplications and divisions performed.

If you work with the instance variables in attractions using constructors, getters, and setters only, you need to change only what happens in constructor, getter, and setter instance methods:

```
public class Attraction {
 // First, define instance variable:
 public double hours;
 // Define zero-parameter constructor:
 public Attraction () {hours = 1.25;}
 // Define one-parameter constructor, presumed to take minutes:
 public Attraction (double m) {hours = m / 60.0;}
 // Define getters:
 public int getMinutes () {
   return (int)(hours * 60);}
 public double getHours () {
   return hours;
 }
 // Define setters:
 public void setMinutes (int m) {
   hours = m / 60.0;
 }
 public void setHours (double h) {
   hours = h;
 }
}
```

235 Suppose, for example, that your program contains statements that read the minutes or hours of a particular attraction, x. If you work with getters, you need to make no change

to that statement to accommodate the switch from a minutes-based class definition to an hours-based class definition:

```
··· x.getMinutes() ···  ⟶  ··· x.getMinutes() ···
··· x.getHours() ···    ⟶  ··· x.getHours() ···
```

On the other hand, if you do not work with the instance variables in attractions using constructors, getters, and setters only, you have to go through your entire program, modifying myriad statements:

```
··· x.minutes ···           ⟶  ··· (int)(x.hours * 60) ···
··· (x.minutes / 60.0) ···  ⟶  ··· x.hours ···
```

Thus, constructors, getters, and setters isolate you from the effects of your efficiency-motivated switch from a minutes-based class definition to an hours-based class definition.

236 In general, constructors, getters, and setters isolate you from the details of how a class is implemented. Once you have written those instance methods, you can forget about how they refer to and assign values; none of the details, such as whether you have a minutes or an hours instance variable, clutter the programs that use attractions.

237 Collectively, constructors, getters, and setters sometimes are called **access methods**. When you move representation detail into a set of access methods, you are said to be practicing **data abstraction**, and you are said to be hiding the details of how data are represented behind a **data-abstraction barrier**.

Good programmers carefully design into their programs appropriate access methods so as to create data-abstraction barriers.

238 Because the virtues of data abstraction parallel those of procedure abstraction, the following discussion of the virtues of data abstraction is much like the previous discussion, in Section 7, of the virtues of procedure abstraction.

The key virtue of data abstraction is that *you make it easy to reuse your work*. You can develop a library of class definitions, and can transfer the entire library to another programmer with little difficulty.

239 A second virtue of data abstraction is that *you push details out of sight and out of mind*, making your methods easy to read and enabling you to concentrate on high-level steps.

240 A third virtue of data abstraction is that *you can easily augment what a class provides*. You can, for example, add information-displaying statements to your getters and setters, as you saw in Section 12.

241 A fourth virtue of data abstraction is that *you can easily improve the way that data are stored*. In this section, you have seen an example in which there is an efficiency-motivated switch from a minutes-based class definition to an hours-based class definition.

242   Most good programmers provide getters and setters for some instance variables, but not for others. The choice is a matter of taste and style. Until you have developed your own taste and style, you should rely on the following heuristic:

- Whenever the detailed implementation of a class may change, provide instance-variable getters and setters to insulate your class-using methods from the potential change.

243   Revise the getters and setters that you defined in Segment 231 for the boxCar class, such
PRACTICE that they display messages when used.

244   Revise the getters and setters for the boxCar class such that class variables are incremented
PRACTICE when corresponding instance methods are called.

245

HIGHLIGHTS

- Constructors, getters, and setters are called access methods. When you move instance-variable evaluations and assignments into access methods, you are practicing data abstraction.

- Data abstraction has many virtues, including the following:

  - Your programs become easier to reuse.

  - Your programs become easier to read.

  - You can easily augment what a class provides.

  - You can easily improve the way that data are stored.

- If you anticipate that the detailed definition of a class may change, then you should provide access methods for the instance variables to isolate the effects of the potential changes.

14 HOW TO PROTECT INSTANCE VARIABLES FROM HARMFUL ACCESS

246   In Section 13, you learned that constructor, getter, and setter instance methods help you to benefit from data abstraction. In this section, you learn how to ensure that all instance-variable evaluations assignments are channeled through such instance methods.

247   The benefits of data abstraction derived from access methods disappear if you or an associate writes methods that include direct instance-variable evaluations or assignments.

If, for example, you decide to switch from a `minutes`-based definition to an `hours`-based definition, then Java no longer can compile any expression that attempts to access the `minutes` instance variable directly. On the other hand, if you prevent direct access to the `minutes` instance variable, no one can accidentally come to rely on expressions that include such access.

248   You prevent direct instance-variable access by marking instance variables with the `private` keyword.

You can, for example, redefine the `Attraction` class as follows, with `minutes` marked with the `private` keyword, rather than with the `public` keyword:

```
public class Attraction {
 // First, define instance variable:
 private int minutes;
 // Define zero-parameter constructor:
 public Attraction () {minutes = 75;}
 // Define one-parameter constructor:
 public Attraction (int d) {minutes = d;}
 // Define getter:
 public int getMinutes () {return minutes;}
 // Define setter:
 public void setMinutes (int d) {minutes = d;}
}
```

With the `Attraction` class so redefined, attempts to access an attraction's instance-variable values from outside the `Attraction` class, via the field-selection operator, fail to compile:

```
x.minutes        ←— Evaluation fails to compile;
                    the minutes instance variable is private
x.minutes = 6  ←— Assignment fails to compile;
                    the minutes instance variable is private
```

249   Note, however, that all instance methods in the `Attraction` class have access to instance variables declared in the private portion of the `Attraction` class definition. Thus, attempts to access an attraction's instance-variable values from outside the `Attraction` class, via public instance methods, are successful:

```
x.getMinutes()      ←── Evaluation compiles;
                        getMinutes is a public method
x.setMinutes(6)     ←── Assignment compiles;
                        setMinutes is a public method
```

250 The public instance variables, with the public instance methods, are said to constitute the class's **public interface**. Once you have marked the `minutes` instance variable `private`, instead of `public`, the only way to get at that `minutes` instance variable from methods defined outside the `Attraction` class is via `Attraction`'s public interface.

251 You can also mark instance methods with the `private` keyword. Thus, instance methods are not necessarily part of the public interface, just as instance variables are not necessarily part of the public interface.

252 Most programmers put the public instance variables and methods first, on the aesthetic ground that what is *public* should be up front and open to view, whereas what is *private* should not be so up front and not so open to view.

253 Data abstraction and the notion of a public interface fit together as follows:

- Channeling instance-variable evaluations and assignments through access methods isolates you from the details of class implementation.

- When you define private instance variables, you force all instance-variable evaluations and assignments to go through the constructors, getters, setters, and other instance methods in the public interface, thus providing a means to ensure that you practice data abstraction.

254 Revise the `boxCar` class that you were asked to define in Segment 231 such that the instance
PRACTICE variables are protected from access, except via getters and setters.

255

HIGHLIGHTS

- Inadvertent instance-variable evaluations and assignments via the field-selection operator can destroy your attempts to practice data abstraction.

- You can prevent inadvertent direct access to instance variables by making such instance variables private.

- Instance methods in general, and constructors, getters, and setters in particular, have complete access to all instance variables declared in the same class.

- The public instance variables and instance methods constitute the class's public interface.

- The public–private dichotomy helps to ensure that you can benefit from data abstraction.

15 HOW TO DEFINE CLASSES THAT INHERIT INSTANCE VARIABLES AND METHODS

256 In this section, you learn that you can tie together classes in hierarchies such that the instance variables declared in one class automatically appear in instances belonging to another. Thus, you learn about the notion of inheritance. Object-oriented programming languages provide for classes, instances, and inheritance, whereas traditional programming languages do not.

257 So far, you have learned how you can define classes for two entertainment types: movies and symphonies. Now, suppose that you want to add information that is common to all entertainment types.

One way to proceed is to start with the classes that you have already defined for movies and symphonies, adding whatever information you need.

You would then have a movie class containing `script`, `acting`, `directing`, and `minutes` instance variables, a `rating` instance method, and a collection of constructors, getters, and setters. You would also have a symphony class containing `music`, `playing`, `conducting`, and `minutes` instance variables, a `rating` instance method, and a collection of constructors, getters, and setters.

The problem with this way of defining movies and symphonies is that the `minutes` instance variable and the `getMinutes` and `setMinutes` instance methods found in the `Movie` and `Symphony` class definitions would be exact duplicates.

258 Maintaining multiple copies of instance variables and instance methods makes software development and maintenance difficult as you try to correct bugs, add features, improve performance, and change behavior. Adding multiple programmers and multiple years to the mix turns mere difficulty into certain failure.

Of course, with just two new instance variables about which to worry, you could cope. In a more complex example, every kind of entertainment—from football to opera—would have a `minutes` instance variable, as well as a variety of other instance variables.

259 Fortunately, Java encourages you to cut down on duplication, thereby easing program developing, debugging, and maintenance, by allowing you to arrange class definitions in hierarchies that reflect natural category hierarchies.

Using Java, you can say, for example, that movies and symphonies are attractions. Then, you can declare a `minutes` instance variable in the `Attraction` class alone, because the `minutes` instance variable will appear in each `Movie` instance and `Symphony` instance, as though `minutes` had been declared in each.

Also, you can define a `getMinutes` and a `setMinutes` instance method in the `Attraction` class alone, because those instance methods will work with every `Movie` instance and `Symphony` instance, as though those methods had been defined in both the `Movie` class and the `Symphony` class.

260 Whenever an instance variable or instance method is made available because of a subclass–superclass relationship, it is said to be **inherited**.

261 In addition to reducing duplication, there are other reasons for exploiting inheritance.

- You may already have defined a fully debugged `Attraction` class. To prevent the gratuitous introduction of bugs, you would want to use that class definition as it stands, rather than, say, copying bits of the `Attraction` class definition into the `Movie` and `Symphony` class definitions.

- You may have decided to purchase code for the `Attraction` class from a vendor, because you anticipate using the elaborate capabilities advertised by that vendor. Because the vendor supplies you with compiled code only, you cannot access the source code, so you cannot copy bits of the vendor's `Attraction` class definition into your `Movie` and `Symphony` class definitions. You can only define new classes that inherit from your purchased classes.

262 Usually, it is a good idea to draw a **class-hierarchy diagram**, such as the following, to see how your classes fit together:

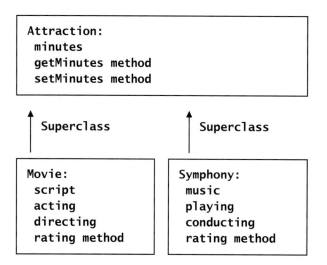

Such a class-hierarchy diagram helps you to see how to distribute instance variables and instance methods among the classes in the hierarchy.

263 Instances inherit instance variables from the class to which they belong, and from all that class's superclasses. Each `Movie` instance, for example, has its own copy of every instance variable declared in the `Movie` and `Attraction` classes.

Similarly, class instances inherit instance methods from the class to which they belong, and from all that class's superclasses. You can, for example, work on a `Movie` instance not only with instance methods defined in the `Movie` class, but also with those defined in the `Attraction` class.

264 As a general rule, you should place instance variables and instance methods in classes such that two criteria are satisfied:

- There is no needless duplication of an instance variable or instance method.

- Each instance variable and instance method is useful in all the subclasses of the class in which the instance variable or instance method is defined.

For example, the minutes instance variable is in the Attraction class, because it is useful for all Attraction subclasses.

On the other hand, there are two rating instance methods, because the way that you compute the rating of a Movie instance is different from the way that you compute the rating of a Symphony instance. There is duplication, because there are two rating methods, but there is no needless duplication.

265 Once you have decided in which classes instance variables and instance methods should be declared and defined, you can proceed to define the classes, and to link them up in a class hierarchy.

You have already seen various definitions of the Attraction class in Section 12. The following version contains the minutes instance variable, a zero-parameter constructor with a statement that announces its use, and a getter and setter for the minutes instance variable:

```
public class Attraction {
  // Define instance variable:
  public int minutes;
  // Define zero-parameter constructor:
  public Attraction () {
    System.out.println("Calling zero-parameter Attraction constructor");
    minutes = 75;
  }
  // Define getter:
  public int getMinutes () {return minutes;}
  // Define setter:
  public void setMinutes (int d) {minutes = d;}
}
```

266 To specify a class's superclass, you insert the keyword extends, and the name of the superclass, just after the name of the class in the class's definition.

For example, as you define the Movie class and the Symphony class, you specify that Attraction is the superclass by inserting the keyword extends, followed by Attraction, just after the class name:

```
public class Movie extends Attraction {
 // Define instance variables:
 public int script, acting, directing;
 // Define zero-parameter constructor:
 public Movie () {
  System.out.println("Calling zero-parameter Movie constructor");
  script = 5; acting = 5; directing = 5;
 }
 // Define three-parameter constructor:
 public Movie (int s, int a, int d) {
  script = s; acting = a; directing = d;
 }
 // Define rating:
 public int rating () {
  return script + acting + directing;
 }
}

public class Symphony extends Attraction {
 // Define instance variables:
 public int music, playing, conducting;
 // Define zero-parameter constructor:
 public Symphony () {
  System.out.println("Calling zero-parameter Symphony constructor");
  music = 5; playing = 5; conducting = 5;
 }
 // Define three-parameter constructor:
 public Symphony (int m, int p, int c) {
  music = m; playing = p; conducting = c;
 }
 // Define rating:
 public int rating () {
  return music + playing + conducting;
 }
}
```

267 Because the Movie class is directly under the Attraction class in the class hierarchy, with no other class in between, the Movie class is said to be the **direct subclass**, relative to the Attraction class, and the Attraction class is said to be the **direct superclass**, relative to the Movie class.

268 Because no direct superclass is specified for the Attraction class, the direct superclass of the Attraction class is taken to be the Object class—a class supplied by Java. Every class is a subclass of Object, but it is not necessarily a direct subclass.

269 You can, if you like, specify explicitly that a class is a direct subclass of the Object class. For example, you can define the Attraction class in either of two equivalent ways:

```
public class Attraction {
  ...
}

public class Attraction extends Object {
  ...
}
```

270   So that the class definitions stay focused on the construction of a class hierarchy, none of the classes defined in this section include private instance variables or private instance methods. Instead, all instance variables and instance methods are in the public interfaces. You could, of course, redefine the classes such that they have private instance variables or instance methods, adding appropriate getters and setters to the public interfaces.

271   In general, the first step taken by any constructor in any class, other than the Object class, is to call the zero-parameter constructor in the direct superclass.

Thus, when you create an instance, all the zero-parameter constructors in the instance's class and its superclasses are called automatically, and each has the opportunity to contribute to the values of the instance variables associated with the new instance.

In Section 18, you learn how to arrange for a constructor to call a constructor other than the zero-parameter constructor.

272   In the following example, print statements in the zero-parameter constructors defined in Segment 265 and Segment 266 tell you when those zero-parameter constructors are executed:

```
public class Demonstrate {
 public static void main (String argv[]) {
  Movie m = new Movie();
  Symphony s = new Symphony();
 }
}
```
———————————————— Result ————————————————
```
Calling zero-parameter Attraction constructor
Calling zero-parameter Movie constructor
Calling zero-parameter Attraction constructor
Calling zero-parameter Symphony constructor
```

273   In Segment 119, you saw that you could define a completely independent JamesBondMovie class. Now, you can see that you can define a JamesBondMovie class that extends the Movie class. Once you have defined such a JamesBondMovie class, you can adjust for your particular attitude toward James Bond movies by defining a special rating method for the JamesBondMovie class:

```
public class JamesBondMovie extends Movie {
 // Define rating:
 public int rating () {
   return 10 + acting + directing;
 }
}
```

274 The following shows how instance variables and the `rating` instance method are distributed for movies.

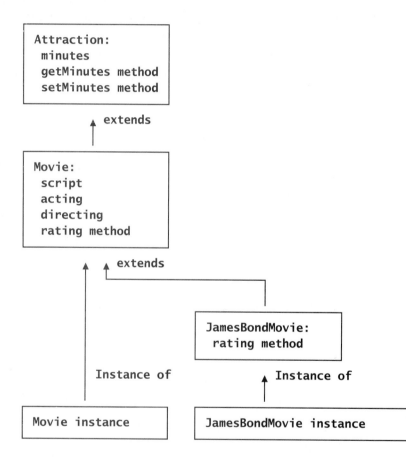

275 To decide which `rating` instance method to use on, say, a `Movie` instance, the Java compiler searches up from the `Movie` instance, through the subclass–superclass chain, to find the first instance method named `rating`. For the `Movie` instance example, the only `rating` instance method that the Java compiler finds is the one in the `Movie` class.

On the other hand, the `rating` instance method selected by the Java compiler to work on `JamesBondMovie` instances is the one in the `JamesBondMovie` class, and the `rating` instance method in the `Movie` class is said to be **shadowed** or **overridden** by that lower-level instance method.

276 Note the distinction between **overloading** and **shadowing** or **overriding**.

- **Overloading** occurs when Java can distinguish two procedures with the same name by examining the number or types of their parameters.

- **Shadowing** or **overriding** occurs when two procedures with the same name, the same number of parameters, and the same parameter types are defined in different classes, one of which is a superclass of the other.

277 *Shadowing* and *overriding* are synonyms. *Shadowing* is used in this book, rather than *overriding*, because similar-sounding terms, such as *overloading* and *overriding*, are easily confused.

278 The `Attraction` class must be defined before you define the `Movie` and `Symphony` classes. You cannot define a direct subclass class until its direct superclass has been defined.

279 The syntax of class definition allows you to specify only one superclass for any class. Accordingly, Java is said to exhibit **single inheritance**.

280
SIDE TRIP Unlike Java, C++ allows **multiple inheritance, absence of.** Because multiple inheritance creates all sorts of complexities, without proportionate benefits, the designers of Java decided to limit Java to single inheritance.

281
PRACTICE Create a class, `tankCar`, for tank cars, patterned on the `boxCar` class that you were asked to define in Segment 254. Include instance variables for the length and radius of each car. Include a `volume` instance method that makes use of the instance variables in the `tankCar` class.

282
PRACTICE Define a `railroadCar` class. Include instance variables for the weight and year of manufacture. Then, redefine the `boxCar` and `tankCar` classes to make them extensions of the `railroadCar` class.

283
HIGHLIGHTS
- Class hierarchies reflect subclass–superclass relations among classes.

- You have several reasons to arrange classes in hierarchies:

  - To parallel natural categories

  - To prevent avoidable duplication and to simplify maintenance

  - To avoid introducing bugs into previously debugged code

  - To use purchased code

- When a subclass–superclass relation is direct, with no intervening classes, the subclass is called the direct subclass, and the superclass is called the direct superclass.

- A class inherits instance variables and instance methods from all its superclasses.

- When a subclass–superclass chain contains multiple instance methods with the same name, argument number, and argument types, the one closest to the target instance in the subclass–superclass chain is the one executed. All others are shadowed.

- **If** you want to create a class hierarchy, **then** draw a diagram that reflects natural categories. Populate the classes in that class hierarchy with instance variables and instance methods such that there is no needless duplication of an instance variable or instance method, and such that each instance variable and instance method is useful in every subclass.

- **If** you want to create a direct-subclass–direct-superclass relation, **then** instantiate the following pattern:

```
public class subclass name extends superclass name {
  ...
}
```

16 HOW TO DEFINE ABSTRACT CLASSES AND ABSTRACT METHODS

284 In this section, you learn how to tell Java that you will never create instances of particular classes, or that you will never call certain methods.

285 Suppose that you intend to create instances of the Movie class and the Symphony class, but that you never intend to create instances of the Attraction class. The only purpose of the Attraction class is to hold an instance variable and associated getter and setter in a place where that instance variable, getter, and setter can be shared by both the Movie class and the Symphony class.

Further suppose that you wish to go beyond intention to ensure that you never can create instances of the Attraction class. To prevent such instance creation, you mark the class definition with the abstract keyword, making the Attraction class an **abstract class**:

```
public abstract class Attraction {
 public int minutes;
 public Attraction () {minutes = 75;}
 public int getMinutes () {return minutes;}
 public void setMinutes (int d) {minutes = d;}
}
```

286 Once you have told Java that a class is abstract, any attempt to create an instance of that class produces a complaint:

```
    ┌─ Attempt to create an instance of an abstract class
    │  fails to compile
    │
    ▼
   ─────────────

new Attraction()
```

287 You can, however, declare an Attraction variable:

```
...
Attraction x;
...
```

The value of such a variable can be either a Movie instance or a Symphony instance, because the value of a variable declared for a particular class can be an instance of any subclass:

```
...
x = new Movie();
...
x = new Symphony();
...
```

288 At some point, you might decide to have a program compute, say, the rating of a `Movie` instance or a `Symphony` instance assigned to an `Attraction` variable. You will run into trouble, however, when you try to work with an expression that computes the rating of such a variable:

```
...
Attraction x;
...
x = new Movie();
...
x.rating();              ←─ BUG!
```

The problem is that you have not defined a `rating` method for the `Attraction` class. To be sure, your program may be written such that the `Attraction` variable may never have a value that is an `Attraction` instance. Nevertheless, Java is not smart enough to conclude that no definition of the `rating` method for the `Attraction` class will be needed; accordingly, Java requires you to define such a method.

289 You could, in principle, define a `rating` method in the `Attraction` class as follows. The method is an instance method, it has the correct return type, has the correct number of arguments, and has an obligatory return statement that returns a value of the correct type:

```
public int rating () {return 0;}        ←─ BAD!
```

The method shown does nothing but return 0, but it could return anything: the method is never actually used because it is always shadowed by the rating method in the `Movie` class or the `Symphony` class.

290 Fortunately, Java allows you to define `rating` to be an **abstract method** in the `Attraction` class. When you mark a method with the `abstract` keyword, you tell Java that the method will always be shadowed by methods in subclasses. Such methods have a semicolon in the place where you normally would expect a body:

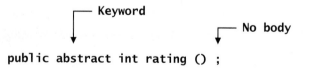

```
public abstract int rating () ;
```

291 With the abstract definition of `rating` installed, the `Attraction` class is defined as follows:

```
public abstract class Attraction {
 public int minutes;
 public Attraction () {minutes = 75;}
 public int getMinutes () {return minutes;}
 public void setMinutes (int d) {minutes = d;}
 public abstract int rating () ;
}
```

292   Note that you can define abstract methods only in abstract classes. The rationale is that, if a class is not abstract, you can create instances of that class, and you should be able to call any instance method of the class on those instances.

293   Once you have defined an abstract method, Java forces you to define corresponding non-abstract methods in certain subclasses of the abstract class in which the abstract method appears. Specifically, you must define nonabstract methods such that Java succeeds in finding a nonabstract method whenever the target is an instance of a subclass of the abstract class.

For example, both the Movie class and the Symphony class must have `rating` methods. On the other hand, if the Movie class were to have subclasses, no `rating` method would be required in those subclasses, because they would inherit the nonabstract `rating` method from the Movie class.

294   With the abstract `rating` method installed in the abstract Attraction class, you can use the `rating` method with an Attraction variable that has a value that is a Movie instance or Symphony instance:

```
public class Demonstrate {
 public static void main (String argv[]) {
   // Movie instance assigned to x:
   Attraction x = new Movie (5, 7, 7);
   System.out.println("The movie's rating is " + x.rating());
   // Symphony instance assigned to x:
   x = new Symphony (7, 5, 5);
   System.out.println("The symphony's rating is " + x.rating());
 }
}
```
———————————————— Result ————————————————
```
The movie's rating is 19
The symphony's rating is 17
```

295   You can mark a class with the `final` keyword, making that class a **final class**. Such classes cannot be extended. Thus, abstract classes can have no instances, and final classes can have no subclasses.

296   All classes form an inverted tree with the Object class at the root. Final classes appear only as leaves.

Abstract classes generally lie high in the tree, because they generally provide instance methods and instance variables that you intend to share among multiple subclasses.

No class can be both abstract and final.

297   In the following illustration, all arrows represent subclass–superclass relations:

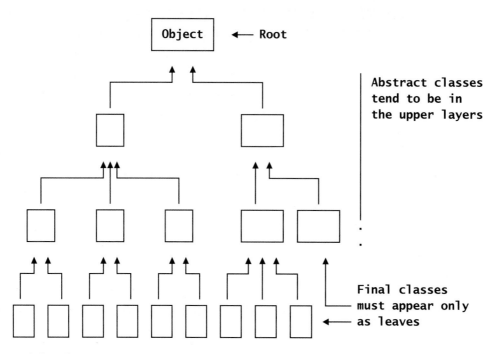

Object ← Root

Abstract classes
tend to be in
the upper layers

Final classes
must appear only
as leaves

298
PRACTICE Redefine the `railroadCar` class that you were asked to define in Segment 282 such that you make the class abstract. Be sure to include an abstract `volume` method.

299
HIGHLIGHTS

- If no instances are to be created for a particular class, **then** you should tell Java that the class is an abstract class by instantiating the following pattern:

  public abstract class `class name` **{**
    ...
  }

- If you want every subclass of an abstract class to define a particular method, **then** you should define an abstract method in the abstract class method by instantiating the following pattern:

  public abstract `return type` `method name` **(** `declarations` **) ;**

17 HOW TO WRITE CONSTRUCTORS THAT CALL OTHER CONSTRUCTORS

300   In Section 11, you learned that constructors are instance methods that you use to construct class instances. In this section, you learn how to arrange for one class's constructor to call another class's constructor explicitly.

301   Suppose that you want to define for the Movie class a constructor that takes four arguments: the familiar script, acting, and directing values, plus the length of the movie in minutes. You want to use the constructor to create new Movie instances as follows:

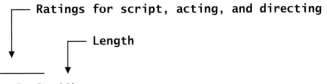

```
new Movie(4, 7, 3, 88)
```

The fourth argument establishes the value of the minutes instance variable inherited from the Attraction class.

302   You could, of course, define the required four-parameter constructor as follows, duplicating the assignment statements of the three-parameter constructor and adding a statement that assigns the minutes instance variable:

```
public class Movie extends Attraction {
 public int script, acting, directing;
 public Movie () {script = 5; acting = 5; directing = 5;}
 public Movie (int s, int a, int d) {
  script = s; acting = a; directing = d;
 }
 public Movie (int s, int a, int d, int m) {
  script = s; acting = a; directing = d;
  minutes = m;
 }
 public int rating () {return script + acting + directing;}
}
```

Duplicates

303   In a small class definition, it does no particular harm for a four-parameter constructor to duplicate the assignment statements of a three-parameter constructor; in general, however, you should avoid duplicating any program fragment on the ground that, when you debug or improve the duplicated program fragment, you must make identical changes in more than one place, which is difficult for the author of a program to do without error, and is completely impracticable for someone else to attempt.

Accordingly, you need a way for the four-parameter constructor not only to do its own unique work, but also to call the three-parameter constructor.

304 Ordinarily, the first action of a constructor is to call the zero-parameter constructor in the direct superclass. Thus, all the constructors in the Movie class, as now defined, call the zero-parameter constructor in the Attraction class.

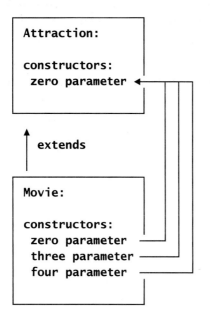

305 Whenever you want a constructor to hand arguments to another constructor in the same class, you modify the constructor's definition by adding a statement consisting of the this keyword followed by an argument list. That added statement must be the first statement in the constructor.

For example, you modify the four-parameter constructor to call the three-parameter constructor as follows:

```
public class Movie extends Attraction {
 public int script, acting, directing;
 public Movie () {script = 5; acting = 5; directing = 5;}
 public Movie (int s, int a, int d) {          ◄────────
  script = s; acting = a; directing = d;                    Call to
 }                                                          three-parameter
 public Movie (int s, int a, int d, int m) {                constructor
  this(s, a, d);   ────────────────────────
  minutes = m;
 }
 public int rating () {return script + acting + directing;}
 }
}
```

306 In any instance method, this can be viewed as a special parameter, not listed with the other parameters, whose value is the instance method's target.

The target of a constructor is the instance under construction. Thus, a constructor-calling expression—such as this(s, a, d)—can be viewed as a method call with a target but no name; that call, by convention, means a call to a constructor. Such expressions are therefore analogous to constructor-calling expressions involving new—such as new Movie(s, a, d); such expressions also can be viewed as method calls with a target, the new movie, but no name.

307 The altered four-parameter constructor calls only the three-parameter constructor. Thus, the four-parameter constructor leaves it to the three-parameter constructor to call the constructor in the Attraction class.

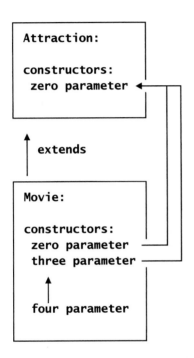

308 Now, suppose that you want to define constructors for the Movie class and for the Symphony class that assigns only the minutes instance variable. You could, of course, define the constructors as follows:

```
public class Movie extends Attraction {
  ...
  public Movie (int m) {minutes = m;}
  ...
}

public class Symphony extends Attraction {
  ...
  public Symphony (int m) {minutes = m;}
  ...
}
```

Duplicates

309 You should avoid duplication, however, even in simple methods—and the `Movie` and `Symphony` constructors shown in Segment 308 are duplicates.

Accordingly, you should define a suitable one-argument, `minutes`-assigning constructor in the `Attraction` class:

```
public class Attraction {
  ...
 public Attraction (int m) {
  minutes = m;
 }
  ...
}
```

Next, you must arrange for one-parameter constructors in the `Movie` and `Symphony` classes to call the new one-parameter constructor in the `Attraction` class. Ordinarily, all constructors call only the zero-parameter constructor in the direct superclass.

310 Whenever you want a constructor to hand one or more arguments to another constructor in the direct superclass, you modify the constructor's definition by adding, as the first statement in that constructor, a statement consisting of the `super` keyword followed by an argument list.

Thus, to modify the one-parameter constructors in the `Movie` class and the `Symphony` class, such that they call the one-parameter constructor in the `Attraction` class, you add `super` constructor calls to both:

```
public class Movie extends Attraction {
  ...
 public Movie (int m) {
  super(m);  ←————————————  Call to one-parameter constructor
 }                           in Attraction class
  ...
}

public class Symphony extends Attraction {
  ...
 public Symphony (int m) {
  super(m);  ←————————————  Call to one-parameter constructor
 }                           in Attraction class
  ...
}
```

311 The one-parameter constructors that make use of `super` call the one-parameter constructor in the `Attraction` class:

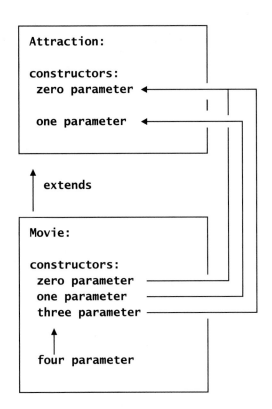

312
SIDE TRIP You cannot arrange for explicit calls to more than one constructor. In this respect, Java differs from C++.

313 Redefine the zero-parameter constructor that you were asked to define for the boxCar
PRACTICE class in Segment 220, such that it calls the three-parameter constructor, also defined in Segment 220.

314

HIGHLIGHTS

- If you want a constructor to call another constructor in the same class explicitly, then instantiate the following pattern:

```
public class name (parameter list) {
 this( arguments for called constructor );
 ...
}
```

- If you want a constructor to call another constructor in the direct superclass explicitly, then instantiate the following pattern:

```
public class name (parameter list) {
 super( arguments for called constructor );
 ...
}
```

18 HOW TO WRITE METHODS THAT CALL OTHER METHODS

315 Ordinarily, you supply an instance method with a class instance by providing the class instance as the target: you write the name of the class instance, followed by the field-selection operator, followed by the name of the instance method.

In this section, you learn how to pass along an instance from a directly called instance method to an indirectly called instance method.

316 Suppose that you want to write an attraction-analysis program that displays a report containing each attraction's category, rating, and length:

```
Movie rated at 14 lasts 88 minutes
Symphony rated at 22 lasts 62 minutes
```

317 To get started, you define the `category` instance method in the Movie class and the Symphony class. Both methods return strings:

```
public class Movie extends Attraction {
 // ... Remainder of Movie definition ...
 // Define rating:
 public int rating () {
  return script + acting + directing;
 }
 // Define category:
 public String category () {
  return "Movie";
 }
}

public class Symphony extends Attraction {
 // ... rest of Symphony definition ...
 // Define rating:
 public int rating () {
  return music + playing + conducting;
 }
 // Define category:
 public String category () {
  return "Symphony";
 }
}
```

Because you expect to assign both Movie instances and Symphony instances to Attraction variables, and you expect to use such variables as category targets, you must define the category method in the Attraction class, as you learned in Segment 288.

Because Attraction is an abstract class, you can create only Movie and Symphony instances; you cannot create Attraction instances. And, because the Movie and Symphony classes both have `category` instance methods, you should define `category` as an `abstract` method in the `Attraction` class:

```
public abstract class Attraction {
 // ... rest of Attraction definition ...
 public abstract int rating () ;
 public abstract String category () ;
}
```

318 Now, you can bring together the `category`, `rating`, and `getMinutes` instance methods to produce the desired output:

```
public class Demonstrate {
 public static void main(String argv[]) {
  Attraction x;
  x = new Movie(4, 7, 3, 88);
  System.out.println(
   x.category() + " rated at "
   + x.rating() + " lasts "
   + x.getMinutes() + " minutes"
  );
  x = new Symphony(10, 9, 3, 62);
  System.out.println(
   x.category() + " rated at "
   + x.rating() + " lasts "
   + x.getMinutes() + " minutes"
  );
 }
}
```
————————————————— Result —————————————————
```
Movie rated at 14 lasts 88 minutes
Symphony rated at 22 lasts 62 minutes
```

319 Suppose that you want to define a `displayAttraction` instance method so that you can write a descriptive line merely by calling `displayAttraction` with a target that is a `Movie` instance or a `Symphony` instance.

320 When you try to define `displayAttraction`, you face a problem: How do you call the `category` and `rating` methods from inside a `displayAttraction` method? Ordinarily, you call instance methods by writing a target, then the field-selection operator, then the method name, and, finally, an empty argument list. But how do you specify that you want the `category` method that is used inside `displayAttraction` to work on the same class instance that was handed over to `displayAttraction`?

The answer is that you use the `category` method with an **implicit target**, as in the following definition of `displayAttraction`:

```
public abstract class Attraction {
 // ... rest of Attraction definition ...
 public abstract int rating () ;
 public abstract String category () ;
 public void displayAttraction () {
  System.out.println(
   category() + " rated at "
   + rating() + " lasts "
   + getMinutes() + " minutes"
  );
 }
}
```

By convention, because the target and the field-selection operator are absent, the `category` and `rating` methods are handed the same class-instance argument that was handed to `displayAttraction`. Thus, `category` and `rating` have an **implicit argument**.

321   The following diagram shows how the various instance variables and methods fit together. The `displayAttraction` method is defined in only the `Attraction` class. The `category` and `rating` methods are defined in all three classes. When they are called, the definitions in the `Movie` and `Symphony` classes shadow the abstract definitions in the `Attraction` class.

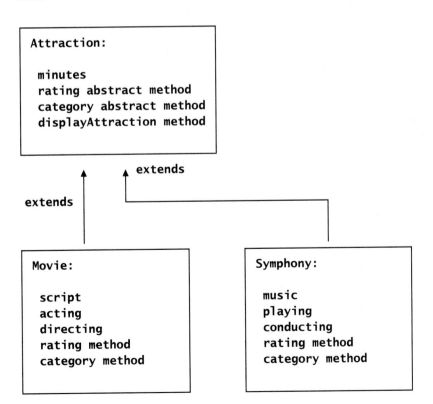

322   Now, you can use `displayAttraction` in a revised version of the program that was shown in Segment 318:

```
public class Demonstrate {
 public static void main(String argv[]) {
  Attraction x;
  x = new Movie(4, 7, 3, 88);
  x.displayAttraction();
  x = new Symphony(10, 9, 3, 66);
  x.displayAttraction();
 }
}
```
———————————————— Result ————————————————
```
Movie rated at 14 lasts 88 minutes
Symphony rated at 22 lasts 66 minutes
```

323   By way of summary, the following are complete definitions of the `Attraction`, `Movie`, and `Symphony` classes that serve for the remainder of this book, save for one small change to `Attraction` made in Section 40. They include all that has been developed so far, plus two additional instance variables, `title` and `poster`, which are needed in Section 30.

```
public abstract class Attraction {
 // First, define instance variables:
 public int minutes;
 public String title, poster;
 // Define constructors:
 public Attraction () {
  minutes = 75;}
 public Attraction (int m) {minutes = m;}
 // Define getters and setters:
 public int getMinutes () {return minutes;}
 public void setMinutes (int d) {minutes = d;}
 // Define rating as an abstract method:
 public abstract int rating () ;
 // Define category as an abstract method:
 public abstract String category () ;
 // Define displayAttraction:
 public void displayAttraction () {
  System.out.println(
   category() + " rated at "
   + rating() + " lasts "
   + getMinutes() + " minutes"
  );
 }
}
```

```
public class Movie extends Attraction {
 // First, define instance variables:
 public int script, acting, directing;
 // Define zero-parameter constructor:
 public Movie () {script = 5; acting = 5; directing = 5;}
 // Define one-parameter constructor:
 public Movie (int m) {super(m);}
 // Define three-parameter constructor:
 public Movie (int s, int a, int d) {
  script = s; acting = a; directing = d;
 }
 // Define four-parameter constructor:
 public Movie (int s, int a, int d, int m) {
  this(s, a, d);
  minutes = m;
 }
 // Define rating:
 public int rating () {return script + acting + directing;}
 // Define category:
 public String category () {return "Movie";}
}

public class Symphony extends Attraction {
 // First, define instance variables:
 public int music, playing, conducting;
 // Define zero-parameter constructor:
 public Symphony () {music = 5; playing = 5; conducting = 5;}
 // Define one-parameter constructor:
 public Symphony (int m) {super(m);}
 // Define three-parameter constructor:
 public Symphony (int s, int a, int d) {
  music = s; playing = a; conducting = d;
 }
 // Define four-parameter constructor:
 public Symphony (int s, int a, int d, int m) {
  this(s, a, d);
  minutes = m;
 }
 // Define rating:
 public int rating () {return music + playing + conducting;}
 // Define category:
 public String category () {return "Symphony";}
}
```

324   As you learned in Segment 306, this can be viewed as a special instance-method parameter whose value is the target of the instance method. If you wish, you can use this as an explicit target. Thus, you can define displayAttraction as follows:

```
public abstract class Attraction {
 // ... rest of Attraction definition ...
 public abstract int rating () ;
 public abstract String category () ;
 public void displayAttraction () {
  System.out.println(
   this.category() + " rated at "
   + this.rating() + " lasts "
   + this.getMinutes() + " minutes"
  );
 }
}
```

Thus, the real result of leaving out an explicit target is that Java takes the target to be the value of the `this` parameter.

325
PRACTICE

Adapt the program that was shown in Segment 323 such that you enable the display of information about boxCar and tankCar instances, rather than about Movie and Symphony instances.

326
HIGHLIGHTS

- If you want to call an instance method from inside another instance method, **and** the called instance method is to work on the same target instance that you handed to the calling method, **then** instantiate the following pattern:

  `instance method ( ordinary arguments )`

- If you prefer to use an explicit target, **then** exploit the assignment of the `this` parameter:

  `this. instance method ( ordinary arguments )`

19 HOW TO DESIGN CLASSES AND CLASS HIERARCHIES

327   At this point, you have learned how to define classes and class hierarchies. In this section, you learn how to design classes and class hierarchies by observing several principles of representation design.

328   The **explicit-representation principle**: Whenever there is a natural category with which your program needs to work, there should be a class in your program that corresponds to that category.

In the attraction domain, for example, there are natural categories corresponding to movies and symphonies.

329   The **modularity principle**: Generally, you should divide your programs into units that you can develop and maintain independently. Programs so divided are said to be **modular**.

One way to achieve modularity is to define your classes such that they reflect naturally occurring categories, exploiting the tendency of human language to divide the world into coherent, relatively independent concepts.

Thus, you define a `Movie` class to reflect the category identified by the word *Movie*; Similarly, you define the `Symphony` class to reflect the category identified by the word *Symphony*.

As you learn in Section 33, another way to achieve modularity, at higher levels, is to organize your classes into functionally coherent compilation units, and to organize your compilation units into functionally coherent packages.

330   The **no-duplication principle**: Instance variables and instance methods should be distributed among class definitions to ensure that there is no needless duplication. Otherwise, duplicate copies are bound to become gratuitously different.

For example, in Segment 323, the `minutes` instance variable resides in the `Attraction` class, rather than in the `Movie` and `Symphony` classes, making that instance variable more generally available.

331   The **look-it-up principle**: A program should look up a frequently needed answer, rather than computing that answer, whenever practicable.

For example, in Segment 323, a `minutes` instance variable was declared in the `Attraction` class, whereas an `hours` instance variable could have been declared. The right choice depends on whether you are more likely to be interested in minutes or in hours.

332   The **need-to-know principle**: Generally, when you design classes to be used by other programmers, your classes will contain more instance variables and methods than you expect to be accessed by the methods written by those other programmers.

By restricting access to your classes to the instance variables and methods in public interfaces, you can revise and improve the other instance variables and methods without worrying about whether other programmers have already come to depend on them.

For example, when you define an Attraction class, you might choose to make the minutes instance variable private, requiring all access to be through public access methods. Your rationale would be that you could change later to an hours-based definition without fear that anyone would have come to depend on direct access to the minutes instance variable. Instead, all users of the Attraction class would have to use the getMinutes and setMinutes methods in the public interface, which you easily could redefine to work with an hours instance variable.

333 **The is-a versus has-a principle:** You learned in Section 9 that instances mirror real-world individuals and classes mirror read-world categories. Accordingly, when you decide to implement a class, you are building a **model** of an aspect of the real world.

Many programmers new to object-oriented programming find it difficult to decide between implementing a new class connection or installing a new instance variable, because the **subclass–superclass relation** is easily confused with the **part–whole relation**.

Generally, if you find yourself using the phrase *an X is a Y* when describing the relation between two classes, then the first class is a subclass of the second. On the other hand, if you find yourself using *X has a Y*, then instances of the second class appear as parts of instances of the first class.

For example, a human is an animal. Accordingly, the **is-a rule** dictates that if you define a Human class, that class should be a subclass of the Animal class. Similarly, a box car is a railroad car, and the BoxCar class should be a subclass of the RailroadCar class.

On the other hand, humans have arms and legs, so the **has-a rule** dictates that the Human class should have arms and legs instance variables. Similarly, a box car has a box, and the BoxCar class therefore should have a box instance variable.

334 Deciding between a subclass–superclass relation and a part–whole relation is not always straightforward, however. For example, you may decide to model a piano as an instrument that has a keyboard, or you may decide to model a piano as a keyboard instrument. If you follow the has-a rule, you implement the Piano class with a keyboard instance variable; if you follow the is-a rule, you implement the Piano class as a subclass of the KeyboardInstrument class.

The rule you should follow is the one that seems to make the most sense in light of the aspects of the real world that you are modeling. If your program is to deal with many types of keyboard instruments, then defining a KeyboardInstrument class probably is the better choice. If your program is to deal with only pianos, then defining a keyboard slot probably is the better choice.

335 The subclass–superclass versus part–whole issue is mercurial, in part, because different applications may view the same objects from different perspectives. For applications that deal with railroads, a box car is best viewed as a railroad car that has a box; for applications that deal with containers, a box car is best viewed as a box that happens to have wheels that run on tracks. Thus, there is no universal right answer to the decision between modeling with the subclass–superclass relation and the part–whole relation.

336
PRACTICE
Design a class hierarchy for a dozen houses and buildings. At the highest level, place an instance variable named `squareFeet` and `age` and `locationMultiplier`. Write an instance method, `appraise`, for the classes in your hierarchy. Include classes such as `bungalow`, `mansion`, `skyscraper`, and `warehouse`.

337
PRACTICE
Design a class hierarchy for a dozen occupations. At the highest level, place an instance variable named `yearsOfExperience` and `locationMultiplier`. Write an instance method, `estimatedSalary`, for the classes in your hierarchy. Include classes such as `physician`, `lawyer`, `engineer`, `athlete`, `ornithologist`, `astrologer`, and `editor`.

338
HIGHLIGHTS

- Programs should obey the explicit-representation principle, with classes included to reflect natural categories.

- Programs should obey the modularity principle, with program elements divided into logically coherent classes and packages.

- Programs should obey the no-duplication principle, with instance methods situated among class definitions to facilitate sharing.

- Programs should obey the look-it-up principle, with class definitions including instance variables for stable, frequently requested information.

- Programs should obey the need-to-know principle, with public interfaces designed to restrict instance-variable and instance-method access, thus facilitating the improvement and maintenance of nonpublic program elements.

- If you find yourself using the phrase *an X is a Y* when describing the relation between two classes, **then** the first class is a subclass of the second.

- If you find yourself using *X has a Y* when describing the relation between two classes, **then** instances of the second class appear as parts of instances of the first class.

20 HOW TO PERFORM TESTS USING PREDICATES

339   In this and the next several sections, you set aside classes and class instances, temporarily, to learn how to do routine testing, branching, iterating, and recursing. You see that Java's mechanisms for accomplishing such tasks are not much different from those that you would find in just about any programming language.

In this section, you learn how to test numbers.

340   Operators and methods that return values representing true or false are called **predicates**. Java offers several operator predicates that test the relationship between pairs of numbers:

Predicate	Purpose
==	Are two numbers equal?
!=	Are two numbers not equal?
>	Is the first number greater than the second?
<	Is the first number less than the second?
>=	Is the first number greater than or equal to the second?
<=	Is the first number less than or equal to the second?

341   The value of the expression 6 != 3, in which the inequality operator appears, is `true`, which is one of the two instances of the `boolean` type. The value of the expression 6 == 3, in which the equality operator appears, is `false`, which is the other instance of the `boolean` type.

342   In general, the value returned by a predicate may be either `true` or `false`.

343   A common error is to write =, the assignment operator, when you intend to check for equality. Be sure to remember that the equality predicate is written as a double equal-to sign, ==.

344   You now know that, whenever the character ! is followed immediately by the character =, the two characters together denote the inequality operator.

The ! character also can appear alone, in which case it denotes the **not operator**. The **not** operator is a unary operator that converts `true` into `false`, and vice versa. Thus, the value of `!false` is `true` and `!true` is `false`. Similarly, the value of `!(6 == 3)` is `true`, meaning that "it is true that '6 is equal to 3' is `false`." Also, the value of `!(6 != 3)` is `false`, meaning that "it is false that '6 is not equal to 3' is `true`."

345   You can declare variables to be **boolean variables**. You can assign either of the **literal boolean values**, `true` or `false`, to such variables.

```
public class Demonstrate {
  public static void main (String argv[]) {
    boolean b;
    b = (2 + 2 == 4);
    System.out.println(b);
  }
}
```

———————————————— Result ————————————————
```
true
```

346   The boolean type is one of the **primitive types,** which you learned about in Segment 185. The **standard default value** of a boolean variable is `false`.

347   In C and C++, `true` and `false` are just alternate names for 1 and 0. In Java, `true` and
SIDE TRIP `false` are distinct values; they are not 1 and 0.

348   Note that you do not need to perform a cast, of the sort you learned about in Segment 94, if you want a program to compare an integer with a floating-point number. Java will perform the cast automatically, as illustrated by the following program:

```
public class Demonstrate {
  public static void main (String argv[]) {
    int i = 50; double d = 50.0;
    System.out.println(i == d);
    System.out.println(i != d);
  }
}
```

———————————————— Result ————————————————
```
true
false
```

349   Occasionally, you need to work with predicates that work on class instances, rather than
SIDE TRIP numbers. For example, if you want to determine if a particular instance is an instance of a particular class, you use the `instanceof` operator. The `instanceof` operator returns `true` if the instance is either a direct instance of the given class or of a subclass of that class.

Suppose, for example, that the `JamesBondMovie` class extends the `Movie` class, which extends the `Attraction` class. Then, a James Bond movie is an instance of all three classes. An ordinary movie is an instance of the `Movie` class as well as the `Attraction` class, but not the `JamesBondMovie` class:

```
public class Demonstrate {
 public static void main (String argv[]) {
  JamesBondMovie j = new JamesBondMovie();
  Movie m = new Movie(1, 1, 1);
  System..out.println(j instanceof Attraction);
  System.out.println(j instanceof Movie);
  System.out.println(j instanceof JamesBondMovie);
  System.out.println(m instanceof Attraction);
  System.out.println(m instanceof Movie);
  System.out.println(m instanceof JamesBondMovie);
 }
}
```

——————————————— Result ———————————————

```
true
true
true
true
true
false
```

350 If you want to determine if two instances are the same instance, you use `equals`, which is
SIDE TRIP a method rather than an operator. Note that the `equals` method determines whether two
instances are the same instance, rather than equivalent instances.

```
public class Demonstrate {
 public static void main (String argv[]) {
  Movie m1 = new Movie(3, 4, 5);
  Movie m2 = new Movie(3, 4, 5);
  Movie m3 = new Movie(4, 5, 6);
  System.out.println(m1.equals(m2));
  System.out.println(m2.equals(m3));
  m3 = m2 = m1;
  System.out.println(m1.equals(m2));
  System.out.println(m2.equals(m3));
 }
}
```

——————————————— Result ———————————————

```
false
false
true
true
```

351 In C and C++, you must perform an explicit cast if you want to compare numbers of
SIDE TRIP different types.

The energy of a moving mass is given by the formula $\frac{1}{2}mv^2$. Write a program that accepts the mass and velocity of two automobiles and that displays `true` if the energy of the first automobile is greater than that of the second; otherwise, your program is to display `false`. Use `double` variables throughout.

- A predicate is an operator or method that returns `true` or `false`, both of which values are instances of the `boolean` type.

- If you want to turn `true` into `false`, and vice versa, **then** use the `!` operator.

21 HOW TO WRITE ONE-WAY AND TWO-WAY CONDITIONAL STATEMENTS

354   In this section, you learn how to use conditional statements when the computation that you want to perform depends on the value of an expression involving a predicate.

355   A **Boolean expression** is an expression that produces a true or false result. Reduced to practice in Java, a Boolean expression is an expression that produces either `true` or `false`.

356   An `if` statement contains a Boolean expression, in parentheses, followed by an embedded statement:

```
if ( Boolean expression )
  embedded statement
```

When the Boolean expression of an `if` statement evaluates to `true`, Java executes the embedded statement; if the Boolean expression evaluates to `false`, Java skips the embedded statement.

357   Suppose, for example, that you want to write a program that displays a message that depends on the length of a movie in minutes. Specifically, if the length is greater than 90 minutes, you want your program to display `It is long!`, and if the length is less than 60 minutes, you want your program to display `It is short!`.

One solution is to write a program that uses an `if` statement in which the embedded statements are display statements:

```
public class Demonstrate {
 public static void main (String argv[]) {
   int length = 95;
   if (length < 60)
     System.out.println("It is short!");
   if (length > 90)
     System.out.println("It is long!");
 }
}
```
———————————— Result ————————————
```
It is long!
```

358   The `if-else` statement is like the `if` statement, except that there is a second embedded statement—one that follows `else`:

```
if ( Boolean expression )
   if-true statement
else
   if-false statement
```

The `if-false` statement is executed if the Boolean expression evaluates to `false`.

359 Either the `if-true` statement or the `if-false` statement, or both, may be embedded `if` statements. Accordingly, another solution to the length-testing problem looks like this:

```
public class Demonstrate {
 public static void main (String argv[]) {
   int length = 95;
   if (length < 60)
     System.out.println("It is short!");
   else
     if (length > 90)
       System.out.println("It is long!");
 }
}
```
————————————— Result —————————————
It is long!

360 The layout of nested `if` statements is a matter of convention. Here is another common arrangement:

```
public class Demonstrate {
 public static void main (String argv[]) {
   int length = 95;
   if (length < 60)
     System.out.println("It is short!");
   else if (length > 90)
       System.out.println("It is long!");
 }
}
```
————————————— Result —————————————
It is long!

361 Suppose that you want more than one statement to be executed when a Boolean expression evaluates to `true`. You need only to combine the multiple statements, using braces, into a single **block**.

In the following `if-else` statement, for example, two display statements are executed whenever the value of `length` is greater than 90:

```
if (length > 90) {
 System.out.println("It is long!");
 System.out.println("It may try your patience");
}
```

362 In the following nested `if` statement, it is not immediately clear whether the question mark should be replaced by `long` or `short`.

```
if (length > 60)
 if (length < 90)
  System.out.println("It is normal!");
 else
  System.out.println("It is ?");
```

As the nested if statement is laid out on the page, it seems that long is the right answer. If the nested if statement were laid out another way, however, you might have the impression that short is the right answer:

```
if (length > 60)
 if (length < 90)
  System.out.println("It is normal!");
else System.out.println("It is ?");
```

Because Java pays no attention to layout, you need to know that Java assumes that each else belongs to the nearest if that is not already matched with an else. Thus, the question mark should be replaced by long.

363   Although you can rely on the rule that else statements belong to the nearest unmatched if, it is better programming practice to use braces to avoid potential misreading.

In the following example, it is clear that the question mark should be replaced by long, because the braces clearly group the else statement with the second if:

```
if (length > 60) {
 if (length < 90)
  System.out.println("It is normal!");
 else
  System.out.println("It is ?");
}
```

On the other hand, in the following example, it is clear that the question mark should be replaced by short, because the braces clearly group the else statement with the first if:

```
if (length > 60) {
 if (length < 90)
  System.out.println("It is normal!");
}
else
 System.out.println("It is ?");
```

364   Many Java programmers use braces in every if statement that they write, even though the braces often surround just one statement. Such programmers argue that the habitual use of braces reduces errors later on when a program is modified. When braces are not used, it is easy to add a second embedded statement to an if statement or else statement, yet to forget that the modification requires the addition of braces.

365 So far, you have learned how to use if-else statements to execute one of two embedded computation-performing *statements*. You should also know about Java's **conditional operator**, which enables you to compute a value from one of two embedded, value-producing *expressions*.

The conditional operator sees frequent service in display statements, where it helps you to produce the proper singular–plural distinctions. Consider, for example, the following program, which displays a length change:

```
public class Demonstrate {
 public static void main (String argv[]) {
  int change = 1;
  if (change == 1) {
   System.out.print("The length has changed by ");
   System.out.print(change);
   System.out.println(" minute");
  }
  else {
   System.out.print("The length has changed by ");
   System.out.print(change);
   System.out.println(" minutes");
  }
 }
}
```

––––––––––––––––––––––– Result –––––––––––––––––
The length has changed by 1 minute

The program works, but most experienced programmers would be unhappy because there are two separate display statements that are almost identical. Such duplication makes programs longer, and the longer a program is, the greater the chance that a bug will creep in.

Accordingly, you can improve such a program by moving the variation—the part that produces either the word *minute* or the word *minutes*—into a value-producing expression inside a single display statement.

366 The following is the pattern for Java's value-producing conditional-operator expression:

Boolean expression ? **if-true expression** : **if-false expression**

In contrast to the operators that you have seen so far, the conditional operator consists of a combination of distributed characters, ? and :, separating three operands—the Boolean expression, the if-true expression, and the if-false expression. Thus, the conditional operator combination is said to be a **ternary operator**.

367 Either the if-true expression or the if-false expression is evaluated, but both are not. Thus, any **side effects**, such as variable assignment or display, called for in the unevaluated expression do not occur.

368   The value of the following expression is the character string, `"minute"`, if the length change is 1 minute; otherwise, the value is the character string, `"minutes"`:

```
Conditional    If-true      If-false
expression     expression   expression
     |             |            |
     v             v            v
_____    _____   _____

change == 1 ? "minute" : "minutes"
```

You can, if you wish, employ parentheses to delineate the Boolean expression, but parentheses are not needed in the example, because the equality operator has precedence higher than that of the conditional operator.

369   Because a conditional-operator expression, unlike an `if` statement, produces a value, you can place it inside another expression. In the following, for example, a conditional-operator expression appears inside a display expression, solving the duplication problem encountered in Segment 365:

```
public class Demonstrate {
 public static void main (String argv[]) {
  int change = 1;
  System.out.print("The length has changed by ");
  System.out.print(change);
  System.out.println(change == 1 ? " minute" : " minutes");
 }
}
```
————————————————— Result —————————————————
```
The length has changed by 1 minute
```
——

370   Write a program that transforms a patient's weight and height into one of three messages:
PRACTICE   "The patient appears to be underweight," "The patient appears to be of normal weight," or "The patient appears to be overweight." Your program's input is three numbers: the patient's weight in kilograms, the patient's height in meters, and a gender code—0 for men and 1 for women. You may assume that a patient's "ideal" weight is proportional to height, and that the overweight and underweight messages should not appear unless the patient's weight differs from the ideal weight by more than 10 percent.

371   Write a program that displays a complete sentence that indicates the deviation from the
PRACTICE   patient's ideal weight, truncated to the nearest integer. Your program's input is three numbers: weight in kilograms, height in meters, and a gender code. Be sure that, if the deviation is just 1 kilogram, the word *kilogram* appears, rather than *kilograms*.

372
HIGHLIGHTS
- If you want to execute a statement only when an expression produces `true`, then use an `if` statement:

     `if (``Boolean expression``)` `statement`

- If you want to execute one statement when an expression evaluates to `true`, and another when the expression evaluates to `false`, **then** use an `if-else` statement:

```
if ( Boolean expression )
   if-true statement
else
   if-false statement
```

- If you want to execute a group of statements in an `if` or `if-else` statement, **then** use braces to combine those statements into a single block.

- If you want to use nested `if-else` statements, **then** use braces to clarify your grouping intention.

- If you want the value of an expression to be the value of one of two embedded expressions, **and** you want the choice to be determined by the value of a Boolean expression, **then** instantiate the following pattern:

```
Boolean expression
 ? if-true expression : if-false expression
```

22 HOW TO COMBINE BOOLEAN EXPRESSIONS

373 In this section, you learn how to combine Boolean expressions to form larger Boolean expressions that contain multiple predicates.

374 The **and operator, &&,** returns `true` if *both* of its operands evaluate to `true`. The **or operator, ||,** returns `true` if *either* of its operands evaluates to `true`.

375 The following expression, for example, evaluates to `true` only if the value of the `length` variable is between 60 and 90:

```
60 < length && length < 90
```

Accordingly, the display statement embedded in the following `if` statement is evaluated only if the value of the `length` variable is inside the 60-to-90 range.

```
if (60 < length && length < 90)
 System.out.println("The length is normal.");
```

376 The evaluation of **&&** and **||** expressions is complicated because certain subexpressions may not be evaluated at all.

In **&&** expressions, the left-side operand is evaluated first: If the value of the left-side operand is `false`, then the right-side operand is ignored completely, and the value of the **&&** expression is `false`.

Of course, if both operands evaluate to `true`, the value of the **&&** expression is `true`.

In **||** expressions, the left-side operand also is evaluated first: If the left-side operand evaluates to `true`, nothing else is done, and the value of the **||** expression is `true`; if both operands evaluate to `false`, the value of the **||** expression is `false`.

377 The **&** and **|** operators also combine Boolean expressions, returning `true` or `false`. But **&**
SIDE TRIP and **|** differ from **&&** and **||** in that **&** and **|** evaluate both arguments, no matter what.

Ordinarily, you would not use **&** and **|** on Boolean operands, because **&&** and **||** are more efficient. You would use **&** and **|** on integral expressions, however, because, when provided integral operands, **&** and **|** perform logical *and* and *or* operations on the bits that constitute the integers. Neither **&** nor **|** is discussed further in this book, because understanding bit manipulation is not a prerequisite to understanding either basic Java programs or the special strengths of the language.

378 Java specifies that operands are always evaluated from left to right. Other languages, such
SIDE TRIP as C and C++, do not insist on left-to-right evaluation in general. In those languages, operators such as **&&** and **||**, which you learned about in this section, and **?:**, which you learned about in Section 21, are exceptions to the general rule.

You might think that it would be possible to use an **&&** expression instead of an **if** statement by exploiting the property that the right-side operand of an **&&** expression is evaluated only if the value of the left-side operand is **true**.

You cannot do so, however, because both the operands surrounding **&&** and **||** operators must be Boolean expressions.

Do not think that this requirement is a handicap, however. Most good programmers object to the use of **&&** and **||** operators to allow or block evaluation. They argue that, when an **&&** or **||** operator is included in an expression, anyone who looks at the expression—other than the original programmer—naturally expects the value produced by the expression to be used. If the value is not used, the person who looks at the program may wonder whether the original programmer left out a portion of the program unintentionally.

Write a method that transforms an athlete's pulse rate into one of three integers: if the rate is less than 60, the value returned by the method is to be **-1**; if the rate is more than 80, the value returned is to be **1**; otherwise, the value returned is to be **0**. Then, write another method that transforms an athlete's body fat as a percentage of weight into one of three integers: if the athlete's body-fat percentage is less than 10, the value returned is to be **-1**; if it is more than 20, the value returned is to be **1**; otherwise, the value returned is to be **0**.

Write a program that accepts two numbers—a pulse rate and a body-fat percentage—and displays "The athlete appears to be in great shape," if both the athlete's pulse rate and body fat are low.

- **If** you want to combine two predicate expressions, **and** the result is to be **true** if the values of *both* expressions are **true**, **then** use **&&**.

- **If** you want to combine two predicate expressions, **and** the result is to be **true** if the value of *either* expression is **true**, **then** use **||**.

- Both **&&** and **||** evaluate their left operand before they evaluate their right operand. The right operand is not evaluated if the value of the left operand of an **&&** expression is **false**, or if the value of the left operand of a **||** expression is **true**.

23 HOW TO WRITE ITERATION STATEMENTS

383   In this section, you learn how to tell Java to repeat a computation by looping through that computation until a test has been satisfied.

384   Java's `while` statement consists of a Boolean expression, in parentheses, followed by an embedded statement or block:

```
while ( Boolean expression )
   embedded statement or block
```

The Boolean expression is evaluated and if it evaluates to `true`, the embedded statement or block is evaluated as well; otherwise, Java skips the embedded statement or block. In contrast to an `if` statement, however, the **test–evaluate loop** continues as long as the Boolean expression evaluates to `true`, and the computation is said to **iterate**.

385   For example, the following method fragment repeatedly decrements n by 1 until n is 0:

```
while (n != 0)
  n = n - 1;
```

Replacement of the single embedded statement, n = n - 1;, by an embedded block enables the `while` statement to do useful computation while counting down n to 0:

```
while (n != 0) {
  n = n - 1;
  ...
}
```

386   Many programmers prefer to use embedded blocks instead of embedded statements in `while` statements, even if the embedded block contains just one statement.

The rationale is that, whenever you use an embedded statement instead of an embedded block, you run a small risk of forgetting to add braces later, should new requirements force you to switch from an embedded statement to an embedded block. Accordingly, in this book, you see mostly embedded blocks.

387   Now suppose, for example, that you want to compute the number of viewers that a movie will have at a given time if the number of viewers doubles each month. Plainly, the number after n months is proportional to 2^n, thus requiring you to develop a method that computes the nth power of 2.

One way to do the computation is to count down a parameter, n, to 0, multiplying a variable, `result`, whose initial value is 1, by 2 each time that you decrement n:

```
public class Demonstrate {
 public static void main (String argv[]) {
  System.out.println(powerOf2(4));
 }
 public static int powerOf2 (int n) {
  int result = 1;                  // Initial value is 1
  while (n != 0) {
    result = 2 * result;           // Multiplied by 2 n times
    n = n - 1;
  }
  return result;
 }
}
```
————————————————— Result —————————————————
16
_____

388 In C and C++, *true* is represented by any integer other than 0, and *false* is represented by

SIDE TRIP 0. In such languages, the value of the Boolean expression n != 0 is false if and only if the value of n is 0.

Accordingly, the following while statement is legitimate in those languages, but is not in Java:

```
while (n) {                 // BUG! Will not work in Java!
  ...
}
```

389 The defect of many while loops is that the details that govern the looping appear in three places: the place where the counting variable is initialized, the place where it is tested, and the place where it is reassigned. Such distribution makes looping difficult to understand. Accordingly, you also need to know about the for statement:

```
for ( entry expression ;
      Boolean expression ;
      continuation expression )
  embedded statement or block
```

The entry expression is evaluated only once, when the for statement is entered. Once the entry expression is evaluated, the Boolean expression is evaluated, and, if the result is true, the embedded statement or block is evaluated, followed by the continuation expression. Then, the test–evaluate loop continues until the Boolean expression eventually evaluates to false.

390 Specialized to counting down a counter variable, the for statement becomes the **counting loop**:

```
variable declaration
for ( counter initialization expression ;
      counter testing expression ;
      counter reassignment expression )
  embedded statement or block
```

391 Many programmers prefer to use only embedded blocks instead of embedded statements in for statements, for the same reasons that many programmers use only embedded blocks in while statements, as explained in Segment 386.

392 Now, you can define the powerOf2 method using a for loop instead of a while loop. The initialization expression, counter = n, assigns the value of the parameter n to counter. Then, as long as the value of counter is not 0, the value of result, whose initial value is 1, is multiplied by 2, and the value of counter is decremented by 1:

```
public class Demonstrate {
 public static void main (String argv[]) {
   System.out.println(powerOf2(4));
 }
 public static int powerOf2 (int n) {
   int counter, result = 1;
   for (counter = n; counter != 0; counter = counter - 1) {
     result = 2 * result;
   }
   return result;
 }
}
```
———————————————— Result ————————————————
16
——

393 **Augmented assignment operators** reassign a variable to a value obtained through a combination of the variable's current value with an expression's value via addition, subtraction, multiplication, or division. The following diagram illustrates how an assignment using an augmented assignment operator differs from an ordinary assignment:

```
variable name  =  variable name  operator  expression
```

```
variable name  operator  =  expression
```

For example, you can rewrite result = result * 2 as follows:

result *= 2

Even though this shorthand gives you a perfectly valid way to multiply and reassign, you may choose to write result = result * 2, which you see throughout this book, on the ground that result = result * 2 stands out more clearly as a reassignment operation.

394

Although augmented assignment operators are not used further in this book, there are situations in which an expression written with an augmented assignment operator produces a faster and smaller program than the corresponding expression without the augmented assignment operator. In Section 27, for example, you learn about Java arrays. In particular, you learn that you can reassign an array element to twice its former value as follows:

`array name` `[ index-producing expression ]`
`= array name` `[ index-producing expression ] * 2`

Alternatively, using an augmented assignment operator, you can write the reassignment expression as follows:

`array name` `[ index-producing expression ] *= 2`

Plainly, if the index-producing expression is complex, the augmented assignment operator offers one way to increase speed, to keep size down, and to avoid a maintenance headache should the expression require modification, because the index-producing expression is written only once and evaluated only once.

395 In principle, you could rewrite `counter = counter - 1`, using an augmented assignment operator, as `counter -= 1`. You are not likely to see such expressions, however, because Java offers a still more concise shorthand for adding 1 to a variable or for subtracting 1 from a variable. To use the shorthand, you drop the equal-to sign altogether, as well as the 1, and prefix the variable with the **increment operator**, ++, or the **decrement operator**, --. Thus, you can replace `counter = counter - 1` by the following expression:

```
--counter
```

396 Using Java's shorthand notations for variable reassignment, you can write the `powerOf2` method as follows:

```
public class Demonstrate {
 public static void main (String argv[]) {
  System.out.println(powerOf2(4));
 }
 public static int powerOf2 (int n) {
  int counter, result = 1;
  for (counter = n; counter != 0; --counter) {
    result = 2 * result;
  }
  return result;
 }
}
```
———————————————— **Result** ————————————————
```
16
```

397 You can embed expressions involving the increment operator, ++, or the decrement operator, --, in larger expressions, such as the following:

```
++x + x
```

In such an expression, the increment operator, ++, is said not only to produce a value, but also to have the **side effect** of incrementing x.

Note that the Java language prescribes that operands are evaluated in left-to-right order. Thus, in the expression ++x + x, the left-side operand, ++x, is evaluated before the right-side operand, x.

398

SIDE TRIP C and C++ do not prescribe the order in which operands are evaluated for many operators, including the + operator. In those languages, the use of side-effect operators, such as ++ and --, can lead to mysterious portability problems.

Other mysterious problems occur because a C or C++ compiler is free to compile some expressions for left-side-first evaluation and others for right-side-first evaluation. Thus, side-effect operands can cause plenty of trouble in those languages.

399 You can, in principle, position two plus signs or two minus signs as suffixes, rather than as prefixes. In either position, the plus signs or minus signs cause a variable's value to change, but, if the incremented or decremented variable is embedded in a larger expression, the value handed over differs. If a variable is prefixed, the value handed over is the new, incremented value; if a variable is suffixed, the value handed over is the old, original value.

Suppose that the value of counter is 3. Then, the value of the expression --counter is 2, and the new value of counter is 2. On the other hand, the value of the expression counter-- is 3, even though the new value of counter is 2.

400 Consider, for example, the following oddball version of powerOf2, in which the decrementing of the counter variable occurs in the Boolean expression, rather than in the normal continuation expression, which is rendered empty. The suffix form, counter--, must be used, rather than the prefix form, --counter, because decrementing is to be done after your program decides whether to go around the loop. Were you to use the prefix form, your program would fail to go around the loop enough times.

```
public class Demonstrate {
 public static void main (String argv[]) {
  System.out.println(powerOf2(4));
 }
 public static int powerOf2 (int n) {
  int counter, result = 1;
  for (counter = n; counter-- != 0;) {
    result = 2 * result;
  }
  return result;
 }
}
```
———————————————— Result ————————————————
16
——

401   There are still other ways to define powerOf2 using a for loop. Here is one in which the initialization of the result variable is included within the for statement, along with the initialization of the counter variable, the two being separated by a comma:

```
public class Demonstrate {
 public static void main (String argv[]) {
  System.out.println(powerOf2(4));
 }
 public static int powerOf2 (int n) {
  int counter, result;
  for (counter = n, result = 1; counter != 0; --counter) {
    result = 2 * result;
  }
  return result;
 }
}
```
——————————————— Result ———————————————
16
———————————————————————————————————

402   You can even, if you wish, bring the reassignment of the result variable within the reassignment part of the for loop, joining it to the reassignment of the counter variable. The result is a for loop with an **empty statement**, which consists of a semicolon only, in place of an ordinary statement or block:

```
public class Demonstrate {
 public static void main (String argv[]) {
  System.out.println(powerOf2(4));
 }
 public static int powerOf2 (int n) {
  int counter, result;
  for (counter = n, result = 1;       // Initialization
       counter != 0;                  // Test
       --counter, result = result * 2) // Reassignment
    ;                                  // Empty statement
  return result;
 }
}
```
——————————————— Result ———————————————
16
———————————————————————————————————

403   The definition of powerOf2 that appears in Segment 401 is the best of the lot in many respects: All initialization is done in the initialization part of the for statement, a simple test of a counter variable occurs in the testing part of the for statement, the counter variable is reassigned in the reassignment part of the for statement, and the computation of the result is separated from the reassignment part. The for statement is deployed straightforwardly; there are no parlor tricks.

404
PRACTICE Write an iterative program that accepts two positive integers, m and n, and computes m^n.

405
PRACTICE Write an iterative program that accepts a positive integer, n, and computes the factorial of n, written $n!$, where $n! = n \times n - 1 \times \ldots \times 1$.

406
HIGHLIGHTS
- If you want to repeat a calculation for as long as a Boolean expression's value is true, then use a `while` loop:

  ```
  while ( Boolean expression )
      embedded statement
  ```

- If you want to repeat a calculation involving entry, Boolean, and continuation expressions, then use a `for` loop:

  ```
  for ( entry expression ;
      Boolean expression ;
      continuation expression )
      embedded statement
  ```

- If you want to repeat a calculation until a variable is counted down to 0, then use a counting loop:

  ```
  variable declaration
  for ( counter-initialization expression ;
      counter-testing expression ;
      counter-reassignment expression )
      embedded statement
  ```

- If you want to increment or decrement the value of a variable by 1, then instantiate one of the following patterns:

  ```
  ++ variable name
  -- variable name
  ```

- If you want to change a variable's value by combining it with the value of an expression via addition, subtraction, multiplication, or division, then consider instantiating the following pattern:

  ```
  variable name  operator = expression
  ```

24 HOW TO WRITE RECURSIVE METHODS

407 In Section 23, you learned how to repeat a computation by using Java's iteration statements. In this section, you learn how to repeat a computation by using recursive method calls.

408 If you are not yet familiar with **recursion**, it is best to see how recursion works through an example involving a simple mathematical computation that you already know how to perform using iteration.

409 Suppose, for example, that you want to write a method, recursivePowerOf2, that computes the nth power of 2 recursively. One way to start is to define recursivePowerOf2 in terms of the powerOf2 method already provided in Section 23:

```
public static int recursivePowerOf2 (int n) {
 return powerOf2(n);
}
```

Once you see that you can define recursivePowerOf2 in terms of powerOf2, you are ready to learn how gradually to turn recursivePowerOf2 into a recursive method that does not rely on powerOf2.

410 First, note that you can eliminate the need to call powerOf2 in the simple case in which the value of recursivePowerOf2's parameter is 0:

```
public static int recursivePowerOf2 (int n) {
 if (n == 0) {
  return 1;
 }
 else {return powerOf2(n);}
}
```

411 Next, note that you can arrange for recursivePowerOf2 to hand over a little less work to powerOf2 by performing one of the multiplications by 2 in recursivePowerOf2 itself, and subtracting 1 from powerOf2's argument:

```
public static int recursivePowerOf2 (int n) {
 if (n == 0) {return 1;}
 else {
  return 2 * powerOf2(n - 1);
 }
}
```

Clearly, recursivePowerOf2 must work as long as one of the following two situations holds:

• The value of the parameter, n, is 0; in this situation, recursivePowerOf2 returns 1.

- The value of n is not 0, but powerOf2 is able to compute the power of 2 that is 1 less than the value of n.

412   Now for the recursion trick: you replace the call to powerOf2 in recursivePowerOf2 by a call to recursivePowerOf2 itself:

```
public static int recursivePowerOf2 (int n) {
  if (n == 0) {return 1;}
  else {
   return 2 * recursivePowerOf2(n - 1);
  }
}
```

The new version works for two reasons:

- If the value of the parameter, n, is 0, recursivePowerOf2 returns 1.

- If the value of n is not 0, recursivePowerOf2 asks itself to compute the power of 2 for a number that is 1 less than the value of n. Then, recursivePowerOf2 may ask itself to compute the power of 2 for a number that is 2 less than the original value of n, and so on, until the recursivePowerOf2 needs to deal with only 0.

413   When a method, such as recursivePowerOf2, is used in its own definition, the method is said to be **recursive**. When a method calls itself, the method is said to **recurse**.

Given a positive, integer argument, there is no danger that recursivePowerOf2 will recurse forever—calling itself an infinite number of times—because eventually the argument is counted down to 0, which recursivePowerOf2 handles directly, without further recursion.

414   There is also no danger that the values taken on by the parameter n will get in one another's way. Each time recursivePowerOf2 is entered, Java sets aside a private storage spot to hold the value of n for that entry.

415   Note that the simple case—the one for which the result is computed directly—is handled by the **base** part of the definition.

The harder case—the one in which the result is computed indirectly, through solution of another problem first—is handled by the **recursive** part of the definition.

416   You can experiment with recursivePowerOf2 in a program such as this:

```
public class Demonstrate {
 public static void main (String argv[]) {
  System.out.print("2 to the 3rd power is ");
  System.out.println(recursivePowerOf2(3));
  System.out.print("2 to the 10th power is ");
  System.out.println(recursivePowerOf2(10));
 }
 public static int recursivePowerOf2 (int n) {
  if (n == 0) {
   return 1;
  }
  else {
   return 2 * recursivePowerOf2(n - 1);
  }
 }
}
```
——————————————— Result ———————————————
```
2 to the 3rd power is 8
2 to the 10th power is 1024
```
——————————————————————————————————————

417 The following diagram shows the four calls involved when the recursivePowerOf2 method is set to work on 3:

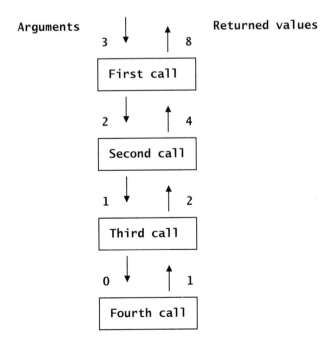

418 The recursivePowerOf2 method is an instance of the **recursive counting pattern,** in which a specified operand is combined by a specified operand with a recursive call:

```
public static int method name (int n) {
  if (n == 0) {
   return result for n equal to 0 ;
  }
  else {
   return combination operand
          combination operator
          method name (n - 1);
  }
}
```

419 Now, suppose that the number of users of your movie-evaluation service is growing like a colony of rabbits. You are asked to predict the number of users there will be a few months from now.

Fortunately, Fibonacci figured out long ago how fast rabbits multiply, deriving a formula that gives the number of female rabbits after n months, under the following assumptions: Female rabbits mature 1 month after birth. Once they mature, female rabbits have one female child each month. At the beginning of the first month, there is one immature female rabbit. Rabbits live forever. And there are always enough males on hand to mate with all the mature females.

420 The following diagram shows the number of female rabbits at the end of every month for 6 months:

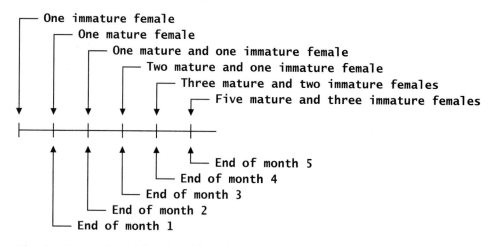

Clearly, the number of female rabbits there are at the end of the nth month is the number of females there were at the end of the previous month plus the number of females that gave birth during the current month. But, of course, the number of females that gave birth during the current month is the number of mature female rabbits at the end of the previous month, which is same as the number of females there were all together at the end of the month before that. Thus, the following formula holds:

$$\text{Rabbits}(n) = \text{Rabbits}(n - 1) + \text{Rabbits}(n - 2)$$

421 Capturing the rabbit formula in the form of a Java method, you have the following:

```java
public class Demonstrate {
 public static void main (String argv[]) {
   System.out.print("At the end of month 3, there are ");
   System.out.println(rabbits(3));
   System.out.print("At the end of month 10, there are ");
   System.out.println(rabbits(10));
 }
 public static int rabbits (int n) {
   if (n == 0 || n == 1) {
     return 1;
   }
   else {return rabbits(n - 1) + rabbits(n - 2);}
 }
}
```
———————————————— Result ————————————
```
At the end of month 3, there are 3
At the end of month 10, there are 89
```

422 The following diagram shows `rabbits` at work on 3, the same argument previously used with `recursivePowerOf2`.

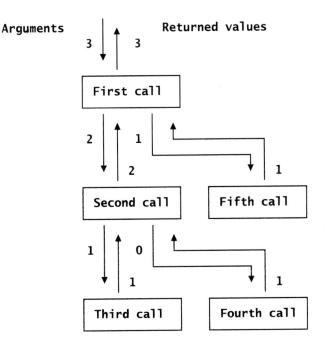

423 Now, suppose that you rewrite the `rabbits` method in terms of two auxiliary methods:

```
public static int rabbits (int n) {
  if (n == 0 || n == 1) {
    return 1;
  }
  else {return previousMonth(n) + penultimateMonth(n);}
}
```

Realizing that previousMonth must return the number of rabbits at the end of the previous month, you see that you can define previousMonth as follows:

```
public static int previousMonth (int n) {return rabbits(n - 1);}
```

Analogous reasoning leads you to the following definition for penultimateMonth:

```
public static int penultimateMonth (int n) {return rabbits(n - 2);}
```

424 Note that, no matter how you arrange the three methods inside the Demonstrate class, at least one method is referred to before it is defined. In the following arrangement, for example, both previousMonth and penultimateMonth are referred to before they are defined:

```
public class Demonstrate {
  public static void main (String argv[]) {
    System.out.print("At the end of month 3, there are ");
    System.out.println(rabbits(3));
    System.out.print("At the end of month 10, there are ");
    System.out.println(rabbits(10));
  }
  public static int rabbits (int n) {
    if (n == 0 || n == 1) {
      return 1;
    }
    else {return previousMonth(n) + penultimateMonth(n);}
  }
  public static int previousMonth (int n) {return rabbits(n - 1);}
  public static int penultimateMonth (int n) {return rabbits(n - 2);}
}
```
—————————————————— Result ——————————————————
```
At the end of month 3, there are 3
At the end of month 10, there are 89
```

Fortunately, because the Java compiler is a **multiple-pass compiler**, such forward references cause no problems, as long as the methods referred to all are defined in the same class.

425 The following diagram shows rabbits and its two auxiliaries working to determine how many rabbits there are at the end of 3 months.

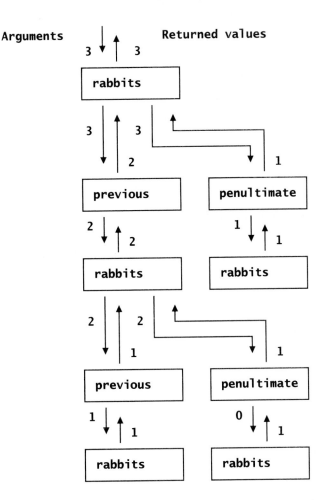

Each of the three cooperating methods can initiate a chain of calls that ends in a call to itself. Thus, the cooperating methods exhibit indirect, rather than direct, recursion.

426   In Segment 424, you learned that you can have forward references to methods, as long SIDE TRIP   as those methods are defined in the same class. In Section 33, you learn also that you can have forward references to methods, as long as those methods are defined in the same compilation unit or package.

427   Many mathematically oriented programmers prefer recursive definitions to iterative defini- SIDE TRIP   tions, when both are possible, believing that there is inherent elegance in defining a method partly in terms of itself.

Other, practically oriented programmers dislike recursive definitions for one or both of two reasons. First, the recursive approach usually produces much slower programs, because each method call takes time. Second, the recursive approach may have problems with large arguments, because the number of method calls in a recursive chain of calls is usually limited to a few hundred. Recursion aficionados counter by creating compilers that handle certain recursive methods in sophisticated ways that avoid such limits.

428
PRACTICE
Write a recursive program that accepts two positive integers, m and n, and computes m^n.

429
PRACTICE
Write a recursive program that accepts a positive integer, n, and computes the factorial of n, written $n!$, where $n! = n \times n - 1 \times \ldots \times 1$.

430
PRACTICE
Temporarily suspending disbelief, convert the program that you wrote in Segment 429 into a program consisting of two cooperating methods, `factorial` and `recurse`. The `recurse` method is to call the `factorial` method.

431
HIGHLIGHTS

- Recursive methods work by calling themselves to solve subproblems until the subproblems are simple enough for them to solve directly.

- The portion of a recursive method that handles the simplest cases is called the base part; the portion that transforms more complex cases is called the recursion part.

- If you want to solve a difficult problem, **then** try to break it up into simpler subproblems.

- If you are writing a recursive method, **then** your method must handle the simplest cases, **and** must break down every other case into the simplest cases.

- If your recursive method is to count down a number, **then** you may be able to instantiate the following recursive counting pattern:

```
public static int method name (int n) {
  if (n == 0) {
   return result for n equal 0 ;
  }
  else {
   return combination operand
          combination operator
          method name (n - 1);
  }
}
```

25 HOW TO WRITE MULTIWAY CONDITIONAL STATEMENTS

432   In this section, you learn how to write programs that decide which of many alternatives to execute on the basis of an expression that returns an integer value.

433   The purpose of a `switch` statement is to execute a particular sequence of statements according to the value of an expression that produces an integer. In most `switch` statements, each anticipated value of the integer-producing expression and the corresponding sequence of statements is sandwiched between a `case` keyword on one end and a `break` or `return` statement on the other, with a colon separating the anticipated value and the statement sequence:

```
switch ( integer-producing expression ) {
  case integer constant 1 : statements for integer 1 break;
  case integer constant 2 : statements for integer 2 break;
  ...
  default: default statements
}
```

When such a switch statement is encountered, the expression is evaluated, producing an integer. That value is compared with the integer constants found following the `case` keywords. As soon as there is a match, evaluation of the following statements begins; execution continues up to the first `break` or `return` statement encountered.

The line beginning with the `default` keyword is optional. If the expression produces an integer that fails to match any of the `case` integer constants, the statements following the `default` keyword are executed.

If there is no match and no `default` keyword, no statements are executed.

434   The version of the `rabbits` method shown in the program in Segment 421 contains an `if-else` statement that determines what to do for any number of rabbits:

```
public class Demonstrate {
 public static int rabbits (int n) {
  if (n == 0 || n == 1) {
   return 1;
  }
  else {
   return rabbits(n - 1) + rabbits(n - 2);
  }
 }
}
```

If you wish, you can rewrite the program without the `||` operator, handling 0 and 1 separately:

```
public class Demonstrate {
 public static int rabbits (int n) {
  if (n == 0) {return 1;}
  else if (n == 1) {return 1;}
  else {return rabbits(n - 1) + rabbits(n - 2);}
 }
}
```

435 If you wish, you can use a switch statement to control recursion. In the following, the first two statement sequences are terminated by return statements, rather than by break statements.

```
public class Demonstrate {
 public static int rabbits (int n) {
  switch (n) {
   case 0: return 1;
   case 1: return 1;
   default: return rabbits(n - 1) + rabbits(n - 2);
  }
 }
}
```

436 When there is no break or return statement to terminate the execution of a sequence of statements, execution is said to **fall through** to the next sequence of statements, where execution continues, once again, in search of a break or return statement.

The reason for the fall-through feature is that you occasionally want to perform the same action in response to any of several conditions.

Note carefully, however, that inadvertently forgetting a break or return statement is a common error.

437 The following switch statement does the work with no duplication of the return statement:

```
public class Demonstrate {
 public static int rabbits (int n) {
  switch (n) {
   case 0: case 1: return 1;
   default: return rabbits(n - 1) + rabbits(n - 2);
  }
 }
}
```

438 The integer constants and the integer-producing expression in switch statements can be any of the integral types. In Section 30, you learn about a program in which the integer constants are characters, and the integer-producing expression produces a character.

Write a program that accepts two numbers, representing a year and a month, and displays the number of days in that month. Use a `switch` statement, and be sure to exploit the fall-through feature. Note that leap years occur in years divisible by 4, except for centenary years that are not divisible by 400.

- If you want a program to decide which of many alternative statements to evaluate, **then** instantiate the following pattern:

```
switch ( integer-producing expression ) {
  case integer constant 1 : statements for integer 1 break;
  case integer constant 2 : statements for integer 2 break;
  ...
  default: default statements
}
```

- In `switch` statements, you can omit the keyword `default:` and the default statements.

- In `switch` statements, the integer-producing expression can produce a value belonging to any of the integral data types, including the `char` data type.

- In `switch` statements, once embedded statement execution begins, execution continues up to the first embedded `break` or `return` statement, or to the end of the `switch` statement, whichever comes first. Bugs emerge when you forget to pair `case` keywords with `break` or `return` statements.

26 HOW TO CREATE FILE STREAMS FOR INPUT

441   So far, you have worked exclusively with wired-in information. In this section, you learn how to work with information stored in files.

442   A **stream** is a sequence of data. The stream that flows from your program to your display is the **standard output stream**; the stream that flows from your keyboard to your program is the **standard input stream**:

```
                Standard                    Standard
                input stream                output stream
Keyboard  ─────────────────────▶ Your program ─────────────────────▶ Display
```

443   To read data from a file, you create an **input stream** that connects an input file to your program. Similarly, to write data into a file, you create an **output stream** that flows from your program to the output file.

```
            File                        File
            input stream                output stream
Input file ─────────────────▶ Your program ─────────────────▶ Output file
```

444   To create an input stream connected to a file, you use an expression that creates an instance of the FileInputStream class, also known as a **file input stream**, for a specified file.

The following is an example in which the file specification happens to be "input.data", and the file input stream is assigned to inputFile:

```
                              File specification ┐
                                                 ▼
                                        _____

FileInputStream inputFile = new FileInputStream("input.data");
```

Of course, the file specification may include a **path**, as in the following example:

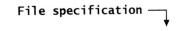

```
FileInputStream inputFile
  = new FileInputStream("/phw/onto/java/input.data");
    _____

                         ↑
                         └─ Path
```

445   Given a file input stream, you can read 1 byte at a time from that stream. You are more likely to want to be able to read complete numbers and strings, however, so you must convert a FileInputStream instance into a StreamTokenizer instance. In the following statement, you declare a StreamTokenizer variable, and create a StreamTokenizer instance from a FileInputStream instance:

```
                    ┌─── StreamTokenizer variable
                    │
                    ▼
StreamTokenizer tokens = new StreamTokenizer(inputFile);
                                                    ▲
                                                    │
                    FileInputStream instance ───────┘
```

StreamTokenizer instances are called **tokenizers**.

446 Tokenizers treat whitespace characters as delimiters that divide character sequences into **tokens**. Thus, a file containing the following characters is viewed as a stream of nine tokens divided by spaces and line-terminating characters:

    4   7   3
    8   8   7
    2 10   5

447 You can think of a tokenizer as though it were a machine that steps through a stream of tokens. The nextToken method moves the machine from one token to the next. Suppose, for example, that you call nextToken with tokens, a StreamTokenizer instance, as the target:

tokens.nextToken()

The first time that Java executes a call to the nextToken method, given that the first token is a number, the value of that token is assigned to the nval instance variable in the tokenizer:

After Java executes the second call to nextToken, the second token is assigned to nval:

448 Because the value of the current token is stored in the nval instance variable of the tokenizer, you obtain the number using the field-selection operator:

tokens.nval

449   Note that the number stored in the nval instance variable is always a floating-point double value, even if what you see in the file is an integer. The rationale is that you can always cast a double value into any other type. Accordingly, if your file contains integers, and you want to work with int values, you need to cast the number that you obtain from the nval instance variable:

```
(int) tokens.nval
```

450   As the token machine moves down a stream of tokens, eventually it reaches the end of the token stream. At that point, the nextToken method returns a special value, which is the same as the value assigned to the TT_EOF instance variable of the tokenizer, where TT is an acronym for token type.

Thus, when nextToken returns a value equal to the value of the TT_EOF instance variable, there are no more tokens to be read. Accordingly, you can read and process all the integer tokens in a token stream with a while loop such as the following:

```
while (tokens.nextToken() != tokens.TT_EOF) {
  ...
  ... (int) tokens.nval ...
  ...
}
```

451   The value of the TT_EOF variable happens to be an integer, so you can assign that value to an int variable. Good programming practice dictates that you should never use the integer in place of the instance variable, because using the instance variable makes it clear, without any inference, that you are testing for the end of the token stream.

452   Before you can do anything with the FileInputStream and StreamTokenizer classes, you must inform Java that you wish to use classes defined in a group of classes called the **input–output package**, also known as the io package.

In general, if you want to use a particular class in a particular package, then you inform Java that you want that class by including a statement such as the following in your class definition:

```
       ┌── Include a class from the io package
       │        ┌── Include the FileInputStream class
       │        │
       ▼        ▼
       ───────  ──────────────
import java.io.FileInputStream;
```

Alternatively, if you want to tell Java to be prepared to use any class in a particular package, then you include an asterisk, instead of a class name, in the import statement:

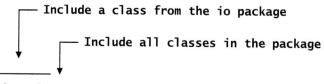

Include a class from the io package

Include all classes in the package

```
import java.io.*;
```

The advantage of using an asterisk is that you can cover all the classes from a single package in one statement; the disadvantage is that your compiler may work slowly.

453   Whenever you create `FileInputStream` and `StreamTokenizer` instances, you must also tell Java what to do in the event that a horrible input–output error occurs: perhaps your program will try to attach a stream to a file that does not exist, or will try to read from an empty stream.

In such horrible situations, Java is said to **throw an exception**. For example, Java throws an exception that is an instance of the `FileNotFoundException` class whenever you try to connect a file input stream to a file that does not exist.

454   To tell Java what to do when exceptions are thrown, you have two choices.

First, you can embed a group of statements, some of which may throw exceptions, in a `try–catch` statement, in which you specify explicitly what Java is to do when particular exceptions are thrown. You learn about this approach in Section 31.

Second, you can indicate that a method contains statements that may throw exceptions with which you do not wish to deal in that method. You so indicate by adding the keyword `throws` and the name of the exception class, or a superclass of the exception class, to the method definition. To handle all sorts of input–output exceptions, including instances of the `FileNotFoundException` class, you use `IOException` as the name of the exception class:

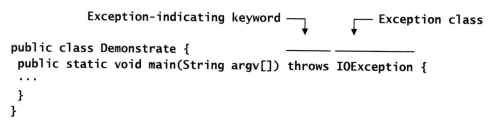

Exception-indicating keyword

Exception class

```
public class Demonstrate {
 public static void main(String argv[]) throws IOException {
 ...
 }
}
```

Java insists that you use either a `try–catch` statement or the `throws` keyword, to force you to think about what you want to happen in the event that a failure occurs.

Of the two approaches, you see the `throws` keyword in this section, because the focus of this section is on streams, not on exception handling. In general, however, using a `try–catch` statement is better programming practice, because such statements place the solution to a problem close to where the problem occurs.

455   At this point, at last, you have all the machinery needed to produce a series of `int` values from the information in a file. When you gather that machinery into a program, you have the following, which simply displays the `int` values, one to a line:

```
import java.io.*;
public class Demonstrate {
 public static void main(String argv[]) throws IOException {
  FileInputStream inputFile = new FileInputStream("input.data");
  StreamTokenizer tokens = new StreamTokenizer(inputFile);
  while (tokens.nextToken() != tokens.TT_EOF) {
    System.out.println("Integer: " + (int) tokens.nval);
  }
 }
}
```

────────────────── Sample Data ──────────────────
```
 4  7  3
```
────────────────── Result ──────────────────
```
Integer: 4
Integer: 7
Integer: 3
```

456 Of course, the program in Segment 455 goes to a lot of trouble to produce int values from the characters in a file, just to display them for you as characters. Accordingly, the next example uses the int values to initialize Movie instances, each of which becomes the target of the ratings method, as defined, for example, in the class definitions provided in Segment 323.

```
import java.io.*;
public class Demonstrate {
 public static void main(String argv[]) throws IOException {
  FileInputStream inputFile = new FileInputStream("input.data");
  StreamTokenizer tokens = new StreamTokenizer(inputFile);
  while (tokens.nextToken() != tokens.TT_EOF) {
    int x = (int) tokens.nval;
    tokens.nextToken(); int y = (int) tokens.nval;
    tokens.nextToken(); int z = (int) tokens.nval;
    Movie m = new Movie(x, y, z);
    System.out.println("Rating: " + m.rating());
  }
 }
}
```

────────────────── Sample Data ──────────────────
```
 4  7  3
 8  8  7
 2 10  5
```
────────────────── Result ──────────────────
```
Rating: 14
Rating: 23
Rating: 17
```

457   When you are finished with an input file stream, you should close it, using the `close` method:

```
inputFile.close()
```

Java generally closes all streams for you, once they no longer can be accessed, but Java may not close a particular stream for a long time. Accordingly, you should close files using the `close` method, as a matter of good programming practice.

458   Of course, a token stream may produce not only number tokens, but also string tokens. Suppose, for example, that movie names are included in the input file, with delimiting double quotation marks:

```
"Apocalypse Now"          4   7   3
"The Sting"               8   8   7
"Bedtime for Bonzo"       2  10   5
```

First, you learn how to recognize and ignore the movie names. In Section 30, you learn how to incorporate them into `Movie` instances.

459   You know that `nextToken` returns the value of the TT_EOF instance variable when there are no more tokens.

In the event that there is a token, the value returned by `nextToken` depends on whether the token is a number or a string. If the token is a number, `nextToken` returns the value of the TT_NUMBER instance variable; if the token is a string, `nextToken` returns the value of the TT_WORD instance variable.

460   Whenever the token is a whitespace-delimited string, that token is assigned to the `sval` instance variable of the tokenizer. For example, if movie names are included in the file, each word in those movie names becomes a value of the `sval` instance variable:

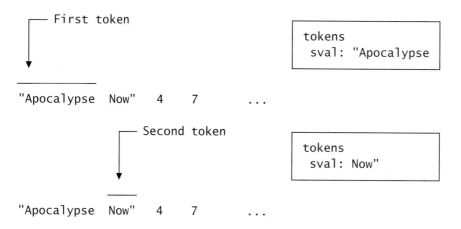

461   You readily can adapt the program in Segment 456 to deal with both numbers and strings. In the following, the value of the `nextToken` method is assigned to a local variable, `next`, which is then compared with the TT_NUMBER and TT_WORD instance variables. In the event

that the value returned by the nextToken method is the value of the TT_WORD instance variable, the token is ignored. A switch statement, of the sort you learned about in Section 25, takes care of responding appropriately to the value:

```java
import java.io.*;
public class Demonstrate {
 public static void main(String argv[]) throws IOException {
  FileInputStream inputFile = new FileInputStream("input.data");
  StreamTokenizer tokens = new StreamTokenizer(inputFile);
  int next = 0;
  while((next = tokens.nextToken()) != tokens.TT_EOF) {
   switch (next) {
    case tokens.TT_WORD: break;
    case tokens.TT_NUMBER:
     int x = (int) tokens.nval;
     tokens.nextToken(); int y = (int) tokens.nval;
     tokens.nextToken(); int z = (int) tokens.nval;
     Movie m = new Movie(x, y, z);
     System.out.println("Rating: " + m.rating());
     break;
   }
  }
  inputFile.close();
 }
}
```

———————————————————— Sample Data ————————————————————

"Apocalypse Now"	4	7	3
"The Sting"	8	8	7
"Bedtime for Bonzo"	2	10	5

————————————————————— Result —————————————————————

Rating: 14
Rating: 23
Rating: 17

462
SIDE TRIP Java's tokenizer mechanisms serve in place of scanf in C and the insertion operator, >>, in C++.

463
PRACTICE Suppose you are hired as a programmer by a baseball team. Your first job is to write a program that reads a file containing opponent names and scores. Your team's score comes first, followed by the opponent's score.

Twins	2	4
Yankees	9	5
Blue Jays	4	3

Your program is to use the information in the file to display your team's won/lost record.

- If you want to tell Java that you intend to work with file input or file output streams, **then** include the following line in your program:

```
import java.io.*;
```

- If you want to read from an input file, **then** instantiate the following pattern:

```
FileInputStream file variable
 = new FileInputStream( file specification );
StreamTokenizer token variable
 = new StreamTokenizer( file variable );
```

- If you want to move a tokenizer to the next token, **then** instantiate the following pattern:

```
token variable .nextToken()
```

- If you want to read from a tokenizer until it is empty, **then** instantiate the following pattern:

```
while( token variable .nextToken() != token variable .TT_EOF) {
...
}
```

- If you want to know whether the current token is a number, **then** compare the value produced by nextToken to the TT_NUMBER instance variable:

```
token variable .nextToken() == token variable .TT_NUMBER
```

- If you want to know whether the current token is a string, **then** compare the value produced by nextToken to the TT_WORD instance variable:

```
token variable .nextToken() == token variable .TT_WORD
```

- If the current token is a number, **and** you want to use the value of that number, **then** instantiate the following pattern:

```
( desired type ) token variable .nval
```

- If the current token is a string, **and** you want to use the value of that string, **then** instantiate the following pattern:

```
token variable .sval
```

- If you have finished reading from an input file stream, **then** close the file by instantiating the following pattern:

```
file variable .close();
```

27 HOW TO CREATE AND ACCESS ARRAYS

465　In this section, you learn how to store information in arrays, and you learn how to retrieve such information.

466　An `Array` instance, also known as an **array** by the convention mentioned in Segment 173, contains a collection of **elements** that Java stores and retrieves using an integer **index**. In Java, the first element is indexed by zero; hence, Java is said to have **zero-based arrays**.

The following, for example, is a one-dimensional array, of length 4, with integer elements:

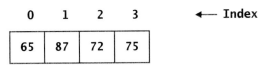

467　The number of bytes allocated for each place in an array is determined by the type of the elements to be stored. If an array is to hold integers of type `short`, for example, Java allocates 2 bytes per integer. On the other hand, if an array is to hold integers of type `int`, Java allocates 4 bytes per integer.

468　To declare a variable with an array as that variable's type, you add brackets to an ordinary variable declaration. For example, to declare `durations` to be a variable to which an integer array will be assigned, you write the following:

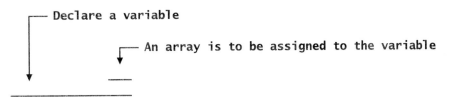

```
int durations [ ];
```

469　Variables typed with arrays are said to be **reference variables**. You learned in Segment 77 that variables typed with classes are also reference variables.

470　To create an array instance, you need to deploy the `new` operator, just as you need to deploy the `new` operator to create any kind of instance.

To signal that the kind of instance to be created is an array, you include a bracketed number that specifies how many elements the array is to hold. For example, to create an array of four integers, you write the following:

        ┌──── Specifies that a new array instance is to be created
        │
        ▼
   ──────────
   new int [4]
        ▲   ▲
        │   └──── Specifies that the instance contains four elements
        │
        └──── Specifies that the new array contains integer elements

471 At this point, you can declare an integer array variable, and can assign an integer array instance to that variable:

```
int durations [];
durations = new int [4];
```

Alternatively, you can combine variable declaration and array creation:

        ┌── Declare   ┌── Create
        │   │
        ▼   ▼
   ──────────────   ──────────
   int durations [] = new int [4];

472 To use an array, once it is created, you need to know how to write into and to read from the various locations in the array, each of which is identified by a numerical index.

Consider durations—the one-dimensional array of integers. To write data into that array, you use assignment statements in which the array name and a bracketed integer index appear on the left side of an assignment operator—the place where you are accustomed to seeing variable names. The following statement, for example, inserts an integer into the place indexed by the value of counter:

```
durations[counter] = 65;
```

473 You can combine array creation and element insertion by using an **array initializer**, in which specific elements appear, separated by commas, and surrounded by brackets:

```
int durations [] = {65, 87, 72, 75};
```

The array initializer shown specifies that an array is to be created, that the array is to have four elements provided, and that the initial values are to be 65, 87, 72, and 75. Thus, one statement takes the place of five:

```
int durations[] = new int [4];
durations[0] = 65;
durations[1] = 87;
durations[2] = 72;
durations[3] = 75;
```

474   To read data from the `durations` array, once the data have been written, you write an expression containing the array name and a bracketed integer index. The following expression, for example, yields the integer stored in the place indexed by the value of `counter`:

```
durations[counter]
```

475   To obtain the length of an array, you can use the field-selection operator to obtain the value of the `length` instance variable:

```
durations.length
```

476   Whenever you create an array of numbers, all the elements in the array are initialized automatically to 0.

477   The following program defines an array of four integers, wires in integers via an array initializer, computes the sum of the integers, and displays the average:

```
public class Demonstrate {
 public static void main (String argv[]) {
   int counter, sum = 0;
   int durations [] = {65, 87, 72, 75};
   for (counter = 0; counter < durations.length; ++counter)
     sum = sum + durations[counter];
   System.out.print("The average of the " + durations.length);
   System.out.println(" durations is " + sum / durations.length);
 }
}
```
———————————————— Result ————————————————
```
The average of the 4 durations is 74
```

478   You can use arrays to store not only numbers, but also class instances. Once you have defined the `Movie` class, for example, you can use the following statement to declare and initialize a `Movie` array variable:

      ┌── **Declare**   ┌── **Initialize**
      ↓   ↓

```
Movie movies [] = new Movie [4];
```

479   To insert a `Movie` instance into an array, you use an assignment statement, in which the array name and a bracketed integer index are followed by the assignment operator, and an expression that yields a `Movie` instance.

                   ┌── **Expression that yields a new Movie instance**
                   ↓

```
movies[counter] = new Movie();
```

480 Once you have inserted `Movie` instances into an array, you can alter the instance variables in that `Movie` instance. For example, to write into an element of the `movies` array, you use assignment statements in which the array name, a bracketed integer index, and the instance-variable name appear on the left side:

```
                    ┌── Instance-variable name

                            ┌── Value to be stored


movies[counter].script = 6;
```

481 To read data from the `movies` array, once the data have been inserted, you simply write an expression containing the array name, a bracketed integer index, and the instance-variable name. The following expression, for example, yields the value of the `script` instance variable of the `Movie` instance stored in the place indexed by the value of `counter`:

```
movies[counter].script
```

482 Whenever you create an array of instances, all the elements in the array are initialized to a value that represents the absence of an instance. That value is denoted as `null`. Thus, if you want a program to determine whether it has written into an array of instances at a particular place, you compare the value obtained from that place with `null`. If the value obtained from a place is `null`, you have yet to write an instance into that place:

```
movies[counter] == null
```

483 To use an array element as an instance method target, you write an expression containing the array name, a bracketed integer index, and the instance-method name and arguments. The following expression, for example, yields the value produced by `rating` when used on the `Movie` instance stored in the place indexed by the value of `counter`:

```
movies[counter].rating()
```

484 You can combine array creation and element insertion when the elements are of type `Movie`, just as you can combine array creation and element insertion when the elements are of type `int`. For example, to create a four-element array of specific movies, you can write the following, in which all `Movie` instances happen to be created with the three-parameter constructor:

```
Movie movies[] = {new Movie(5, 6, 3), new Movie(8, 7, 7),
                  new Movie(7, 2, 2), new Movie(7, 5, 5)};
```

485 The following is a program in which an array of four `Movie` instances is defined, data are wired in via an array initializer, the sum of the ratings is determined in a `for` loop, and the average of those ratings is reported via a print statement. The `Movie` class involved is the one defined in Segment 323:

```
public class Demonstrate {
 public static void main (String argv[]) {
  Movie movies[] = {new Movie(5, 6, 3),
                    new Movie(8, 7, 7),
                    new Movie(7, 2, 2),
                    new Movie(7, 5, 5)};
  int counter, sum = 0;
  for (counter = 0; counter < movies.length; ++counter)
    sum = sum + movies[counter].rating();
  System.out.print("The average rating of the " + movies.length);
  System.out.println(" movies is " + sum / movies.length);
 }
}
```

———————————————— Result ————————————————
```
The average rating of the 4 movies is 16
```

486 Now, suppose that you have defined the Attraction class, the Movie class, and the Symphony class as in Segment 323. If you then declare an array for instances of the Attraction class, you can place Movie instances and Symphony instances in that array, because the value of an element of an array declared for a particular class can be an instance of any subclass of that class.

For example, you can compute the average rating of a mixed array of Movie and Symphony instances:

```
public class Demonstrate {
 public static void main (String argv[]) {
  int counter, sum = 0;
  Attraction attractions[] = {new Movie(4, 7, 3),
                              new Movie(8, 8, 7),
                              new Symphony(10, 9, 3),
                              new Symphony(9, 5, 8)};
  for (counter = 0; counter < attractions.length; ++counter) {
    sum = sum + attractions[counter].rating();
  }
  System.out.print("The average rating of the " + attractions.length);
  System.out.println(" attractions is " + sum / attractions.length);
 }
}
```

———————————————— Result ————————————————
```
The average rating of the 4 attractions is 20
```

487 Many programmers find it helpful—albeit not absolutely necessary—to understand, in general terms, how arrays are implemented.

In Java, integer arrays contain a length instance variable and 4 bytes of memory for every int instance in the array:

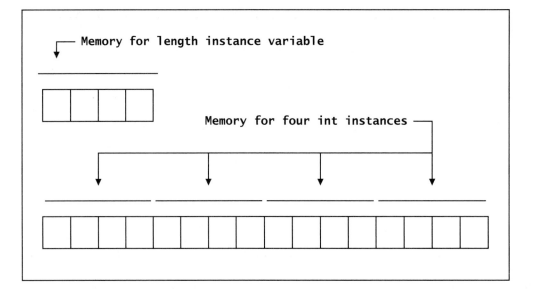

The 4-byte chunks are arranged consecutively in memory. If you want to know the address of the first byte occupied by the nth integer, you add the address of the first byte of the zeroth integer to $4 \times n$.

488   All other arrays of primitive types are arranged the same way. The location of the nth element is always the sum of the address of the first byte of the zeroth element and n times the number of bytes occupied by each element.

489   Instances of a reference type cannot be stored so straightforwardly, because the number of bytes required for each element may vary.

For example, an instance of the Attraction class will need fewer bytes than will instances of the Movie and Symphony classes, both of which are subclasses of the Attraction class. Yet instances of the Movie and Symphony classes are valid occupants of an Attraction array.

Accordingly, you cannot store mixtures of Array, Movie, and Symphony instances consecutively, expecting that the nth element will be offset from the beginning of the array by n times a constant number of bytes.

490   In Java, Attraction arrays each contain a length instance variable and several bytes of memory for the **address** of every Attraction instance in the array.

Even though the instances may occupy different amounts of space, the instance addresses occupy the same amount of space. Hence, the address of the nth instance address will be offset from the beginning of the array by n times a constant number of bytes.

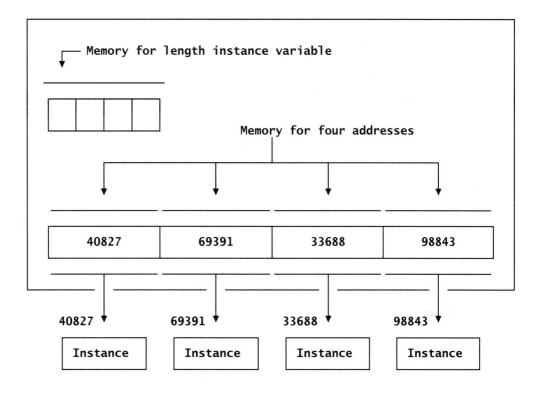

Memory for length instance variable

Memory for four addresses

| 40827 | 69391 | 33688 | 98843 |

40827   69391   33688   98843

| Instance | Instance | Instance | Instance |

491   Whenever you assign a new instance to an array, displacing an existing element, and that displaced instance is not an element of any other array or the value of any variable, then the memory for that instance is returned to the free-storage list via the garbage-collection process described in Segment 191.

492   The addresses that connect arrays to class instances are called pointers. Java moves through
SIDE TRIP   the pointers to the instances for you automatically, so you do not need to know even that pointers exist.

C and C++ provide elaborate tools for pointer manipulation. Accordingly, proponents of those languages consider the pointer-manipulation tools to be a strength of the language.

Explicit pointer manipulation by programmers can be a source of system-endangering bugs, because you can chase an errant pointer into the wrong part of memory, or even, in extreme cases, into some other program. Accordingly, proponents of Java consider the absence of pointer-manipulation tools to be a strength of the language.

Proponents of Java sometimes say that Java has no pointers when what they mean is that Java provides no access to pointers.

493   In C++, you are allowed to create arrays of class instances, as well as arrays of pointers to
SIDE TRIP   class instances. If you have an array of class instances, all the elements must be instances of the class, rather than instances of the class's subclasses, because only enough room is reserved for instances of the class itself.

Accordingly, if you want to place subclass instances in an array, you must use a pointer array, which, in C++, requires you to understand pointer dereferencing and virtual functions.

By uniformly implementing reference arrays with automatically handled pointers, Java avoids the need for both pointer dereferencing and virtual functions.

494
SIDE TRIP

When you create an array of class instances, memory is set aside for addresses, but memory for the class instances is not set aside until those class instances are created. Accordingly, if you should overestimate the number of elements that you need, you waste only the memory required by the unnecessary addresses, not the memory that would be required if memory were set aside for the unnecessary class instances.

In general, setting aside memory for addresses leads to far less memory waste than the alternative approach of setting aside memory for class instances.

495
PRACTICE

You easily can define arrays with more than one dimension: you simply add more bracketed dimension sizes. For example, to define a `double` array with 2 rows and 100 columns, you proceed as follows:

```
double 2DArray [] [] = new double[2][100];
```

Amend the program you were asked to write in Segment 463 such that it writes scores into an array with 2 rows and 160 columns. Then, display not only the won/lost record, but the average difference between your team's score and the opponent's score for games won and for games lost.

496
HIGHLIGHTS

- If you want to declare and initialize a one-dimensional array, **then** instantiate the following pattern:

  `data type` `array name` `[]` =
  `new` `data type` `[` `number of elements` `]`;

- If you have an array, **and** you want to write a value into the array at a specified position, **then** instantiate the following pattern:

  `array name` `[` `index` `]` = `expression` ;

- If you want to know whether an array has been assigned a value at a specified position, **then** instantiate the following pattern:

  `array name` `[` `index` `]` == `null`

- If you have a value stored in an array at a specified position, **and** you want to read that value, **then** instantiate the following pattern:

  `array name` `[` `index` `]`

- If you want to know the length of an array, **then** instantiate the following pattern:

```
array name .length
```

28 HOW TO MOVE ARRAYS INTO AND OUT OF METHODS

497　In Section 26, you learned how to use tokenizers to read integers and strings from a file. In Section 27, you learned how to store information in arrays.

Now, you can combine what you learned about files with what you learned about arrays to read movie-rating information from a file, to create movie instances, and to store those instances in an array.

498　You probably do not know exactly how many Movie instances you need to store. Accordingly, you need to define an array that is sure to be large enough to hold all the elements that you can possibly encounter.

If you cannot determine a maximum size for an array because the number of needed elements is too unpredictable, you probably should store your information in a vector. You learn about vectors in Section 29.

499　The following program creates an array that can hold up to 100 Movie instances. Then, it fills part or all of that array with Movie instances:

```java
import java.io.*;
public class Demonstrate {
 public static void main(String argv[]) throws IOException {
   FileInputStream inputFile = new FileInputStream("input.data");
   StreamTokenizer tokens = new StreamTokenizer(inputFile);
   int movieCounter = 0;
   Movie movies [] = new Movie [100];
   while (tokens.nextToken() != tokens.TT_EOF) {
     int x = (int) tokens.nval;
     tokens.nextToken(); int y = (int) tokens.nval;
     tokens.nextToken(); int z = (int) tokens.nval;
     movies [movieCounter] = new Movie(x, y, z);
     ++movieCounter;
   }
   inputFile.close();
 }
}
```

500　To make the file-reading and array-writing program in Segment 499 generally useful, you must repackage that program as a method defined in its own class, rather than retaining it as part of main in the Demonstrate class. Accordingly, you need to know how to specify that a parameter is an array and that a returned value is an array.

501　To specify that a parameter is an array, you include brackets with the parameter type specification. Similarly, to specify that a method produces an array value, you include brackets with the return-value type specification.

502 Suppose, for example, that you decide to repackage the file-reading and array-storing apparatus into a method named `readData`. You write `readData`, a class method that both accepts and returns an array of `Movie` instances:

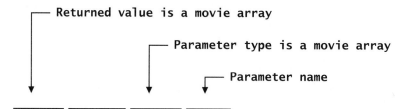

```
public static Movie[] readData(Movie[] movies) throws IOException {
  ...
}
```

Equivalently, you can place the brackets behind the parameter name, with or without an intervening space:

```
                                                    ┌── Optional space
public static Movie[] readData(Movie movies []) throws IOException {
  ...
}
```

503 Now, you can create a movie array in `main`, and can hand that array to the `readData` class method, defined in the `Auxiliaries` class. Evidently, the `readData` method adds elements to the array and returns it, whereupon a `for` loop prints ratings. Note that the `main` program determines that there are no more movies with which to deal by looking for `null`, as explained in Segment 482:

```
import java.io.*;
public class Demonstrate {
 public static void main(String argv[]) throws IOException {
  Movie mainArray [] = new Movie [100];
  mainArray = Auxiliaries.readData(mainArray);
  int counter;
  Movie m;
  for (counter = 0; (m = mainArray[counter]) != null; ++counter) {
   System.out.println(m.rating());
  }
 }
}
```

504 The required definition for the `readData` method is as follows:

```
import java.io.*;
public class Auxiliaries {
 public static Movie[] readData(Movie movies []) throws IOException {
   FileInputStream inputFile = new FileInputStream("input.data");
   StreamTokenizer tokens = new StreamTokenizer(inputFile);
   int movieCounter = 0;
   while (tokens.nextToken() != tokens.TT_EOF) {
    int x = (int) tokens.nval;
    tokens.nextToken(); int y = (int) tokens.nval;
    tokens.nextToken(); int z = (int) tokens.nval;
    movies [movieCounter] = new Movie(x, y, z);
    ++movieCounter;
   }
   inputFile.close();
   return movies;
 }
}
```

505 Curiously, the following pair of methods also works, although, at first glance, it might seem that nothing is returned from `readData`, inasmuch as `readData` has the `void` keyword, instead of a return type, and the call to `readData` does not appear in an assignment statement:

```
import java.io.*;
public class Demonstrate {
 public static void main(String argv[]) throws IOException {
   Movie mainArray [] = new Movie [100];
   Auxiliaries.readData(mainArray);
   // ... remainder as in Segment 503 ...
 }
}
```

```
import java.io.*;
public class Auxiliaries {
 public static void readData(Movie movies []) throws IOException {
   FileInputStream inputFile = new FileInputStream("input.data");
   StreamTokenizer tokens = new StreamTokenizer(inputFile);
   int movieCounter = 0;
   // ... while loop as in Segment 504 ...
   inputFile.close();
   // Return statement deleted here
 }
}
```

506 To understand why the program in Segment 505 works, you need to know that, when an array is assigned to a variable, the value is represented as an address of a chunk of memory representing an array instance:

mainArray, in main

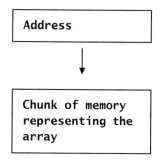

When you hand `mainArray` to `readData`, the value of the parameter, `movies`, becomes a copy of the address of `mainArray`, because Java's parameters are **call-by-value** parameters, which you learned about in Segment 135.

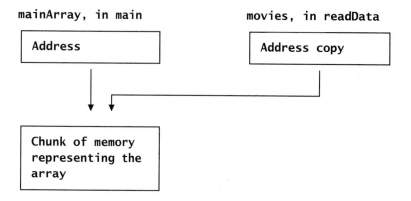

Note, however, that only the address is copied; the contents of the chunk of memory representing the array are not copied. Accordingly, any changes to the elements of the array inside `readData` are retained after `readData` returns. In this respect, the argument–parameter relationship of an array is like the argument–parameter relationship of an instance, as described in Segment 190.

507 So far, you have seen two ways to write the `main`–`readData` combination:

- You create an array in `main`. The address of the memory representing the array is assigned to a variable in `main`. Then, you hand over the address to `readData`, where it is assigned to a parameter. On return, the address is handed back, and again is assigned to the variable in `main` from whence it came.

- You create an array in `main`. The address of the memory representing the array is assigned to a variable in `main`. Then, you hand over the address to `readData`, where it is assigned to a parameter. Nothing is returned, but the changes to the array stick, because only the address is copied on entering `readData`, and the array elements are not copied.

There is another alternative:

- You only declare an array variable in `main`. Thus, there is no array to hand to `readData`. Instead, you create the array in `readData`, and hand it back as the value of `readData`.

508 The following program illustrates the approach that creates the array in the called method. In this version, the file name is passed from `main` to `readData`:

```
import java.io.*;
public class Demonstrate {
 public static void main(String argv[]) throws IOException {
  Movie mainArray [] = Auxiliaries.readData("input.data");
  // ... remainder as in Segment 503 ...
 }
}
```

```
import java.io.*;
public class Auxiliaries {
 public static Movie[] readData(String fileName) throws IOException {
  FileInputStream inputFile = new FileInputStream(fileName);
  StreamTokenizer tokens = new StreamTokenizer(inputFile);
  Movie movies [] = new Movie [100];
  int movieCounter = 0;
  // ... while loop as in Segment 504 ...
  inputFile.close();
  return movies;
 }
}
```

509 Now that you understand how to declare array parameters, you are, at last, ready to understand why the `main` method has a parameter declared by `String arg[]`.

Evidently, the `main` method has just one parameter, `arg`, which is assigned, when the method is called, to an array of `String` instances. The length of the array is equal to the number of command-line arguments provided; each element corresponds to one command-line argument.

Thus, the following program displays all the command-line arguments provided when the `Demonstrate` program is called:

```
public class Demonstrate {
 public static void main(String argv[]) {
  int counter;
  int max = argv.length;
  for (counter = 0; counter < max; ++counter) {
   System.out.println(argv[counter]);
  }
 }
}
```

Suppose that you run the program by typing the following command line:

```
java Demonstrate This is a test
```

Then, the program displays the arguments, one to a line:

```
This
is
a
test
```

510 You are free, of course, to use the strings provided by the command line in any way you wish.

Frequently, you may wish the strings were numbers, rather than strings. Fortunately, you can convert strings to integers using the parseInt class method of the Integer class.

Thus, if you want to supply rating information as a set of command-line arguments, you can produce integers from those arguments as illustrated in the following program, which computes a movie rating:

```
public class Demonstrate {
  public static void main(String argv[]) {
    Movie m = new Movie(Integer.parseInt(argv[0]),
                        Integer.parseInt(argv[1]),
                        Integer.parseInt(argv[2]));
    System.out.println("The rating is " + m.rating());
  }
}
```

Suppose that you run the program by typing the following command line:

```
java Demonstrate 4 7 3
```

Then, the program displays the movie rating:

```
The rating is 14
```

511 Typing data is tedious; even skilled typists make mistakes. Accordingly, suppose you
PRACTICE decide to have two typists independently create files for your baseball team's season record. Assume both typists use the format shown in Segment 463.

To use both files, you decide to write two methods: readScores and verifyScores. The readScores method is to take a file-name argument and return a two-dimensional array of the sort you learned about in Segment 495. The verifyScores method is to take two arguments: a file name and the array produced by readScores. The verifyScores method is to display information about every score for which the two files differ, and return true only if there are no discrepancies.

512
HIGHLIGHTS
- If you want to specify that a parameter is an array, **then** include brackets with the parameter type specification.

- **If** you want to specify that a method produces an array value, **then** include brackets with the return-value type specification.

- When you hand an array argument to a method, the array address is copied, and is assigned to the corresponding method parameter. The array itself is not copied.

29 HOW TO STORE DATA IN EXPANDABLE VECTORS

513   You learn about vectors in this section. You learn that vectors are useful alternatives to arrays, especially when you are unsure about how much information you need to be able to store.

514   An instance of the `Vector` class, also known as a **vector** by the convention mentioned in Segment 173, contains elements that are stored and retrieved in several ways. For example, you can store and retrieve the elements of a vector using an integer **index**, just as you can store and retrieve the elements of an array.

515   Instances of the `Vector` class differ substantively from those of the `Array` class, however:

- You can store any number of elements in any vector. Vectors are not of fixed size.
- You can add elements to the front or back of a vector, or even insert elements into the middle without replacing an existing element.
- You can store only class instances in vectors. Vectors cannot hold elements of primitive type.

516   The `Vector` class is one of many offerings provided in Java's `util` package; `util` is, of course, an acronym for **util**ities.

517   You declare `Vector` variables just as you would any variable to which class instances are assigned. For example, to declare v to be a variable to which a vector will be assigned, you write the following:

```
┌─ Declare a Vector variable
▼
─────────
Vector v;
```

To create a vector instance, you deploy the new operator:

```
┌─ Create a Vector instance
▼
─────────
new Vector()
```

Both to declare a vector variable and to create an instance, you combine variable declaration and vector creation:

```
Vector v = new Vector();
```

518 To add elements to the back end of a vector, you use the `addElement` method. For example, if a `Movie` instance is assigned to a variable m, you add that movie instance to a vector assigned to v as follows:

```
          ┌── A vector
          │              ┌── A movie instance
          │              │
          ▼              ▼
v.addElement(m)
```

519 To insert an element at a particular place, you use the `insertElementAt` method, providing an instance and an integer index as arguments. Thus, if you want to add elements to the front end of a vector, displacing all other elements, you use `insertElementAt` with an index of 0:

```
v.insertElementAt(m, 0)
```

520 To remove an element from a particular place, you use the `removeElementAt` method, providing an integer index as the argument. Thus, if you want to remove the first element of a vector, displacing all the other elements to fill in the hole, you use `removeElementAt` with an index of 0:

```
v.removeElementAt(0)
```

521 To read the element at the front end of a vector, you use the `firstElement` method:

```
v.firstElement()
```

To read the element at the back end of a vector, you use the `lastElement` method:

```
v.lastElement()
```

522 Using the `addElement`, `firstElement`, and `removeElementAt` methods, you can use vectors to represent **first-in, first-out (FIFO) queues:**

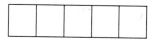

```
          ┌── firstElement reads elements from the front
          │
          ├── removeElementAt removes elements from the front
          │
          ▼
    ┌───┬───┬───┬───┬───┐
    │   │   │   │   │  ╱│
    └───┴───┴───┴───┴───┘
                    ▲
                    └── addElement adds elements at the back
```

Similarly, you can use vectors to represent **last-in, first-out (LIFO) push-down stacks** by using the `insertElementAt`, `firstElement`, and `removeElementAt` methods:

firstElement reads elements from the front

removeElementAt removes elements from the front

insertElementAt adds elements to the front

523   Once an element has been placed in a vector, you can retrieve that element using the `elementAt` method with an integer argument. For example, the following expression retrieves the element identified by an integer variable, `counter`, from the vector, v:

```
v.elementAt(counter)
```

Similarly, you can replace an element using the `setElementAt` method. For example, the following expression replaces the element identified by the value of an integer variable, `counter`, by the instance assigned to the instance variable, m:

```
v.setElementAt(m, counter)
```

Thus, `elementAt` and `setElementAt` allow you to use a vector as though it were an array.

524   The definition of the `addElement`, `insertElementAt`, and `setElementAt` methods specify that the element added shall be an instance of the `Object` class. Because all classes descend from the `Object` class, you can add any class instance to an array.

525   To obtain the number of elements in a vector, you use the `size` method:

```
v.size()
```

Note that `size` is a method; it is not an instance variable.

526   Having stored `Movie` instances in a vector, you might think that you could calculate the rating of one of those instances, using the `rating` method, as follows:

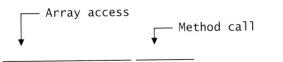

Array access

Method call

BUG!
Object instance has
no rating method

```
(v.firstElement()).rating()
```

The reason such an expression does not work is that the elements of a vector always appear to be instances of the `Object` class, and no `rating` method is defined for the `Object` class.

527   In Segment 94, you learned that you can convert a value of one arithmetic type into another by **casting**. You can also convert an instance of one class into another by casting.

For example, you can work with an element of a vector by casting that element, an `Object` instance, into a `Movie` instance:

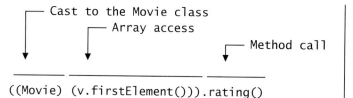

```
((Movie) (v.firstElement())).rating()
```

528   The following combination is based on the combination shown in Segment 508, and reads the same sort of data file, but differs in that a vector, rather than an array, stores `Movie` instances. The highlighted expressions and statements identify the principle differences.

```
import java.io.*;
import java.util.*;
public class Demonstrate {
 public static void main(String argv[]) throws IOException {
  Vector mainVector = Auxiliaries.readData("input.data");
  int counter;
  int size = mainVector.size();
  for (counter = 0; counter < size; ++counter) {
   System.out.println(
    ((Movie) mainVector.elementAt(counter)).rating()
   );
  }
 }
}

import java.io.*;
import java.util.*;
public class Auxiliaries {
 public static Vector readData(String fileName) throws IOException {
  FileInputStream inputFile = new FileInputStream(fileName);
  StreamTokenizer tokens = new StreamTokenizer(inputFile);
  Vector v = new Vector();
  while (tokens.nextToken() != tokens.TT_EOF) {
   int x = (int) tokens.nval;
   tokens.nextToken(); int y = (int) tokens.nval;
   tokens.nextToken(); int z = (int) tokens.nval;
   v.addElement(new Movie(x, y, z));
  }
  inputFile.close();
  return v;
 }
}
```

529   If you use a vector, you do not need to worry about how many `Movie` instances there may be; no matter how many there are, the vector will hold them, unlike an array of fixed size.

530   Because all vector elements must be instances, you might wonder how you could possibly
SIDE TRIP   make a vector of, say, `int` values, inasmuch as `int` values are not instances of a class.

The answer is that you use an instance of the `Integer` class. All such instances have an instance variable to which an integer is assigned. Because instances of the `Integer` class are instances, in contrast to `int` values, those instances are valid vector elements.

Because the purpose of `Integer` instances is to surround `int` values in a way that enables those `int` values to enter into vectors, `Integer` instances are called **wrappers**.

The `Long`, `Float`, and `Double` class serves as wrapper classes for other arithmetic types.

531   Another reason for using a wrapper is that a wrapper can be the target of method calls,
SIDE TRIP   whereas an arithmetic value, for example, cannot be such a target.

532   You get information into and out of wrappers as illustrated for the `Integer` wrappers:
SIDE TRIP

```
                    ┌── An int value
                    ↓
    new Integer(n)          ←── Create a wrapper from the int value
                                 using the new operator


                        ┌── A String instance
                        ↓
    Integer.valueOf(s)       ←── Create a wrapper from the String instance
                                 using a class method


                  ┌── An Integer instance
                  ↓
    i.intValue()            ←── Obtain embedded int value
                                 using an instance method
```

533   Write a method, `readScoreVector`, that records baseball scores in a vector. You are to
PRACTICE   obtain the scores from a file, as specified in Segment 463. Each vector element is to be an instance of a class named `Game`, which you also are to define. Instance variables are to hold your team's score and your opponent's score.

534
HIGHLIGHTS

- If you want to store instances, **but** you cannot predict how many there will be, **then** use a vector, rather than an array.

- If you want to implement a queue or a push-down stack, **then** use a vector.

- If you want to declare a vector variable and to create a vector instance, **then** instantiate the following pattern:

```
Vector vector name = new Vector();
```

- If you want to add elements to the front or back of a vector, or insert an element into a vector, **then** instantiate one of the following patterns:

  `vector name` `.insertElementAt(` `instance` `, 0)`
  `vector name` `.addElement(` `instance` `)`
  `vector name` `.insertElementAt(` `instance` `,` `index` `)`

- If you want to retrieve an element from the front or back of a vector, **then** instantiate one of the following patterns:

  `vector name` `.firstElement()`
  `vector name` `.lastElement()`

- If you want to retrieve an element from a vector, or to replace an element in a vector as though the vector were an array, **then** instantiate one of the following patterns:

  `vector name` `.elementAt(` `index` `)`
  `vector name` `.setElementAt(` `index` `)`

- If you want to know how many elements a vector contains, **then** instantiate the following pattern:

  `vector name` `.size()`

- If you want to use a vector element as a target for a method belonging to a particular class, **and** that vector element is known to be an instance of the class, **then** you can cast the vector element to the class by instantiating the following pattern:

  `((` `class name` `)` `vector element` `)`

30 HOW TO WORK WITH CHARACTERS AND STRINGS

535   In this section, you learn how to deposit both Movie and Symphony instances in a vector, using a code character added to each line of information in a file.

You also learn how to work with strings, so that you can deposit title information in Movie and Symphony instances.

536   Imagine that your data file has not only information about script, acting, and directing, but also code characters, with M indicating a Movie instance and S indicating a Symphony instance:

```
┌── Type code
↓

M  4  7  3      ←── Script, acting, and directing ratings
M  8  8  7      ←── Script, acting, and directing ratings
S 10  9  3      ←── Music, playing, and conducting ratings
```

537   You learned in Segment 460 that tokenizers read strings, such as the single character string, "M", which become the value of the tokenizer's sval instance variable. Accordingly, you can easily extract strings from a file.

538   Once you have a string, you can determine its length using the length method. For example, if codeString has a string assigned to it, you can obtain the length of the string as follows:

```
┌── Variable with a string assignment
│
│        ┌── length method
↓        ↓
─────────  ────────
codeString.length()
```

Note the contrast with arrays and vectors: to obtain the length of an array, you examine the length instance variable, rather than calling a method; to obtain the length of a vector, you deploy the size method.

539   Strings are constants. You can concatenate two strings to produce a new, longer string, but you cannot add, delete, insert into, or delete from any particular string.

540   When you wish to extract a particular character from a string, you use the charAt method, with the argument indicating the character that you wish to extract. A 0 argument indicates that you want the first character, because all string indexing is zero based, as it is with arrays:

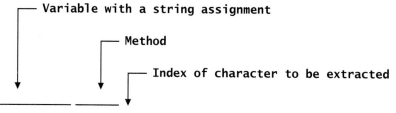

Variable with a string assignment

Method

Index of character to be extracted

```
codeString.charAt(0)
```

541   You denote a particular character by surrounding that character with single quotation marks, thus distinguishing the character from, say, a variable name. For example, you denote the character *M* by writing 'M'.

If you want to see whether you have extracted a particular character, you compare what you have extracted with that character. Then, if you wish, you can center an `if` statement on that comparison, as in the following example, which executes the block only if the first character in the string is *M*:

```
if (codeString.charAt(0) == 'M') {
  ...
}
```

542   As you learned in Segment 438, you can also use characters in `switch` statements, because characters are considered integral types:

```
switch (codeString.charAt(0)) {
  case 'M': ... break;
  ...
}
```

In this example, the integer-producing expression actually produces a character, and the integer constants actually are characters.

543   You can declare variables to be character variables. You can assign any **literal character**, such as 'X', to such variables:

```
char c = 'X';
```

544   The character type is one of the **primitive types**, which you learned about in Segment 185. The **standard default value** of a character variable is the **null character**, denoted by '\u000'.

545   You see strings and characters at work in the following program. This program differs from the one in Segment 528 in two key ways. First, the program reads strings from a file, as well as integers, and interprets the first character of those strings as a code letter. Second, the program uses the code letter to determine whether it should create a `Movie` instance or a `Symphony` instance.

```java
import java.io.*;
import java.util.*;
public class Demonstrate {
 public static void main(String argv[]) throws IOException {
  Vector mainVector;
  mainVector = Auxiliaries.readMixture("input.data");
  int counter;
  int size = mainVector.size();
  for (counter = 0; counter < size; ++counter) {
   System.out.println(
    ((Attraction)mainVector.elementAt(counter)).rating()
   );
  }
 }
}


import java.io.*;
import java.util.*;
public class Auxiliaries {
 public static Vector readMixture(String fileName) throws IOException {
  FileInputStream inputFile = new FileInputStream(fileName);
  StreamTokenizer tokens = new StreamTokenizer(inputFile);
  Vector v = new Vector();
  while (tokens.nextToken() != tokens.TT_EOF) {
   String codeString = tokens.sval;
   tokens.nextToken(); int x = (int) tokens.nval;
   tokens.nextToken(); int y = (int) tokens.nval;
   tokens.nextToken(); int z = (int) tokens.nval;
   switch (codeString.charAt(0)) {
    // First character indicates a movie:
    case 'M': v.addElement(new Movie(x, y, z)); break;
    // First character indicates a symphony:
    case 'S': v.addElement(new Symphony(x, y, z)); break;
   }
  }
  inputFile.close();
  return v;
 }
}
```

546
SIDE TRIP
Java's strings differ from the strings of C and C++, because Java's strings are instances of the String class, rather than arrays of characters. In Java, the length of a string is determined by the length method.

In C and C++, you determine length by looking for the first null character in the array. Most programmers believe that Java's approach is simpler from the conceptual perspective, and is easier to work with from the practical perspective.

547　As an illustration of other features of tokenizers, suppose that you have a file that supplies not only movie titles and rating information, but also, optionally, names of poster files, expressed in a form that you learn about in Section 39:

```
"Apocalypse Now"        4  7  3      "file:///e:/phw/onto/java/apnow.jpg"
"Bedtime for Bonzo"     8  8  7
```

An ordinary tokenizer ignores carriage returns and provides you with one title word at a time. Accordingly, you need to learn how to alter a tokenizer such that it will recognize carriage returns. You also need to learn how to use double quotation marks to delimit strings with embedded spaces.

548　You tell a tokenizer to use a particular character as a delimiter by using the `quoteChar` method.

For example, to revise the `tokens` tokenizer to use double quotation marks to delimit strings, you write the following:

```
tokens.quoteChar((int) '"')
```

Note that the double quotation character, ", must be cast to an `int` before you hand that character over as the argument to `quoteChar`.

549　The reason that `quoteChar` requires an integer argument is that the low-level methods
SIDE TRIP　that read from files actually read bytes from those files, and those bytes are immediately translated into integer values. Tokenizers translate the integer values into characters only later, after the delimiters have done all their work.

550　You tell a tokenizer to recognize carriage returns using the `eolIsSignificant` method with `true` as the argument:

```
tokens.eolIsSignificant(true);
```

551　Now, you can write the following movie-reading program, which captures movie names, ratings, and poster files, if any:

```
import java.io.*;
import java.util.*;
public class Demonstrate {
 public static void main(String argv[]) throws IOException {
  Vector mainVector;
  mainVector = Auxiliaries.readMovieFile("input.data");
  int counter;
  int size = mainVector.size();
  for (counter = 0; counter < size; ++counter) {
   System.out.println(
     ((Movie) mainVector.elementAt(counter)).rating()
   );
  }
 }
}
```

```
import java.io.*;
import java.util.*;
public class Auxiliaries {
 public static Vector readMovieFile(String fileName) throws IOException
{
  FileInputStream inputFile = new FileInputStream(fileName);
  StreamTokenizer tokens = new StreamTokenizer(inputFile);
  tokens.quoteChar((int) '"');
  tokens.eolIsSignificant(true);
  Vector v = new Vector();

  while (tokens.nextToken() != tokens.TT_EOF) {
   String nameString = tokens.sval;
   tokens.nextToken(); int x = (int) tokens.nval;
   tokens.nextToken(); int y = (int) tokens.nval;
   tokens.nextToken(); int z = (int) tokens.nval;
   Movie m = (new Movie(x, y, z));
   m.title = nameString;
   if (tokens.nextToken() == tokens.TT_EOL) {}
   else {m.poster = tokens.sval; tokens.nextToken();}
   v.addElement(m);
  }
  inputFile.close();
  return v;
 }
}
```

552
SIDE TRIP
Occasionally you need to denote various special characters. You denote the space character, straightforwardly, as ' '. The others are denoted by a combination of a **backslash**, \, and a code. In such combinations, the backslash is said to be the **escape character**:

\t	tab
\r	carriage return
\n	line feed
\f	form feed
\b	backspace
\"	double quote
\'	single quote
\\	backslash

The backslash itself appears in the table because you need a way to denote the backslash when you really want a backslash, rather than the escape character.

553
PRACTICE
Generalize the program you were asked to write in Segment 533 such that it records not only scores, but also opponent names. You are to assume the data file includes comments

as in the following illustration. Have your program record those comments as well.

```
Twins         2    4      Nearly rained out
Yankees       9    5      Very exciting
Blue Jays     4    3      Close
```

- Strings are constants. You cannot add, delete, or change the characters in strings.

- If you want to determine the length of a string, **then** instantiate the following pattern:

  `string .length()`

- If you want to extract a character from a string, **then** instantiate the following pattern:

  `string .charAt( index )`

- If you want to concatenate two strings, creating a third string, **then** instantiate the following pattern:

  `first string + second string`

- If you want to denote a character, **then** surround that character with single quotation marks.

- If you want a tokenizer to return a token for the end of a line, **then** instantiate the following pattern:

  `token variable .eolIsSignificant(true);`

- If you want to know if the current token represents the end of a line, **then** compare the value produced by nextToken to the TT_EOL instance variable:

  `token variable .nextToken() == token variable .TT_EOL`

- If you want a tokenizer to use the double quotation mark to delimit strings with embedded spaces, **then** instantiate the following pattern:

  `token variable .quoteChar((int) '"');`

- You can use character values in switch statements, because char is an integral type.

31 HOW TO CATCH EXCEPTIONS

555   In Section 26, you learned that Java expects you to acknowledge that a method may lead to an error, such as an attempt to open a nonexistent file. Your acknowledgment may appear in the method in the form of the keyword throws and the name of the exception class associated with the error. Such an acknowledgment merely passes the problem up to the calling method, which must itself acknowledge the possibility of an error.

In this unit, you learn about a way not only to acknowledge that a method may lead to exceptional behavior, but also to specify the appropriate response to that behavior.

556   If an error does occur, that error is said to be **exceptional behavior** that **throws an exception**. Whenever an expression has the potential to throw an exception, you can embed that expression in a try–catch statement, in which you specify explicitly what Java is to do when an exception actually is thrown.

557   Suppose, for example, that you want to open a file for reading using a FileInputStream instance. You can acknowledge that the attempt may throw an exception by embedding the reading expressions in a block following the try keyword.

Java stops executing statements in the try block as soon as an exception is thrown.

```
try {
 ...   ←── An attempt to attach a stream to a file occurs here
}
```

558   You specify what to do in the event that the exception is an instance of the IOException class by writing the keyword catch, followed by a parameter typed by IOException, surrounded by parentheses, followed by another block.

```
catch (IOException e) {
 ...
}
```

559   Typically, when Java catches a thrown exception, you want Java to announce the nature of the problem. Accordingly, you write display statements that include the exception parameter in the catch block:

```
catch (IOException e) {
 System.out.println(e);
}
```

Such statements produce informative comments, such as the following:

┌── Name of missing file

```
java.io.FileNotFoundException: input.data
```

560 Note that exceptions form a class hierarchy. The exception actually thrown when a file does not exist is an instance of the `FileNotFoundException` class:

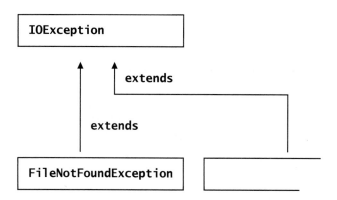

Because the `IOException` class is a superclass of the `FileNotFoundException` class, the `FileNoteFoundException` instance is also an instance of the `IOException` class, enabling the `IOException` catch block to catch instances of the `FileNotFoundException` class.

561 If you like, you can write multiple `catch` blocks so that you can handle different exceptions differently. The `catch` block actually invoked is the one with a parameter typed by the most specific class of which the exception is an instance.

562 Thus, in the following example, failure to find a file would activate the block associated with the `FileNotFoundException` class, rather than the one associated with the `IOException` class:

```
try {

          ←— An attempt to attach a stream to a file occurs here

}
// More specific exception caught:
catch (FileNotFoundException e) {
 System.out.println(
   "Evidently the input file does not exist."
 );
}
// More general exception caught:
catch (IOException e) {
 System.out.println(
   "Evidently an input--output error occurred."
 );
}
```

563   The catch blocks in the following revised version of the readMovieFile program, last seen in Segment 551, announce where an exception is caught and explain that exception's nature.

```java
import java.io.*;
import java.util.*;
public class Auxiliaries {
 public static Vector readMovieFile(String fileName) {
  Vector v = new Vector();
  try {
    FileInputStream inputFile = new FileInputStream(fileName);
    StreamTokenizer tokens = new StreamTokenizer(inputFile);
    tokens.quoteChar((int) '"');
    tokens.eolIsSignificant(true);
    while (tokens.nextToken() != tokens.TT_EOF) {
      String nameString = tokens.sval;
      tokens.nextToken(); int x = (int) tokens.nval;
      tokens.nextToken(); int y = (int) tokens.nval;
      tokens.nextToken(); int z = (int) tokens.nval;
      Movie m = (new Movie(x, y, z));
      m.title = nameString;
      if (tokens.nextToken() == tokens.TT_EOL) {}
      else {m.poster = tokens.sval; tokens.nextToken();}
      v.addElement(m);
    }
    inputFile.close();
  }
  catch (FileNotFoundException e) {
    System.out.println(e);
  }
  catch (IOException e) {
    System.out.println(e);
  }
  return v;
 }
}
```

This version of the Auxiliaries definition, which contains a definition of readMovieFile serves for remainder of this book.

564   If a program fails to find a file, the reason may be that the file has not yet appeared, and the right approach to take is to try again.

For example, the following variation on the program shown in Segment 563 loops if the file does not exist, because the catch expression continues to reset the tryAgain variable to true.

177

```
import java.io.*;
import java.util.*;
public class Auxiliaries {
 public static Vector readMovieFile(String fileName) {
  boolean tryAgain = true;
  Vector v = new Vector();
  while (tryAgain) {
   try {
    tryAgain = false;
    // ... rest of try expression same as shown in Segment 563 ...
   }
   catch (FileNotFoundException e) {
    tryAgain = true;
   }
   catch (IOException e) {
    System.out.println(e);
   }
  }
  return v;
 }
}
```

565   The Java compiler attempts to be smart, anticipating potential exceptions and forcing you to acknowledge those potential exceptions.

Sometimes, however, Java does not detect a potential exception at compile time, but encounters an exception at run time nevertheless. Java compiles the following demonstration program without complaint, but throws an ArrayIndexOutOfBoundsException, because the array has no element indexed by 3:

```
public class Demonstrate {
 public static void main(String argv[]) {
  int [] threeElements = {1, 2, 3};
  int counter;
  for (counter = 0; counter < 4; ++counter) {
   System.out.println(threeElements[counter]);
  }
 }
}
```

566   As you work with Java programs, you are likely to encounter other exception instances that you will either have to acknowledge or want to deal with. Such exceptions include, for example, instances of the NegativeArraySizeException class, thrown by attempts to create arrays with a negative number of elements, and instances of the ArithmeticException class, thrown by attempts to divide by zero.

567   If you want a program to stop when an exception is thrown, you use exit—a class method of the System class, to which you supply an argument of 0:

```
catch (IOException e) {
 System.exit(0);
}
```

When executed, the `exit` statement terminates the program and returns its argument either to the calling program or, if there is no calling program, to the operating system. By general convention, an argument of 0 is taken by the calling program or the operating system to mean that no special action is to be taken.

568   Occasionally, you may want to have a block of statements executed after a `try` statement, whether or not an exception is thrown, activating a `catch` block.

Accordingly, Java provides for `finally` blocks, which are executed after the `try` block is executed, along with any `catch` block that happens to be executed:

```
try {
 ...
}
catch ( exception-class name e) {
 ...
}
finally {
 clean up statements
}
```

569   You can create and throw your own exceptions. To create an exception, you extend the `Exception` class, as illustrated in the following example:

```
public class StrangeDataException extends Exception {
}
```

Once you have defined an exception class, you can throw instances:

```
throw (new StrangeDataException())
```

Those instances are caught by corresponding catchers:

```
catch (StrangeDataException e) {
 ...
}
```

570   Amend the program you were asked to write in Segment 553 such that it creates and throws
PRACTICE   instances of the `StrangeDataException` class whenever a baseball score is negative or more than 50. Have your program catch such exceptions and respond by displaying a brief explanation and then terminating your program.

- If you want to catch an exception, **then** instantiate the following pattern:

```
try {
  ...
  Statement with potential to throw exception
  ...
}
catch (exception-class name  parameter) {
  Exception-handling code
}
```

- If you want to catch input–output exceptions, **then** write a `try–catch` statement focused on the `FileNotFoundException` or `IOException` class.

- If you want to shut a program down, **then** write the following statement:

```
System.exit(0);
```

- If you want to add clean up statements to a `try` statement, **then** add a `finally` block by instantiating the following pattern:

```
finally {
  clean up statements
}
```

32 HOW TO CREATE FILE STREAMS FOR OUTPUT

572   In Section 26, you learned how to read information from an input file. Now, you learn to write information into an output file.

573   Much of the required machinery for writing into a file runs parallel to the required machinery for reading from a file.

First, you connect to an output file by creating an instance of the `FileOutputStream` class, also known as a **file output stream**, for a specified file. The following is an example in which the file specification happens to be `"output.data"`, and the file output stream is assigned to `outputFile`:

File specification ⌐
                ↓
               —————————

`FileOutputStream outputFile = new FileOutputStream("output.data");`

574   It is good programming practice to close output streams when you are finished writing to them. You close output streams with the same sort of `close` statement that you use to close input streams:

`outputFile.close();`

575   Given a `FileOutputStream` instance, you can write 1 byte at a time to that stream. You are more likely to want to be able to write `String` instances to the stream, however, so you must declare a `PrintStream` variable and create a `PrintStream` instance from a `FileOutputStream` instance:

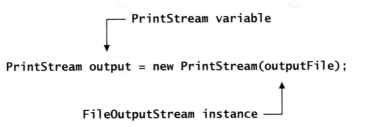

           ┌─ **PrintStream variable**
           ↓

`PrintStream output = new PrintStream(outputFile);`

                             ↑
FileOutputStream instance ─┘

576   Once you have a `PrintStream` instance, you can write strings to that stream, using the `print` and `println` methods.

577   You can use the program in Segment 563 to read movie script, acting, and directing ratings from file. Then, in the following program, you can write overall movie ratings into another file.

```
import java.io.*;
import java.util.*;
public class Demonstrate {
 public static void main(String argv[]) throws IOException {
  FileOutputStream outputFile = new FileOutputStream("output.data");
  PrintStream output = new PrintStream(outputFile);
  Vector mainVector;
  mainVector = Auxiliaries.readMovieFile("input.data");
  int counter;
  int size = mainVector.size();
  for (counter = 0; counter < size; ++counter) {
   output.println(
     ((Movie) mainVector.elementAt(counter)).rating()
   );
  }
  outputFile.close();
  System.out.println("File written");
 }
}
```
─────────────────── Sample Data ───────────────────
```
"Apocalypse Now"      4  7  3      "file:///e:/phw/onto/java/apnow.jpg"
"Bedtime for Bonzo"   8  8  7
```
─────────────────── Result ───────────────────
```
File written
```
──

Once the `main` method is executed, the file, `output.data`, contains the following data:

```
14
23
```

578   Amend the program you were asked to write in Segment 570. Have your amended program
PRACTICE   catch all exceptions of the `StrangeDataException` class and respond by writing a brief
explanation into an error file. Your program is not to stop when it encounters an error,
however; instead it is to record all legitimate scores in a vector.

579

HIGHLIGHTS

- If you want to tell Java that you intend to work with file input or file output
  streams, **then** include the following line in your program:

  ```
  import java.io.*;
  ```

- If you want to write to an output file, **then** instantiate the following pattern:

  ```
  FileOutputStream  file variable
    = new FileOutputStream( file specification );
  PrintStream  print-stream variable
    = new PrintStream( file variable );
  ```

- If you want to write data to a `PrintStream` instance, **then** instantiate one of the following patterns:

  `stream name` `.print(` `information to be printed` `);`
  `stream name` `.println(` `information to be printed` `);`

- If you have finished writing to an output file stream, **then** close the file by instantiating the following pattern:

  `file stream variable` `.close();`

33 HOW TO MODULARIZE PROGRAMS USING COMPILATION UNITS AND PACKAGES

580 In Section 19, you learned about how to organize, into inheritance hierarchies, classes that share instance variables and instance methods. In this section, you learn how to organize, into modular compilation units and packages, classes that work together to solve problems.

581 The demonstration program has five classes. The Attraction class, along with the Movie class and Symphony class, form a class hierarchy that extends the Object class. The Auxiliaries and Demonstration classes, which stand apart from the Attraction class hierarchy, also extend the Object class.

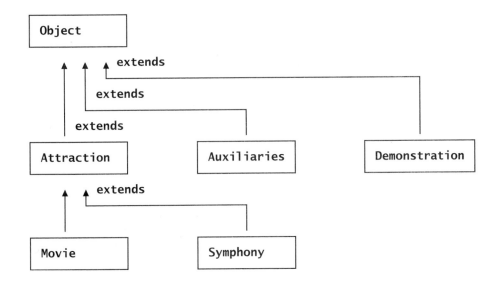

582 Whenever multiple classes can be viewed as part of some sort of natural category—such as the category of classes that support entertainment applications—you should use one of Java's mechanisms that enable you to bring together those classes into a unit that you can develop and maintain independently.

As you learned in Segment 329, programs that are divided into units that can be developed and maintained separately are said to be **modular**.

583 One way to bring together classes is to define them in the same file. Note, however, that only one such class can be public—the one whose name is the same as the name of the file.

You could, for example, bring the Demonstrate, Auxiliaries, Attraction, Movie, and Symphony classes into one file, named Demonstrate, with only Demonstrate marked as public.

Because all classes in a file are compiled together, with all class names accessible in all other classes, files are said to be **compilation units**.

584 The argument against bringing together many classes into one compilation unit is that only one of the classes is universally accessible. Accordingly, most Java programmers place each class in its own compilation unit, or, said another way, they ensure that each file contains just one class definition.

585 Another way to bring together classes is to place the corresponding compilation units into a common **package**, using a package statement at the beginning of each compilation unit.

In general, the package names that appear in package statements consist of **components** separated by dots:

```
package onto.java.entertainment;
public abstract class Attraction {
 // ... rest of class definition ...
}

package onto.java.entertainment;
public class Movie extends Attraction {
 // ... rest of class definition ...
}

package onto.java.entertainment;
public class Symphony extends Attraction {
 // ... rest of class definition ...
}

package onto.java.entertainment;
import java.io.*;
import java.util.*;
public class Auxiliaries {
 // ... rest of class definition ...
}
```

586 The components of package names always correspond to the final components of the path that specifies the location of the corresponding compilation units. The initial components of the path name are taken from the value of CLASSPATH, an **operating-system environment variable**.

Suppose, for example, that you are working in a Windows environment, and that the value of the CLASSPATH environment variable includes the c:\phw path and the package name for your program is onto.java.entertainment. Then, the compilation units of the package reside in the c:\phw\onto\java\entertainment directory:

```
      ┌─ From the CLASSPATH variable

            ┌─ From the package name
      │     │
      ▼     ▼
      ─────  ──────────────────────
c:\phw\onto\java\entertainment
```

If you are working in a UNIX environment and the value of the CLASSPATH environment variable includes /usr/phw and the package name is onto.java.entertainment, then the compilation units of the package are in the /usr/phw/onto/java/entertainment directory.

587
SIDE TRIP On machines that run Windows operating systems, you set the CLASSPATH variable as follows:

```
set CLASSPATH=c:\phw;c:\java\lib;c:\java\bin
```

On machines running the most popular versions of UNIX, you set the CLASSPATH variable as follows:

```
setenv CLASSPATH /usr/phw/:/java/lib:/java/bin
```

588 When you set the CLASSPATH environment variable, you must provide for all the directories that contain classes in the value of the CLASSPATH variable, including the directory that is the current directory when you are testing programs. Accordingly, the following is a typical value for the CLASSPATH variable in a Windows environment:

```
           ┌─ One author has many package names relative to c:\phw
          ↓
    ──────────

c:\phw;c:\phw\onto\java\test
      ───────────────────────
         ↑
         └─ Same author has a directory for testing programs
```

589 The correspondence between package names and path names enables Java to find compilation units specified in import statements. Java simply combines the value of the CLASSPATH variable with the package name to locate the package's compilation units.

Dots are used in package names, rather than path-name separators, so as to ensure portability. The translation from package names to path names is done locally in an operating-system–dependent way.

590 You learned about import statements in the context of single-class compilation units in Segment 452. Now that you have learned about multiple-class compilation units, you can refine what you learned.

When you use a package name in an import statement, you tell Java to load all the package's public classes, and the compilation units in which they appear, as follows:

```
                         ┌─ No compilation unit mentioned;
                         │  all compilation units available
                        ↓
import onto.java.entertainment.*
```

Alternatively, you can specify a specific public class, and the compilation unit in which it appears, in place of the asterisk:

┌─ A compilation unit mentioned;
│   one compilation unit available
↓

```
import onto.java.entertainment.Attraction
```

591 Once you have imported an entire package, or just one compilation unit, from a package, you can refer to the single public class in each compilation unit by name. For example, once you have loaded the onto.java.entertainment package, you can refer to the various public classes found in the compilation units:

```
import onto.java.entertainment.*;
import java.io.*;
import java.util.*;
public class Demonstrate {
 public static void main(String argv[]) {
  Vector mainVector;
  mainVector = Auxiliaries.readMovieFile("input.data");
  int counter;
  int size = mainVector.size();
  for (counter = 0; counter < size; ++counter) {
   System.out.println(
     ((Movie) mainVector.elementAt(counter)).rating()
   );
  }
 }
}
```

592 An import statement is not required if you prepend package names to your class names:

```
import java.io.*;
import java.util.*;
public class Demonstrate {
 public static void main(String argv[]) {
  Vector mainVector;
  mainVector =
    onto.java.entertainment.Auxiliaries.readMovieFile("input.data");
  int counter;
  int size = mainVector.size();
  for (counter = 0; counter < size; ++counter) {
   System.out.println(
     ((onto.java.entertainment.Movie)
      mainVector.elementAt(counter)).rating()
   );
  }
 }
}
```

Add the Game class you were asked to write in Segment 533 to the Entertainment package. Incorporate the file-reading method, readScoreVector, which you were asked to write in Segment 533, into the Auxiliaries class defined in the Entertainment package.

- If you want to bring classes together, **then** you can define them in one file, producing a compilation unit. Only one class in a compilation unit can be public, however.

- If you want to bring classes together, **then** you can define them in one directory, declaring them to be part of the same package with a package statement:

  package package name ;

- If you want to construct a package name, **then** note that package names consist of dot-separated components; each component corresponds to a component of the path that leads to the directory that contains the package's compilation units from the end of the path specified in the value of the CLASSPATH operating-system variable.

HOW TO USE PROTECTED AND PRIVATE VARIABLES AND METHODS

595 One principle of software engineering is that you should try to protect both data and methods from misuse. In this section, you learn how to protect instance variables and instance methods from misuse by using Java's private, protected, and public categories.

596 Consider the following version of the Attraction class, which has been stripped down, for use in this section only, so as to focus on the minutes instance variable:

```
public abstract class Attraction {
  // Declare instance variable:
  public int minutes;
  // Define one-parameter constructor:
  public attraction (int d) {minutes = d;}
}
```

As written, the instance variable, minutes, is marked by the public keyword. Accordingly, you can read and write the minutes instance variable directly from anywhere in the class, the compilation unit, the package, or some other package, using the field-selection operator:

```
instance .minutes                    ← Read
instance .minutes =  new value       ← Write
```

597 As explained in Section 14, you may want to require all access to the minutes variable to go through the access methods, thus hiding an implementation detail. Such hiding makes it easier, for example, to switch to an hours-based implementation later on.

If you decide to require users of Attraction instances to access the minutes variable only through the access methods, you replace the public keyword with private. By convention, variables and methods marked with the public keyword are said to be in the **public part** of the class definition, and those marked with the private keyword are said to be in the **private part**.

```
public class Attraction {
  // Declare instance variable:
  private int minutes;
  // Define one-parameter constructor:
  public Attraction (int d) {minutes = d;}
  // Define getter:
  public int getMinutes () {return minutes;}
  // Define setter:
  public void setMinutes (int d) {minutes = d;}
}
```

Once you have moved the minutes instance variable to the private part of the class definition, access to that variable is possible only via methods defined in the Attraction class, which includes only the one-parameter constructor and the access methods.

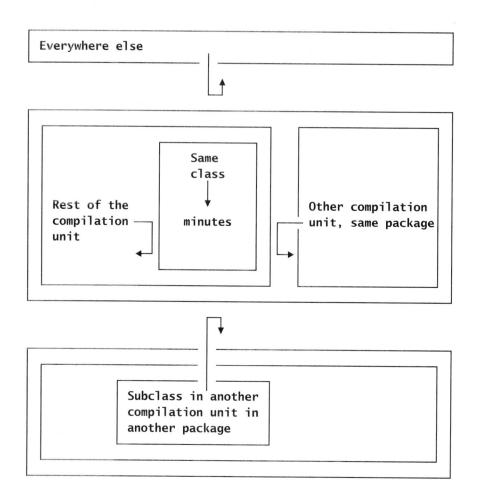

598   Because access to the private part of a class definition is restricted, most Java programmers move the private part of each class definition to the end, making that part less immediately visible, and, hence, more private.

```
public class Attraction {
 // Define one-parameter constructor:
 public Attraction (int d) {minutes = d;}
 // Define getter:
 public int getMinutes () {return minutes;}
 // Define setter:
 public void setMinutes (int d) {minutes = d;}
 // Declare instance variable:
 private int minutes;
}
```

599   Using the private variable and public getters, you can access the private variable indirectly from anywhere in the class, the compilation unit, the package, or some other package:

```
instance .getMinutes()                    ←— Read
instance .setMinutes( new value )         ←— Write
```

Because only instance methods in the attraction class can access the now-private minutes instance variable, no instance method of any other class can write directly into or read directly from the minutes instance variable; all writing and reading must go through the argument-bearing constructor and the access methods, getMinutes and setMinutes, defined in the Attraction class.

600   If you decide that an assignment of the minutes instance variable never changes once the Attraction instance is constructed, you can reflect that decision by removing the setter, setMinutes. Then, only the constructor can assign a value to the minutes instance variable:

```
public class Attraction {
 // Define one-parameter constructor:
 public Attraction (int d) {minutes = d;}
 // Define getter:
 public int getMinutes () {return minutes;}
 // No setter defined here
 // Declare instance variable:
 private int minutes;
}
```

Because getMinutes is defined publicly in the Attraction class, the value of the minutes instance variable is accessible via getMinutes everywhere. Once construction is complete, however, the minutes instance variable cannot be written everywhere, because there is no publicly defined setter.

601   Alternatively, instead of defining getters to expand access to instance variables, you can expand access, without providing totally public access, by marking the instance variables with the protected keyword, rather than with the public or private keywords. Variables so marked are said to be in the **protected part** of the class definition, which, by convention, generally is defined between the public and private parts of the class definition.

```
public class Attraction {
 // Define one-parameter constructor:
 public Attraction (int d) {minutes = d;}
 // Declare instance variable:
 protected int minutes;
}
```

602   Instance variables and instance methods in the protected part of a class definition are accessible from instance methods that are defined in the same class, compilation unit, or package. Protected instance variables and methods are also accessible from any subclass of the class in which they are declared, whether or not that subclass is in the same package. They are not, however, generally accessible from other packages:

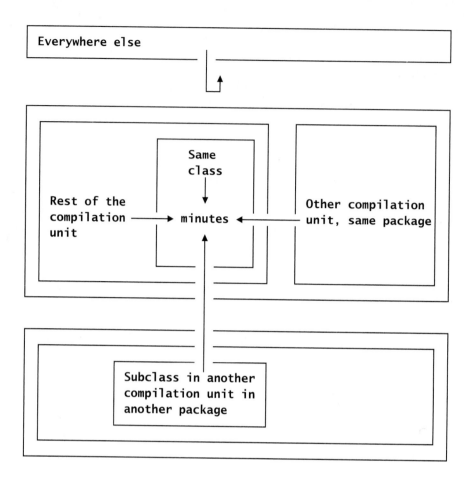

603 The protected minutes instance variable is available not only to methods defined in the Attraction class definition, but also to methods defined in the Movie and Symphony classes, because those classes are subclasses of the Attraction class and because both are defined in the same package as the Attraction class. The minutes instance variable is also accessible to methods defined in the Auxiliaries class, because that class is in the same package as the Attraction class.

604 If you mark the minutes instance variable with the protected keyword, all the instance methods defined in the Movie, Symphony, and Auxiliaries classes can write values into the minutes instance variable, as well as can read from it.

605 If you like, you can combine the virtues of private and protected placement. First, you return the minutes instance variables to the private part of the Attraction class definition, to prevent accidental writing by instance methods defined outside the Attraction class. Second, you provide access to the minutes instance variable's value through a getter defined in the protected part of the Attraction class definition:

```
public class Attraction {
  // Define one-parameter constructor:
  public Attraction (int d) {minutes = d;}
  // Define getter:
  protected int getMinutes () {return minutes;}
  // Declare instance variable:
  private int minutes;
}
```

Because the instance variable is in the private part of the Attraction class definition, it is accessible to only those instance methods defined in the Attraction class. Because the getter is in the protected part of the Attraction class definition, it is accessible to instance methods defined in the entertainment package and to instance methods defined in subclasses of the Attraction class.

606 One other possibility remains: if you use none of the protection keywords—public, protected, or private—you provide access to the rest of the compilation unit and to the rest of the package, but to nothing else.

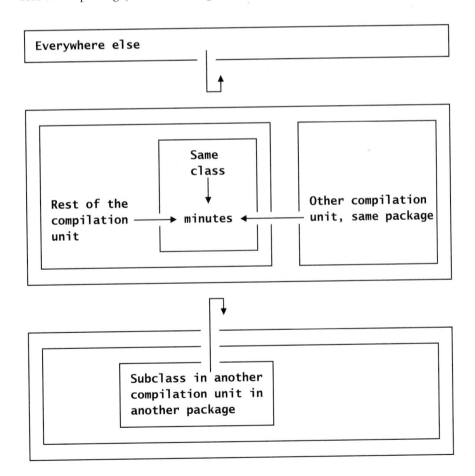

Explain what happens when you run the following program:

```
public class Demonstrate {
 public static void main (String argv[]) {
  new Test();
 }
}
class Test {
 Test () {
  System.out.println("Creating a Test instance");
 }
}
```

Then, explain what happens if you mark the zero-parameter constructor with the private keyword.

- If you want to provide universal access to instance variables and methods, **then** mark them with the public keyword.

- If you want to limit access to instance variables and methods to the package in which they are introduced and to subclasses of the class in which they are introduced, **then** mark them with the protected keyword.

- If you want to limit access to instance variables and methods to the class in which they are introduced, **then** mark them with the private keyword.

- If you want to limit access to instance variables and methods to the package in which they are introduced, **then** do not mark them with the public, protected, or private keywords.

35 HOW TO USE INTERFACES TO IMPOSE REQUIREMENTS

609 Each class in Java, other than the `Object` class, has exactly one direct superclass. Accordingly, Java does not provide for multiple inheritance.

In this section, you learn how interfaces provide the key benefits of multiple inheritance, without any of the disadvantages.

610 Suppose that you decide to display rating information using a star system, with no stars representing the worst possible rating, and 10 representing the best possible rating, as in the following illustration:

```
*           The Last House on the Left
********    Gone with the Wind
```

You need a method that produces a string of zero to 10 stars from an integer between 0 and 10.

611 Suppose that you further decide that you want your integer-to-stars method to be generally available, expecting that you will find uses for the method far outside the world of movies. You therefore decide to implement `starString` as a static method in a utility class that you name `Display`:

```java
public class Display {
 static String starString (int n) {
  String s = "";
  int counter;
  for (counter = 0; counter < 10; ++counter) {
   if (counter < n) {
    s = s + "*";
   }
   else {
    s = s + " ";
   }
  }
  return s;
 }
}
```

With the given definition of `starString` and the definition of `Attraction` given in Segment 323, you can produce the desired display as follows, with the star-controlling statements highlighted:

```
import java.io.*;
import java.util.*;
public class Demonstrate {
 public static void main(String argv[]) {
  Vector mainVector = Auxiliaries.readMovieFile("input.data");
  int counter, size = mainVector.size();
  for (counter = 0; counter < size; ++counter) {
   Attraction x = ((Attraction) mainVector.elementAt(counter));
   int n = x.rating() / 3;
   String stars = Display.starString(n);
   System.out.println(stars + " " + x.title);
  }
 }
}
```

─────────────────── Sample Data ───────────────
"The Last House on the Left"   0 0 0
"Gone with the Wind"   10 10 10
─────────────────── Result ───────────────
                The Last House on the Left
********** Gone with the Wind
──

612   Now, suppose that you want to make a simple change to your starString method: you want to supply starString with an instance, rather than with an integer, somehow arranging for starString to get the required star count from the instance itself:

```
import java.io.*;
import java.util.*;
public class Demonstrate {
 public static void main(String argv[]) {
  Vector mainVector = Auxiliaries.readMovieFile("input.data");
  int counter, size = mainVector.size();
  for (counter = 0; counter < size; ++counter) {
   Attraction x = ((Attraction) mainVector.elementAt(counter));
   String stars = Display.starString(x);
   System.out.println(stars + " " + x.title);
  }
 }
}
```

─────────────────── Sample Data ───────────────
"The Last House on the Left"   0 0 0
"Gone with the Wind"   10 10 10
─────────────────── Result ───────────────
                The Last House on the Left
********** Gone with the Wind
──

198

613 One way to accommodate the desired change in the Demonstrate class is to introduce a star-computing method into the Attraction class:

```
public abstract class Attraction {
 // Define interface method:
 public int starCount () {return rating() / 3;}
 // ... rest of the class definition goes here ...
}
```

Then, with the revised definition of the Attraction class, you modify the starString method, as defined in Segment 611, making the highlighted changes:

```
public class Display {
 static String starString (Attraction x) {
   String s = "";
   int counter;
   int n = x.starCount();
   for (counter = 0; counter < 10; ++counter) {
    if (counter < n) {s = s + "*";}
    else {s = s + " ";}
   }
   return s;
 }
}
```

614 Unfortunately, the starString class accepts only Attraction instances, thus confounding your established desire for the starString class to be available to work in all sorts of circumstances, rather than just in an entertainment-rating program.

615 If Java were to support multiple inheritance, you could define the starCount method abstractly in an abstract class, say StarProvider. Then, you could arrange for multiple classes to impose requirements on the attraction class:

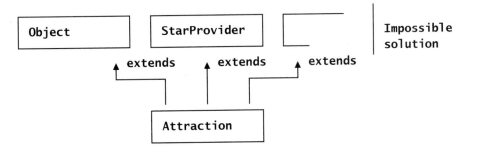

With this arrangement, you could work out a solution to the problem posed in Segment 614 as follows:

- Specify that the Attraction class is to have not only Object, but also StarProvider, as direct superclasses.

- Because the `Attraction` class inherits the abstract `starCount` method from the abstract `StarProvider` class, require either the `Attraction` or both of its subclasses to implement the `starCount` method.

- Declare the parameter of the `starString` class to be a `StarProvider` parameter, to ensure that the `starCount` method works with the value of that parameter as the target.

Java does not provide multiple inheritance, however, so this suggestion is not a solution.

616 The designers of Java deliberately did not provide for multiple inheritance, because multiple
SIDE TRIP inheritance introduces problems as well as benefits. For example, if multiple branches in an inheritance hierarchy provide an instance method or instance-variable value, then language designers have to face the issue of which branch dominates the others. C++ resolves the problem by complaining about such situations at compile time. Other languages, such as Lisp, resolve the problem through an elaborate ordering mechanism called topological-sorting.

617 Fortunately, Java does allow you to impose requirements on a class from multiple classlike **interfaces**. An interface is like an abstract class in that it can hold abstract method definitions that force other classes to implement ordinary methods, but an interface is unlike an abstract class for two important reasons:

- No ordinary methods can be defined in an interface.

- Many interfaces can impose requirements on the same class.

618 You define an interface as you would define a class, except that the keyword `interface` appears, instead of the `class` keyword. All methods in an interface are abstract, whether or not you mark them so. Good programming practice suggests that you make the abstract nature of the methods explicit.

For example, the following definition of the `starInterface` interface determines that the interface imposes a method requirement on all classes that use the interface. Specifically, such classes must implement the `starCount` method:

```
public interface StarInterface {
 public abstract int starCount () ;
}
```

619 To indicate that the `StarInterface` class is to impose its requirements on the `Attraction` class, you specify that the `Attraction` class is to implement the interface by adding the keyword `implements` and interface's name as illustrated:

```
public abstract class Attraction implements StarInterface {
 // Define interface method:
 public int starCount () {return rating() / 3;}
 // ... Rest of the class definition goes here ...
}
```

620   At this point, you have defined an interface, StarInterface, and you have used that interface to ensure that the Attraction class will implement the starCount method. You have done all that you need to do to enable Java to allow a parameter or variable to be typed with an interface name, instead of with a class name. Such typing ensures that the parameter or variable will have instance assignments that belong to classes that implement the requirements imposed by the interface.

For example, you can rewrite the method shown in Segment 613 such that the parameter is typed by StarInterface, rather than by Attraction.

```
public class Display {
  static String starString (StarInterface i) {
    String s = "";
    int counter;
    int n = i.starCount();
    for (counter = 0; counter < 10; ++counter) {
     if (counter < n) {s = s + "*";}
     else {s = s + " ";}
    }
    return s;
  }
}
```

621   Now, you can use the starString method on any instance of a class that implements the StarInterface interface, rather than on only attraction classes, thus providing the desired general availability.

622   You can see, then, that an interface has two purposes:

- An interface can impose requirements, without forcing those requirements into the ordinary superclass–subclass chain.

- An interface can serve as a type indicator.

623   Because interfaces define only abstract methods, there is no possibility that a method defined in an interface can conflict with a method inherited from a class.

624   A class can implement multiple interfaces, all of which are listed following the implements keyword.

625   Interfaces are called interfaces because they require classes to define prescribed methods in the classes's public interfaces.

626   Another possible, albeit undesirable, approach to the requirement problem discussed in
SIDE TRIP   this section would be to create an abstract StarProvider class containing an abstract starCount method. Then, every class that you want to require to have the starString method would extend the StarProvider class, rather than the Object class:

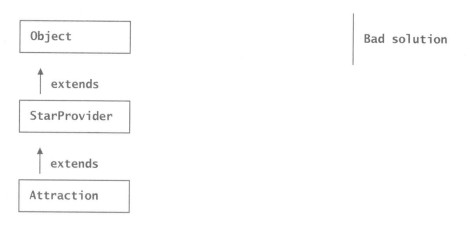

Such a solution is undesirable aesthetically, because attractions are not star providers in any natural sense. Such a solution also is undesirable technically, because you cannot combine requirements from multiple classes without arranging those classes in a chain of extends relations, which makes it impossible to impose requirements from the classes at the bottom of the hierarchy without imposing requirements from the top of the hierarchy as well.

627
PRACTICE

Suppose that you want to be able to force class definitions to define a rating method. Define an interface that imposes such a requirement on classes that implement that interface.

Then, suppose you have defined a University class. Explain what interfaces you would require that class to implement such that you can be sure you can use instances of the University class as targets for the stars method.

628
HIGHLIGHTS

- Interfaces are similar to classes, except that all methods defined in interfaces are automatically abstract.

- If you want to require a class to implement certain methods, **and** those requirements are not appropriate for an abstract class in the ordinary inheritance chain, **then** you should define an interface.

- If you want to define a public interface, **then** instantiate the following pattern:

  ```
  public interface interface name {
    ...
  }
  ```

- If you want an interface to impose requirements on a particular class using an interface, **then** instantiate the following pattern:

  ```
  public class class name implements interface name {
    ...
  }
  ```

- You can use interfaces as method-parameter declarations.

36 HOW TO DRAW LINES IN WINDOWS

629 Programs that have graphical user interfaces seem much more powerful than programs that provide services via character-only interfaces. Accordingly, to please users, you need to learn how to build graphical user interfaces.

In this section, you learn how to create windows, and how to draw lines of the sort needed to produce a meterlike drawing, which eventually becomes part of a movie-rating display.

630 Much of the work involved in constructing a graphical user interface, or GUI, is centered on the creation of rectangular **windows**, with attached menus, buttons, choice boxes, text fields, text editors, and drawing canvases. Each such attachment is called a **component**, or equivalently, a **widget**.

631 To support GUI development, Java provides a set of classes that collectively constitutes the awt package, where awt is taken from abstract window toolkit. By using classes in the awt package, you endow your program with sophisticated graphical-interaction capability.

632 The awt package is a key part of Java's application programmer's interface (API).

633 The awt package is platform independent. If you use the awt package to construct a GUI for a program, that program will run without change under UNIX, Windows, or Macintosh operating systems, and you can adapt the program to run as an applet hosted by a web browser.

634 The following is a simple program that creates a small, titled window and nothing more—the program does not even provide a means for eliminating the window from your display.

```java
import java.awt.*;
public class Demonstrate {
 public static void main (String args []) {
 Frame f = new Frame("Meter-Display Window");
  f.resize(300, 100);
  f.show();
 }
}
```

The argument of the Frame constructor, "Meter Display Window", supplies the title for the window. The resize method fixes the size of the window using width and height arguments. The show method displays the window, which otherwise would exist, but would not be visible.

635   The program shown in Segment 634 produces the following window:

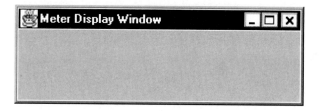

636   The program shown in Segment 634 does not terminate, because it starts to look for mouse movements, button clicks, and key presses. But because the program is so rudimentary, the **close button**—the one in the right corner of the **title bar** at the top of the window—is not connected to the Java mechanism that terminates programs and eliminates windows. The program, like the sorcerer's apprentice, has no way to shut operations down; instead, it continues to look for mouse movements, button clicks, and key presses indefinitely.

637   To arrange for proper program termination and window erasure, you must understand that the Frame class inherits an important method, handleEvent, that Java calls automatically whenever an event, such as a mouse click, occurs. That handleEvent method then decides what, if anything, to do. For example, when you click on the close button, the handleEvent method decides to do nothing.

Accordingly, you need to arrange for something to be done when you click on the close button by augmenting the behavior produced by the handleEvent method.

You might think you could augment the behavior of the handleEvent method by editing the method's definition. You cannot alter the classes that Java provides, however.

You would not want to alter the definition of handleEvent, even if you could, because the proper response to particular events will vary from window to window.

Thus, you augment the handleEvent method by creating a subclass of the Frame class in which you define your own handleEvent method. Your definition shadows the method provided by the Frame class.

638   Suppose, for example, that you decide to call your subclass of the Frame class MeterFrame.

In your definition of the MeterFrame class, you define a constructor that calls the one-parameter constructor of the Frame class, fixes the size of the window, and displays the window:

```
import java.awt.*;
public class MeterFrame extends Frame {
 public MeterFrame(String title) {
  super(title);
  resize(300, 100);
  show();
 }
 // ... handleEvent method definition goes here ...
}
```

To call the one-parameter constructor of the superclass, you use the Java convention that the first statement in a constructor can be a call to another constructor. You learned in Segment 310 that `super(title)` calls the one-parameter `Frame` constructor, which provides the title of the window to the `Frame` constructor.

639 Next, you must define a `handleEvent` method that shadows the `handleEvent` method in the `Frame` class. To define `handleEvent`, you need to know that the type returned by the `handleEvent` method is `boolean`, and the type of the single parameter is `Event`. Java creates instances of the `Event` class in response to events, such as mouse clicks, and hands those instances to the `handleEvent` method.

```
import java.awt.*;
public class MeterFrame extends Frame {
 // ... One-parameter constructor definition goes here ...
 public boolean handleEvent(Event e) {
   ...
 }
}
```

640 Instances of the `Event` class have an important instance variable, `id`. The value of the `id` variable indicates what event actually occurred. To interpret the value of the `id` variable, you compare that value with the values of various class variables provided by the `Event` class.

For example, if the value of the `id` variable of an `Event` instance is the same as the value of the `WINDOW_DESTROY` class variable of the `Event` class, then you have clicked on the close button:

```
import java.awt.*;
public class MeterFrame extends Frame {
 // ... One-parameter constructor definition goes here ...
 public boolean handleEvent(Event e) {
   switch (e.id) {
    // Respond to click on close button:
    case Event.WINDOW_DESTROY: ···
    // Respond to all other events:
    default: ···
   }
  }
}
```

641 If the close button has been clicked, the response is straightforward: you want your program to exit. To make it exit, as you learned in Segment 567, you call the `exit` method of the `System` class, and, to satisfy Java's demand that the `handleEvent` method appear to return a `boolean` value, you return `true`.

```
import java.awt.*;
public class MeterFrame extends Frame {
  // ... One-parameter constructor definition goes here ...
  public boolean handleEvent(Event e) {
    switch (e.id) {
      // Respond to click on close button:
      case Event.WINDOW_DESTROY: System.exit(0); return true;
      // Respond to all other events:
      default: ...
    }
  }
}
```

642   If the event is something other than a click on the close button, you want Java to do whatever would have been done had you not written a shadowing handleEvent method at all. You do not want to copy the handleEvent method to handle all the other events that may occur, however.

Fortunately, you can call the handleEvent method supplied via the Frame class from the handleEvent method defined in the MeterFrame class. Just as you can call a constructor in a direct superclass using the super keyword, you can call a method in a direct superclass using that same super keyword. The super keyword in the target position tells Java to skip over the handleEvent method defined in the current class, so as to initiate a search for another handleEvent method starting with the direct superclass:

```
import java.awt.*;
public class MeterFrame extends Frame {
  // ... One-parameter constructor definition goes here ...
  public boolean handleEvent(Event e) {
    switch (e.id) {
      // Respond to click on close button:
      case Event.WINDOW_DESTROY: ...
      // Respond to all other events:
      default: return super.handleEvent(e);
    }
  }
}
```

643   All the ideas explained in connection with the MeterFrame class appear together in the following definition:

```
import java.awt.*;
public class MeterFrame extends Frame {
  public MeterFrame(String title) {
    super(title);
    resize(300, 100);
    show();
  }
```

```
public boolean handleEvent(Event e) {
  switch (e.id) {
   // Respond to click on close button:
   case Event.WINDOW_DESTROY:
    System.exit(0); return true;
   // Respond to all other events:
   default: return super.handleEvent(e);
  }
 }
}
```

644 Now, you can use the MeterFrame class to create a window that you can close using the close button:

```
public class Demonstrate {
 public static void main (String args []) {
  new MeterFrame("Meter Display Window");
 }
}
```

645 Usually, you expect your programs to generate many instances from each defined class, but the main method defined in Demonstrate in Segment 644 generates only one instance of the MeterFrame class.

In general, you launch applications by generating a sole instance of an application-defining class.

646 Instead of using a separate Demonstrate definition to create a MeterFrame instance, you can move the main method into the MeterFrame class itself:

```
import java.awt.*;
public class MeterFrame extends Frame {
 public static void main (String args []) {
  new MeterFrame("Meter Display Window");
 }
 public MeterFrame(String title) {
  super(title);
  resize(300, 100);
  show();
 }
 public boolean handleEvent(Event e) {
  switch (e.id) {
   case Event.WINDOW_DESTROY:
    System.exit(0); return true;
   default: return super.handleEvent(e);
  }
 }
}
```

647　You can use the value of the `id` instance variable to recognize many kinds of events. The following list indicates some possible values and the meanings associated with those values:

- `Event.WINDOW_DESTROY`: The close button has been clicked.
- `Event.MOUSE_MOVE`: The mouse has moved.
- `Event.MOUSE_ENTER` or `Event.MOUSE_EXIT`: The mouse has moved into or out of the window.
- `Event.MOUSE_DOWN` or `Event.MOUSE_UP`: One of the mouse buttons has been pressed or released in the window.
- `Event.KEY_PRESS` or `Event.KEY_ACTION`: A key has been pressed or released.
- `Event.WINDOW_ICONIFY`: The mouse has been clicked on the iconify button.
- `Event.WINDOW_MOVED`: The window has been moved.
- `Event.WINDOW_EXPOSE`: A previously hidden portion of the window has become exposed.

Note that the final two values indicate that the window's contents, or a portion of those contents, should be redrawn.

648　Instances of the `Event` class contain instance variables in addition to `id`. For example, the value of the `when` instance variable provides the time when the event occurred, and, if the event involves the mouse, the values of the `x` and `y` instance variables identify where the mouse was when the event occurred. In Segment 828, you learn about the `target` instance variable.

649　At this point, you know how to display an empty window. Your next task is to learn to draw in that window. Ultimately, you will learn how to use the sort of drawing operations that you need if you want to develop a reusable meter that can be incorporated into an entertainment program to show the rating associated with a movie:

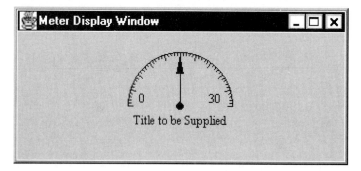

Before you can undertake anything so elaborate, you naturally have to learn how to draw lines in a window.

650　The `Frame` class extends the `Window` class. Both the `Window` class and the `Panel` class descend from the `Container` class, which in turn extends the `Component` class. The `Applet` class, which you learn about in Section 38, extends the `Panel` class.

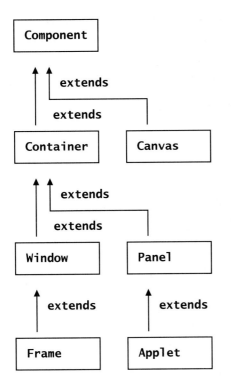

651   By the convention explained in Segment 173, an instance of the Window class is also known as a **window**. Thus, the word *window* can mean either a Window instance or a rectangular area on a display. In this book, however, the word *window* always refers to a rectangular area on a screen.

652   Instances of the component class, or that class's subclasses, are called **components** or **widgets**. Because Java has a class named Component, it is more natural to use *component* than it is to use *widget* when discussing Java.

You can attach any component to any container. For example, you can attach a canvas to a frame.

In the following segments, you learn how to draw lines on canvases attached to frames.

653   Just as you create subclasses of the Frame class so that you can shadow the handleEvent method in the Frame class, you create subclasses of the Canvas class so that you can shadow the paint method of the Canvas class.

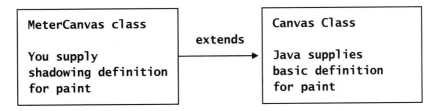

654   You know that Java calls the `handleEvent` method, with an `Event` instance argument, whenever Java determines that an event needs to be handled.

Analogously, Java calls the `paint` method whenever Java determines that a window should be drawn or redrawn.

The argument to a paint method is an instance of the `Graphics` class:

```
import java.awt.*;
public class MeterCanvas extends Canvas {
  String title = "Title to be Supplied";
  int minValue = 0, maxValue = 30, value = 15;
  // ... setters to be defined ...
  public void paint(Graphics g) {
    ...
  }
}
```

655   The `MeterCanvas` class defined in Segment 654 contains four instance variables that will determine exactly what is displayed: `title`, `minValue`, `maxValue`, and `value`. In this section, all have wired-in values that serve as defaults.

The `MeterCanvas` class also contains setters that are defined in Segment 681. In that segment, you learn that the setters initiate the painting process.

656   A `Graphics` instance, also known as a **graphics context**, acts as a controller that determines exactly how graphical commands affect the canvas.

```
                        Graphics context
Graphical        ─────────────────────────
commands         ────────────────────────────────→  The canvas
                 ─────────────────────────
```

You soon learn, in Segment 669, that you can tell a graphics context to have all lines drawn in blue. You then learn, in Segment 678, that you can tell a graphics context to have all text printed in Helvetica.

657   Should you want to draw a simple line, at position (0, 50), with width equal to 100, you use the graphics context as the target of the `drawLine`:

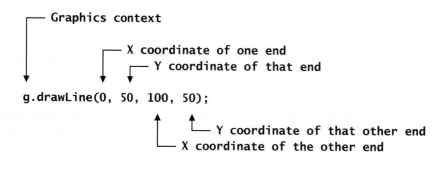

212

658   The drawLine method appears in the paint method of the MeterCanvas class:

```
import java.awt.*;
public class MeterCanvas extends Canvas {
 String title = "Title to be Supplied";
 int minValue = 0, maxValue = 30, value = 15;
 // ... setters to be defined ...
 public void paint(Graphics g) {
   g.drawLine(0, 50, 100, 50);
   ...
 }
}
```

659   Java draws lines using a coordinate system associated with the frame in which the canvas is a component.

The origin of a frame's coordinate system is the upper-left corner of the window produced by the frame. Familiarly, the value of the x coordinate increases from 0 as you move right from the left edge of the window. Strangely, the value of the y coordinate increases from 0 as you move down from the top edge.

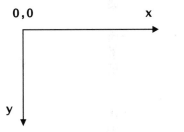

660   You easily can add a short vertical line such that the position of the vertical line along the horizontal line represents the value of the currentValue variable.

```
import java.awt.*;
public class MeterCanvas extends Canvas {
 String title = "Title to be Supplied";
 int minValue = 0, maxValue = 30, value = 15;
 // ... setters to be defined ...
 public void paint(Graphics g) {
   g.drawLine(0, 50, 100, 50);
   g.drawLine(50, 50, 50, 40);
 }
}
```

The maximum value of the variable is presumed to be 30, so the wired-in value, 15, dictates that the vertical line should be at the midpoint of the horizontal line:

661   To see what the `paint` method draws on a canvas, you have to **attach** the canvas to a frame. To attach a canvas to a frame, you use the `add` method, with the frame as the target, and two arguments.

The first argument of the `add` method stipulates where the canvas is to be placed relative to the frame's window; the second argument supplies the canvas itself.

Thus, you need to alter the definition of the `MeterFrame` class provided in Segment 646 by adding an initialization statement that creates a canvas and an `add` statement that attaches the canvas:

```
import java.awt.*;
public class MeterFrame extends Frame {
 public static void main (String args []) {
  new MeterFrame("Meter Display Window");
 }
 MeterCanvas meterCanvas = new MeterCanvas();
 public MeterFrame(String title) {
  super(title);
  add("Center", meterCanvas);
  resize(300, 100);
  show();
 }
// ... definition of handleEvent, like that in Segment 646 ...
}
```

The first argument of the `add` method, `"Center"`, arranges for the canvas to appear in the center of the window.

662   Each `Container` instance—and hence each frame—is associated with a **layout manager** that specifies how the attached components should be arranged. The **default layout manager** used with a frame, the **border layout manager**, allows five components to be added at positions identified by `"Center"`, `"North"`, `"East"`, `"South"`, and `"West"`.

If you like, you can specify that you want a frame to use the border layout explicitly. You first create an instance of `BorderLayout`; then, you add a `setLayout` statement to the frame constructor to tie the new border layout to the frame:

```
import java.awt.*;
public class MeterFrame extends Frame {
 public static void main (String args []) {
  new MeterFrame("Meter Display Window");
 }
 MeterCanvas meterCanvas = new MeterCanvas();
```

```
  public MeterFrame(String title) {
    super(title);
    setLayout(new BorderLayout());
    add("Center", meterCanvas);
    resize(300, 100);
    show();
  }
// ... definition of handleEvent, like that in Segment 646 ...
}
```

663   For a layout manager to place components in a container at the places that you want those components, you may have to define minimumSize or preferredSize methods for the components. Java uses minimumSize and preferredSize methods, when defined, to help determine the ultimate size of each component.

For example, to place the MeterCanvas component instance in a surrounding MeterFrame container instance, with other components, you may want to define minimumSize and preferredSize methods, as is done in the following illustration.

```
import java.awt.*;
public class MeterCanvas extends Canvas {
  String title = "Title to be Supplied";
  int minValue = 0, maxValue = 30, value = 15;
  // ... setters to be defined ...
  public void paint(Graphics g) {
    g.drawLine(0, 50, 100, 50);
    g.drawLine(50, 50, 50, 40);
  }
  public Dimension minimumSize() {return new Dimension(150, 100);}
  public Dimension preferredSize() {return new Dimension(150, 100);}
}
```

664   The minimumSize and preferredSize methods return an instance of the Dimension class, produced by a call to the Dimension class's constructor with width and height arguments:

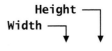

```
public Dimension minimumSize() {return new Dimension(150, 100);}
```

665
SIDE TRIP   Many programmers avoid defining minimumSize and preferredSize methods on the ground that layout managers should be smart enough to do a good job without advice, and providing advice, in the form of definitions for minimumSize and preferredSize methods, robs the layout manager of the potentially useful flexibility.

Other programmers believe that, without a bit of meddling, layout managers act too mysteriously. In this book, we meddle, having found in developing the examples that we need minimumSize and preferredSize to prevent certain components, in certain positions, from failing to appear.

666 Whenever you iconify, deiconify, or expose a window, Java calls the `paint` method of all canvases attached to the corresponding frame, as you can see by adding the following to the `paint` method:

```
System.out.println("Painting again");
```

667 Once you understand how canvases work with frames, it is time for you to learn to produce more sophisticated drawings. To produce more sophisticated drawings, you often take advantage of the information stored in the instance variables provided by the graphics context.

For example, you can obtain an instance of the `Dimension` class using the `size` method. Then, from the `width` and `height` instance variables of the `Dimension` instance, you can obtain the current width and height of the canvas.

With the width and height variables in hand, you can draw not just a meterlike horizontal line with a simple pointerlike vertical line, but a combination that fills out the window and stays centered, even as you move, or change the size of, the window:

```
import java.awt.*;
public class MeterCanvas extends Canvas {
  String title = "Title to be Supplied";
  int minValue = 0, maxValue = 30, value = 15;
  // ... setters to be defined ...
  public void paint(Graphics g) {
   // Obtain Dimension instance:
   Dimension d = size();
   // Draw:
   int meterWidth = d.width * 3 / 4;
   int dialPosition
     = meterWidth * (value - minValue) / (maxValue - minValue);
   int xOrigin = (d.width - meterWidth) / 2;
   int yOrigin = d.height / 2;
   g.drawLine(xOrigin, yOrigin, xOrigin + meterWidth, yOrigin);
   g.drawLine(xOrigin + dialPosition, yOrigin,
              xOrigin + dialPosition, yOrigin - 10);
  }
  public Dimension minimumSize() {return new Dimension(150, 100);}
  public Dimension preferredSize() {return new Dimension(150, 100);}
}
```

Thus, the graphics context is not just a conduit. It is a repository for state information, including information about the current window size.

668 Using the definition of the `MeterCanvas` class provided in Segment 667, and the definition of the `MeterFrame` class provided in Segment 661, produces the following display:

216

669   You can set state information in the graphics context, as well as get state information. For example, if you should want to draw a blue line, rather than a black one, you easily can modify the example of Segment 667 by adding a statement that provides the graphics context with an instance of the Color class.

The definition of the Color class includes class variables with values that are instances of the Color class itself. One such class variable is the blue variable; the value of the blue variable is a Color instance associated with the color blue.

You use the setColor method to provide the graphics context with a color:

```
import java.awt.*;
public class MeterCanvas extends Canvas {
 String title = "Title to be Supplied";
 int minValue = 0, maxValue = 30, value = 15;
 // ... setters to be defined ...
 public void paint(Graphics g) {
  // Set color:
  g.setColor(Color.blue);
  // Obtain Dimension instance and draw:
  Dimension d = size();
  int meterWidth = d.width * 3 / 4;
  int dialPosition
   = meterWidth * (value - minValue) / (maxValue - minValue);
  int xOrigin = (d.width - meterWidth) / 2;
  int yOrigin = d.height / 2;
  g.drawLine(xOrigin, yOrigin, xOrigin + meterWidth, yOrigin);
  g.drawLine(xOrigin + dialPosition, yOrigin,
             xOrigin + dialPosition, yOrigin - 10);
 }
 public Dimension minimumSize() {return new Dimension(150, 100);}
 public Dimension preferredSize() {return new Dimension(150, 100);}
}
```

670   Whenever you make a change to the value of a graphics context variable, you should first obtain the current value, and you should restore that value later. For example, you can use the getColor method to obtain the current Color instance associated with the graphics context. Then, you can change to another Color instance temporarily. Finally, you can use the setColor method again, this time to restore the graphics context to the original state:

```
import java.awt.*;
public class MeterCanvas extends Canvas {
  String title = "Title to be Supplied";
  int minValue = 0, maxValue = 30, value = 15;
  // ... setters to be defined ...
  public void paint(Graphics g) {
    // Obtain current Color instance:
    Color colorHandle = g.getColor();
    // Reset color temporarily:
    g.setColor(Color.blue);
    // ... obtain dimension instance and draw, as was done in Segment 669
...
    // Restore color:
    g.setColor(colorHandle);
  }
  public Dimension minimumSize() {return new Dimension(150, 100);}
  public Dimension preferredSize() {return new Dimension(150, 100);}
}
```

671   The Color class provides class variables for common colors, such as white, gray, black, blue, green, and red.

672   You can create your own Color instances via the three-parameter Color constructor. The
SIDE TRIP   three arguments specify the intensity of red, green, and blue in the color, on a scale that ranges from 0 to 255. In the following example, the Color constructor produces a Color instance corresponding to dark blue.

```
          ┌── Red intensity
          │   ┌── Green intensity
          │   │   ┌── Blue intensity
          │   │   │
          ↓   ↓   ↓
new Color(0,  0,  100)
```

You would evaluate new Color(0, 0, 0) to create an instance corresponding to black. Similarly, you would evaluate new Color(255, 255, 255) to create an instance corresponding to white.

673   The search for mouse movements, button clicks, and key presses is handled by an inde-
SIDE TRIP   pendent thread. You learn about threads in Section 43.

674   Using the MeterCanvas class in Segment 670 as a guide, define a class, Thermometer,
PRACTICE   that produces a drawing that looks like a thermometer with a reading halfway between maximum and minimum. Use the fillOval method to draw the bulb. Use the drawRect and fillRect methods to draw the rest of the thermometer. All three methods take four arguments: x, y, width, and height.

675   Define a class, TrafficLight, that produces a drawing that looks like a traffic light. Use
PRACTICE   drawOval, fillOval, and drawRect. All three methods take four arguments: x, y, width, and height. Arrange for each circle to have the proper color.

- If you want to display a window, **then** create a subclass of the Frame class, by instantiating the following pattern, and create a new instance of that subclass.

```
import java.awt.*;
class subclass name extends Frame {
 subclass name (String title) {
  super(title);
  resize(width, height);
  show();
 }
 public boolean handleEvent(Event e) {
  switch (e.id) {
   case Event.WINDOW_DESTROY:
    System.exit(0); return true;
   default: return super.handleEvent(e);
  }
 }
}
```

- If you want to know what sort of event has occurred, **then** examine the id instance variable of the Event instance that Java hands to the handleEvent method defined in the Frame class and that class's subclasses.

- If you want to draw in a window, **then** create a subclass of the Canvas class, by instantiating the following pattern:

```
import java.awt.*;
public class subclass name extends Canvas {
 ...
 public void paint(Graphics g) {
  drawing statements
 }
}
```

  then, attach a new instance of the subclass to a frame by adding the following statement to the frame constructor:

```
add(position, subclass instance);
```

  The position can be "Center", "North", "East", "South", or "West".

- If you want to draw a line, **then** add a drawLine statement to the paint method defined in a subclass of the Canvas class.

- If you want to get the state of the graphics context established by Java for the paint method defined in the Canvas class and its subclasses, **then** use getters such as size and getColor.

- **If** you want to set the state of the graphics context established by Java for the `paint` method defined in the `Canvas` class and its subclasses, **then** use setters such as `setColor`.

37 HOW TO WRITE TEXT IN WINDOWS

677   In Section 36, you learned how to draw lines on canvases. In this section, you learn how to write text on canvases.

678   The following version of `paint` uses the `drawString` method to write the string assigned to the `title` variable, `"To be Supplied"`, with the left side of the T located at x = 100 and the bottom of the T located at y = 50:

```
import java.awt.*;
public class MeterCanvas extends Canvas {
  String title = "Title to Be Supplied";
  int minValue = 0, maxValue = 30, value = 15;
  // ... setters to be defined ...
  public void paint(Graphics g) {
    g.drawString(title, 100, 50);
  }
  public Dimension minimumSize() {return new Dimension(150, 100);}
  public Dimension preferredSize() {return new Dimension(150, 100);}
}
```

Naturally, Java allows you to use a variety of **fonts**, such as **Roman** and **Helvetica**. Java also allows you to use a variety of font **styles**—namely **plain**, **bold**, and **italic**. And Java allows you to use a variety of font **sizes**.

To control the font, style, and size, you create instances of the `Font` class and you use the `setFont` method to associate those instances with the graphics context.

For example, the following version of the `print` method writes a string using a 12-point Helvetica bold font:

```
import java.awt.*;
public class MeterCanvas extends Canvas {
  String title = "Title to Be Supplied";
  int minValue = 0, maxValue = 30, value = 15;
  public void paint(Graphics g) {
    g.setFont(new Font("Helvetica", Font.BOLD, 12));
    g.drawString(title, 100, 50);
  }
}
```

If you want a plain font, substitute `PLAIN` for `BOLD`. If you want an italic font, substitute `ITALIC` for `BOLD`.

679   When you write strings, the strings are placed on a **baseline**. Portions of all characters appear above the baseline. Characters such as g have **descenders** that appear below the baseline.

The distance by which a font extends above the baseline is that font's **height**, whereas the distance by which the font's characters extends below the baseline is the font's **descent**.

The getFontMetrics method returns an instance of the FontMetrics class. That instance provides height and descent information, via the getHeight and getDescent methods, for the font currently associated with a graphics context. The FontMetrics instance also provides string-width information, via the stringWidth method, for a string argument. The stringWidth method returns the width that the string would occupy if the string were displayed in the font associated with the FontMetrics instance.

You can use information about height, descent, and width to position where you draw a string. In the following example, the string is centered on a baseline located three-quarters of the way down from the top of the window:

```java
import java.awt.*;
public class MeterCanvas extends Canvas {
 String title = "Title to Be Supplied";
 int minValue = 0, maxValue = 30, value = 15;
 // ... setters to be defined ...
 public void paint(Graphics g) {
  Dimension d = size();
  // Write title:
  g.setFont(new Font("Helvetica", Font.BOLD, 12));
  FontMetrics f = g.getFontMetrics();
  int stringWidth = f.stringWidth(title);
  int xOrigin = (d.width - stringWidth) / 2;
  int yOrigin = d.height * 3 / 4;
  g.drawString(title, xOrigin, yOrigin);
 }
 public Dimension minimumSize() {return new Dimension(150, 100);}
 public Dimension preferredSize() {return new Dimension(150, 100);}
}
```

680   The program shown in Segment 679 produces the following result:

681   Now it is time to combine the definition for the MeterFrame class provided in Segment 667 with the definition provided in Segment 679. The following definition not only includes drawing statements from both of the previous definitions, but also adds setters for the title and currentValue methods that call the repaint method.

The repaint method tells Java to call the paint method, just as window movements and resizings tell Java to call the paint method.

```java
import java.awt.*;
public class MeterCanvas extends Canvas {
 String title = "Title to Be Supplied";
 int minValue = 0, maxValue = 30, value = 15;
 // Set the title:
 public void setTitle(String s) {
  title = s;
  repaint();
 }
 // Set the current value:
 public void setValue(int v) {
  value = v;
  repaint();
 }
 // Paint:
 public void paint(Graphics g) {
  // Obtain Dimension instance and draw:
  Dimension d = size();
  int meterWidth = d.width * 3 / 4;
  int dialPosition = meterWidth * (value - minValue)
                        / (maxValue - minValue);
  int xOrigin = (d.width - meterWidth) / 2;
  int yOrigin = d.height / 2;
  g.drawLine(xOrigin, yOrigin, xOrigin + meterWidth, yOrigin);
  g.drawLine(xOrigin + dialPosition, yOrigin,
          xOrigin + dialPosition, yOrigin - 10);
  // Write title:
  g.setFont(new Font("Helvetica", Font.BOLD, 12));
  FontMetrics f = g.getFontMetrics();
  int stringWidth = f.stringWidth(title);
  xOrigin = (d.width - stringWidth) / 2;
  yOrigin = d.height * 3 / 4;
  g.drawString(title, xOrigin, yOrigin);
 }
 // Assist in sizing:
 public Dimension minimumSize() {return new Dimension(150, 100);}
 public Dimension preferredSize() {return new Dimension(150, 100);}
}
```

682 Using the definition in Segment 681 and the definition of MeterFrame in Segment 661 produces the following display:

683   Now that you know how to produce simple displays, such as the one in Segment 682, you can create more elaborate displays, such as the meter display shown in Segment 649.

The difference between the simple meter of Segment 682 and the complex meter of Segment 649 is quantitative, rather than qualitative, as you can see by examining the definition of the `MeterCanvas` class provided in Appendix B.

684
SIDE TRIP When you define `Frame` and `Canvas` subclasses that define shadowing `handleEvent` and `print` methods, you are said to practice the **framework style** of programming, because you build on the powerful framework supplied by Java's awt package.

The framework style of programming differs from the **callback style** of programming, a style often supported by programming languages that are not object oriented, such as C.

When using the callback style, you attach programs to hooks provided for each sort of event associated with each sort of component. Unfortunately, however, you cannot create component subclasses, each with a refined way of handling events, because languages that are not object oriented do not offer inheritance.

685
PRACTICE Using the `MeterCanvas` class in Segment 681 as a guide, augment the `Thermometer` definition you were asked to write in Segment 674 by including appropriate setters. Use `drawString` to place `Max` and `Min` labels at the ends of the thermometer, and have the thermometer display the value set.

686
HIGHLIGHTS

- If you want to write a string, **then** add a `drawString` statement to the `paint` method defined in a subclass of the `Canvas` class, by instantiating the following pattern:

  `graphics context`.drawString(`a string`, `x`, `y`);

- If you want to determine the height or descent of a font, **then** create an instance of the `FontMetrics` class using the graphics context and examine that instance's instance variables by instantiating the following pattern:

  ```
  FontMetrics f = graphics context.getFontMetrics();
  ...
  f.getHeight()                    ⟵ Fetch height
  ...
  f.getDescent()                   ⟵ Fetch decent
  ...
  f.stringWidth( a string );       ⟵ Fetch width of given string
  ```

224

- **If** you want to change to a different font, **then** instantiate the following pattern:

```
graphics context .setFont(new Font(" name ", style , size ));
```

The name could be, for example, `Helvetica`. The style could be, for example, `Font.BOLD` for a bold font. The size could be, for example, `12`, for a 12-point font.

38 HOW TO DEFINE APPLETS

687 The raison d'etre of Java is that Java allows you to access programs via a web browser, such as Netscape Browser. In this section, you learn how to prepare applets for such web browsers.

688 **Applets** differ from ordinary, standalone programs in several respects:

- Applets are meant to be used by web browsers via references inserted into HTML files, which are explained in Section 39.

- Every applet class extends the `Applet` class, which is defined in the `applet` package.

- Java creates an applet in response to a request issued by a web browser.

- As Java creates an applet, Java calls the `init` method and then the `start` method, both with the new applet as the target. There is no role for a `main` method.

- No applet has a title bar; hence, there is no title in `Applet` constructors.

- No applet has a close button; hence, there is no `handleEvent` method in `Applet` classes.

- No applet should call `resize` to establish size, because size is determined by the web browser in cooperation with the HTML file that references the applet, as explained in Section 39.

689 Suppose that you want to transform into an applet the `MeterFrame` class defined in Segment 661. You need to make six changes:

First, add an `import` statement that provides access to the `applet` package:

```
import java.applet.*;
```

Second, change the class name from `MeterFrame` to `MeterApplet`, and define the class to extend the `Applet` class, rather than the `Frame` class:

```
public class MeterApplet extends Applet {
...
}
```

Third, remove the definition of the `main` method.

Fourth, define an `init` method, and move into the `init` method the statements in the constructor that make associations between a new `MeterApplet` instance and the surrounding container.

Also, specify that the border layout manager is to be used: you need an explicit border-layout statement because the default layout for applets is not the border layout:

```
public void init() {
  setLayout(new BorderLayout());
  add("Center", canvas);
}
```

Fifth, transform the one-parameter constructor, which passes along a title to the constructor in the direct superclass, into a zero-parameter constructor. Eliminate the calls to the superclass constructor and to the resize and show methods. Then, noting that there is nothing left in the constructor, eliminate it entirely.

Sixth, remove the definition of handleEvent, because applets have no close button.

690
SIDE TRIP The default layout for panels is the flow layout, which you learn about in Section 45, where several layout alternatives are discussed.

691
SIDE TRIP The reason statements that make associations between a new MeterApplet instance and the surrounding container must appear in init method, rather than in the constructor, is that web browsers may not make preparations to deal with attachment and painting until the constructor has finished its work.

692   With all the changes in place, you have the following definition of the MeterApplet class.

```
import java.applet.*;
import java.awt.*;
public class MeterApplet extends Applet {
  // ... Definition of main removed ...
  MeterCanvas meterCanvas = new MeterCanvas();
  public void init () {
    setLayout(new BorderLayout());
    add("Center", meterCanvas);
  }
  // Definition of constructor commented out:
  // public MeterApplet () {
  //   super(title);
  //   resize(300, 100);
  //   show();
  // }
  // ... Definition of handleEvent removed ...
}
```

693   Ordinarily, you look at applets through a web browser, via a special kind of file, as explained in Section 39. For debugging, however, you may wish to take advantage of the fact that the Applet class is a subclass of the Panel class, as shown in Segment 650; that fact allows you to attach an applet to a frame. In particular, you can define in an applet a main method that constructs a frame, attaches the applet to the frame, and shows the result.

To use the applet-is-a-panel approach, you might want to define AppletTestorFrame, a bare-bones subclass of the Frame class. The AppletTestorFrame differs from the Frame class mainly in that the `AppletTestorFrame` class enables the close button actually to terminate tests:

```
import java.awt.*;
public class AppletTestorFrame extends Frame {
  // Zero-parameter constructor:
  public AppletTestorFrame () {super("Applet Test");}
  // One-parameter constructor:
  public AppletTestorFrame (String t) {super(t);}
  public boolean handleEvent(Event e) {
    switch (e.id) {
      case Event.WINDOW_DESTROY:
        System.exit(0); return true;
      default: return super.handleEvent(e);
    }
  }
}
```

694　Given the definition of `AppletTestorFrame` presented in Segment 693, you can readily insert a definition of `main` into the definition of `MeterApplet` presented in Segment 692.

```
import java.applet.*;
import java.awt.*;
public class MeterApplet extends Applet {
  // The main method is included for testing only
  public static void main (String args []) {
    AppletTestorFrame atf = new AppletTestorFrame();
    MeterApplet m = new MeterApplet(); m.init();
    atf.add("Center", m); atf.resize(300, 200);  atf.show();
  }
  MeterCanvas meterCanvas = new MeterCanvas();
  public void init () {
    setLayout(new BorderLayout());
    add("Center", meterCanvas);
  }
}
```

695　In Segment 661, the calls to `add`, `resize`, and `show` did not require an explicit target, because, in the `MeterFrame` constructor, the desired target is the instance under construction. In Segment 694, the calls to `add`, `resize`, and `show` do require an explicit target, because, in the `main` method, the desired target is the value of the variable `m`.

696　The `main` method is ignored during the ordinary use of the applet provided via a web browser. The `main` method is called only when you use the applet as a standalone application.

Conversely, the init method is ignored during the use of the applet in a standalone program unless you call init explicitly. The init method is called automatically only when you use the applet via a web browser.

697 Seen as a standalone application, activated via the main method, the MeterApplet program produces the following display, when used with the version of the MeterCanvas class defined in Appendix B:

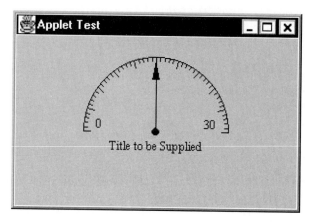

698 Create an applet, ThermometerApplet, based on the applet shown in Segment 694. Ac-
PRACTICE tivate your new applet via a call to main.

699
HIGHLIGHTS

- The Applet class is a subclass of the Panel class especially designed for use by a web browser.

- If you want to create an applet, then create a new instance of the Applet class.

- When an applet is created, the init method is called. Attachment commands should be placed in an init method.

- If you want to test an applet, then you may want to define a main method that creates an instance of the applet, attaches that applet to a frame, and calls init with the applet as the target.

HOW TO ACCESS APPLETS FROM WEB BROWSERS

700 In Section 38, you learned how to define applets for web browsers. In this section, you learn how to place references to applets in the sort of files with which web browsers work. Thus, you learn how to access applications over the Internet.

701 Web browsers look at text files that are **marked up** according to the conventions of the hypertext markup language (HTML). HTML is derived from the standard generalized markup language (SGML).

702 When you mark up a text file, you insert **formatting tags** that dictate appearance and provide for special effects. Text files with HTML formatting tags are often called **HTML files,** and HTML files typically have html file-name extensions.

703 HTML tags consist of **directives** surrounded by angle brackets. The <P> tag, for example, terminates paragraphs. The <HR> tag places a horizontal rule in the text.

704 HTML is not case sensitive. Thus, <p> does the same work as <P>, and <hr> does the same work as <HR>.

705 Some HTML tags are one-half of a pair that surrounds a block of text. The second tag is like the first, except that it carries a forward slash just inside the first angle bracket. For example, the <TITLE>–</TITLE> pair surrounds that portion of the file intended to serve as the file's title. Similarly, the <BODY>–</BODY> pair surrounds the file's body.

Thus, the following is a simple HTML file that contains nothing but a title, two horizontal rules, and a few lines of text:

```
<TITLE>Welcome to a Text-Only HTML File</TITLE>
<BODY>
<HR>
This text can be viewed by a web browser.<P>
It consists of only text, arranged in two
paragraphs, between horizontal rules.
<HR>
</BODY>
```

706 Instead of, or in addition to, referring to text, HTML files can refer to applets using <APPLET>–</APPLET> pairs. The <APPLET> tag includes width and height specifications, as well as the name of the applet file; the file is presumed to be in the same directory as the HTML file:

```
<TITLE>Welcome to the Meter Applet Demonstration</TITLE>
<BODY>
<HR>
<APPLET CODE="MeterApplet.class" width=300 height=200></APPLET>
<HR>
</BODY>
```

707   Once you have created an HTML file containing an applet, you can view that file, and its applet, via a web browser, provided your computer is running a **World Wide Web server**, also known as a **web server** or as a **WWW server**.

If your computer is running a web server, you can access your HTML file, and its applet, from your own computer, or from any other computer on the Internet, by providing a web browser with an appropriate network address in the location field displayed in your web browser:

Location: | `appropriate network address`

708   An appropriate address is in the form of a **uniform resource locator (URL)**. The general form for a URL for an HTML file accessed via a network includes several parts:

- The first part, `http:` specifies that the URL follows the hypertext transfer protocol (HTTP).

- The second part, separated from the **http scheme** specification by two slashes, specifies an Internet address, such as `www.ascent.com`. Such specifications consist of the name of the computer running a web server, such as `www`, and the name of the domain with which that computer is associated, such as `ascent.com`, separated by a period. Domain names usually consist of organization names, such as `ascent`, and types, such as `com`, separated by a period.

- The third part, separated from the Internet address by a slash, specifies a path to your HTML file, relative to a root path established by the web server. If the web server specifies a root path of `/network/`, and you supply `books/java/meter.html`, the location of your file on the computer is `/network/books/java/meter.html`.

The following—with all necessary colons, slashes, and periods—illustrates what a URL typically looks like for a file located on a UNIX system:

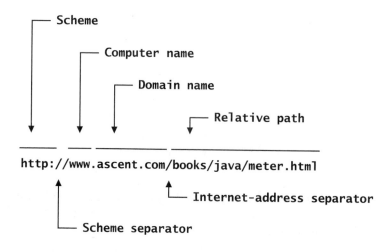

232

Note that the computer name used by many organizations for their web servers is, appropriately enough, www—but it can be any name.

709   If the web server happens to be running on the same computer as your web browser, then you can leave out the Internet address, producing a URL with three slashes in a row:

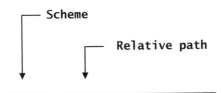

```
http:///books/java/meter.html
```

710   Note that the relative-path part of the URL is generally case sensitive. The rest, however, is generally not case sensitive. Thus, the following URL is equivalent to the one in Segment 708:

```
HTTP://WWW.ASCENT.COM/books/java/meter.html
```

711   If a URL ends in a slash, then the web server provides a default file name and extension. Typical web servers use `index.html` for the default file name and extension, but some web servers use other default names and extensions, such as `homepage.html` and `home.html`.

712   If you do not happen to be running a web server on your computer, you can still access an HTML file using a URL that follows the **file scheme**. The following illustrates what such a URL typically looks like for a file located on a Windows system. The key change is that `http` is replaced by `file`.

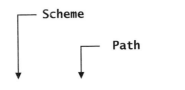

```
file:///e:/phw/onto/java/meter.html
```

713   Using the file scheme, you can view via a web browser the HTML file described in Segment 706 and named `meter.html`. Because that HTML file references the applet defined in Segment 694, you see the following result:

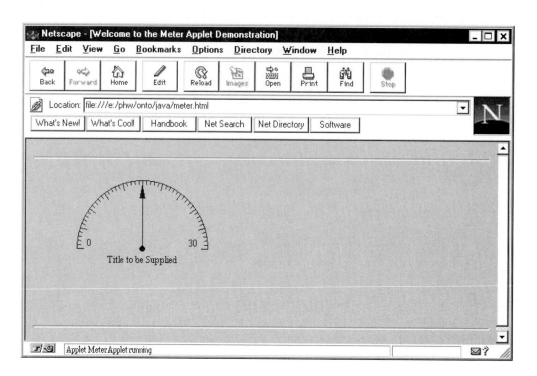

714　You specify the desired width and height of an applet in only the HTML file. Basically, you provide a hole into which the applet squeezes itself. It is as though you had created a window and had used your mouse to resize that window to the size specified in the HTML file.

715　Note that, if an applet reads a file in the course of doing its work, that file must be specified by a URL, and that URL must be identical to the URL provided to the web browser, except for the file name and extension:

Viewer provided: http://www.ascent.com/books/java/meter.html

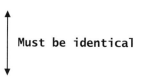

Must be identical

Applet reads:　　http://www.ascent.com/books/java/general.movies

716　As shown in the following program, changing to URL addresses requires making small modifications to methods, such as readMovieFile, that read files.

Instead of using FileInputStream to create a file stream, you must import the net package, create a URL instance, and then use that URL instance as the target of the openStream method, thus producing a **URL input stream**. The URL input stream is handed to the StreamTokenizer constructor inside readMovieURL.

```java
import java.net.*;
import java.io.*;
import java.util.*;
public class Auxiliaries {
 public static Vector readMovieURL(String fileURL) {
  Vector v = new Vector();
  try {
   // Next two statements commented out:
   // FileInputStream inputFile = new FileInputStream(fileName);
   // StreamTokenizer tokens = new StreamTokenizer(inputFile);
   // Next two statements added:
   URL url = new URL(fileURL);
   StreamTokenizer tokens = new StreamTokenizer(url.openStream());
   tokens.quoteChar((int) '"');
   tokens.eolIsSignificant(true);
   while (tokens.nextToken() != tokens.TT_EOF) {
    String nameString = tokens.sval;
    tokens.nextToken(); int x = (int) tokens.nval;
    tokens.nextToken(); int y = (int) tokens.nval;
    tokens.nextToken(); int z = (int) tokens.nval;
    Movie m = (new Movie(x, y, z));
    m.title = nameString;
    if (tokens.nextToken() == tokens.TT_EOL) {}
    else {m.poster = tokens.sval; tokens.nextToken();}
    v.addElement(m);
   }
   // Next statement commented out:
   // inputFile.close();
  }
  catch (FileNotFoundException e) {
  }
  catch (IOException e) {
  }
  return v;
 }
}
```

717 There is no equivalent to closing a file when you are reading a file via a URL. The reason is that the entire file is read all at once into a buffer.

718 Any exceptions thrown in the course of applet execution shut down the applet. Thus, the catch expressions in Segment 716 do nothing. Many programmers like to include statements that display a brief obituary.

719 Java insists that the URL provided to the web browser match the URL that identifies the file to be read for security reasons. By insisting on a URL match, Java prevents an applet

obtained via a network from opening, reading, or writing local files, yet allows that applet to open, read, and write files that reside in the place from which the applet came.

Insisting on a URL match helps you to prevent accidental or malicious damage to your local files; it also prevents applet providers from poking around in your files to gather information.

720   Note an important asymmetry: In ordinary standalone applications, you can access information either via URL input streams or via ordinary file streams; in applets, however, you must use URL input streams.

721   For debugging, you can use Java's **applet viewer** to view an applet embedded in an HTML file. You type the following command line:

```
appletviewer file:///e:/phw/onto/java/meter.html
```

When you use the applet viewer, with the `meter.html` file given in Segment 706, you see only the applet; you do not see the other entries in the HTML file:

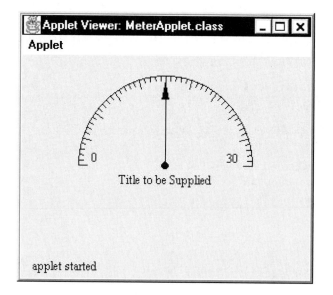

722   You can refer within your HTML file to another HTML file by placing a **link** in your HTML file. Links consist of URLs embedded in the first tag of an **address-tag pair**.

Network browsers generally highlight the text between the two tags in some way that marks that text as a **hypertext link**: if you click on that text, your web browser will switch to the HTML file referenced. For example, the following text contains a link:

```
<TITLE>Welcome to the Link Demonstration</TITLE>
<BODY>
<HR>
This file contains only a link to the
<A HREF="file:///e:/phw/onto/java/meter.html">
meter-applet demonstration.
</A>
<HR>
</BODY>
```

When displayed, the link-containing HTML file produces the following:

723
SIDE TRIP You learn in Appendix C how to arrange for HTML files to pass parameter values to applets.

724
SIDE TRIP You have learned that applets obtained via a network cannot, in general, open, read, or write local files. Advanced techniques, however, allow you to specify limited access via entries in a special file.

725
SIDE TRIP HTTP is but one of the protocols spoken by web browsers and other network-oriented applications: for example, FTP transfers files; GOPHER browses menu hierarchies on foreign computers; and SMTP exchanges electronic mail.

726
SIDE TRIP The HTML language offers a great deal of flexibility, yet the essentials are easy to learn. Many HTML users do not even bother to look at any of the many tutorials on the subject. Instead, they see a display they like in their web browser, and then they examine the related HTML file, typically by clicking on **view** and then on **document source**.

Activate the applet you were asked to create in Segment 698 via an HTML file using a web browser and using the applet viewer.

- Formatting tags are provided by the hypertext markup language, HTML.

- If you want to embed an applet in an HTML file, **then** instantiate the following pattern:

  `<APPLET CODE=" applet name .class" width= width  height= height >`
  `</APPLET>`

- If you want to view an applet using a web browser, **then** provide the web browser with the URL address of the HTML file that contains the applet:

  `http:// machine and domain name / path to file`

- If you want to view an applet embedded in an HTML file for debugging, **then** you may want to use the command-line applet viewer by instantiating the following pattern:

  `appletviewer  URL address`

- Java's security mechanism requires all files read by an applet to be accessed via the URL mechanism. The URL of any file read by an applet must match the URL by which the applet was accessed.

40 HOW TO USE THE MODEL–VIEW APPROACH TO INTERFACE DESIGN

729 In this section, you learn about the model–view approach to building graphical user interfaces, and about the classes that Java provides to support the model–view approach.

730 Maintaining consistency becomes an enormous problem in complex systems unless you adopt an orderly, methodical approach to graphical user interface design.

Java encourages you to use an orderly, methodical approach to graphical user interface design that tells you to identify particular classes with one of two groups. One group, the **observable** group, contains classes, such as the Movie class, whose instances correspond to those domain entities that contain displayed information. The other group, the **observer** group, contains classes, such as the MeterCanvas class, whose instances control your display.

731 Another term for observable is **model**, and another term for observer is **view**. Accordingly, when you divide classes into observable classes and observer classes, you are said to use the **model–view approach** to graphical user interface design.

732 In a system designed using the model–view approach, you maintain consistency by adhering to the following division of responsibility:

- Each model keeps track of the views that display the model's instance-variable values.

- Whenever a model's instance variable's value changes, all the dependent views are notified that a change has occurred.

- Each dependent view, in response to a change notification, interrogates the model's instance-variable values to determine what should be done to the portion of the display for which the view is responsible.

733 To support the model–view approach, Java provides one key class and one key interface. To implement models, Java provides the Observable class, which defines several key methods for managing change:

- The addObserver method attaches views.

- The deleteObserver method detaches views.

- The setChanged method establishes that a noteworthy change has occurred.

- The notifyObservers method announces to viewers that a noteworthy change has occurred, provided that the setChanged method has been called since the most recent call to the notifyObservers method.

To support the model–view approach on the view side, Java provides the Observer interface. The Observer interface imposes the requirement that each implementing class must implement one key method:

- The `update` method prescribes what is to be done when a view receives a change notification from a model.

734   If you want to see how the model–view approach works in general, it is instructive to see how to add model capability to `Movie` instances and viewer capability to `MeterCanvas` instances.

You start by modifying the `Movie` class. Then, you modify `MeterCanvas` class. Finally, you place a particular movie instance and a particular meter-canvas instance in a model–viewer relationship.

735   At this point, the `Attraction` class no longer serves to introduce new ideas, so assume that you start with the following `Movie` class definition, which extends `Object`, rather than `Attraction`:

```
public class Movie {
 // Define instance variables:
 String title, poster;
 int script = 5, acting = 5, directing = 5;
 // Define three-parameter constructor:
 public Movie (int s, int a, int d) {
  script = s; acting = a; directing = d;
 }
 // Define four-parameter constructor:
 public Movie (int s, int a, int d, String t) {
  this(s, a, d);
  title = t;
 }
 // Define rating:
 public int rating () {
  return script + acting + directing;
 }
}
```

736   To adapt the `Movie` class to the model–view methodology, you need to unhook the `Movie` class from the `Object` class, which the `Movie` class extends. Then, you have the `Movie` class extend the `Observable` class, which is found in the `util` package. Henceforward, `Movie` instances are also `Observable` instances.

Next, so that particular movies can notify particular views when any change to an instance variable's value occurs, you need to have all instance-variable value changes flow through setters that call the `changed` method.

Finally, the `changed` method calls the `setChanged` method, to establish that a change has occurred, and the `notifyObservers` method, to broadcast to viewers that a change has occurred:

```java
import java.util.*;
public class Movie extends Observable {
 // Define instance variables:
 String title, poster;
 int script = 5, acting = 5, directing = 5;
 // Define three-parameter constructor:
 public Movie (int s, int a, int d) {
  script = s; acting = a; directing = d;
 }
 // Define four-parameter constructor:
 public Movie (int s, int a, int d, String t) {
  this(s, a, d);
  title = t;
 }
 // Define setter and getter for script:
 public void setScript (int s) {
  script = s;
  changed();
 }
 public int getScript () {
  return script;
 }
 // ... analogous definitions for other setters and getters ...
 // Call methods inherited from Observable class:
 public void changed () {
  setChanged();
  notifyObservers();
 }
 // Define rating:
 public int rating () {
  return script + acting + directing;
 }
}
```

737 Now, you need to modify the MeterCanvas class such that its instances can be viewers of movies:

- First, the MeterCanvas class must not only extend the Canvas class, but also implement the Observer interface, which, like the Observable class, is found in the util package.

- Second, like all classes that implement the Observer interface, the MeterCanvas class must define an update method. The responsibility of the update method is to adjust the display in response to a change in the model.

- Third, the MeterCanvas class must declare an instance variable to which a Movie instance, the model, can be assigned by a setter, attachObservable, and that setter must be defined.

738 The update method has the responsibility of reacting when the MeterCanvas instance, the view, receives a change notification. Straightforwardly, update responds by using MeterCanvas setters to reset instance variables in the meter, which, in turn, call repaint:

```
import java.util.*;
import java.awt.*;
public class MeterCanvas extends Canvas implements Observer{
  Movie movie;
  String title = "Title to be Supplied";
  int minValue = 0, maxValue = 30, value = 15;
  // Set the title:
  public void setTitle(String s) {title = s; repaint();}
  // Set the current value:
  public void setValue(int v) {value = v; repaint();}
  // ... attachObservable defined here ...
  public void update (Observable o, Object x) {
    Movie m = (Movie) o;
    setTitle(m.getTitle());
    setValue(m.rating());
  }
  // ... paint defined here ...
  // ... minimumSize and preferredSize defined here ...
}
```

739 Calling notifyObservers in an attached model causes Java to hand two arguments to update. For generality, the type of the first argument is Observable; in the example, however, the instance handed over is a Movie instance.

Instances of the Observable class cannot be targets of methods defined in the Movie subclass, however. The Object class parameter must be cast to a Movie instance before getTitle and rating can be called:

```
         ┌─ Parameter, an Object instance
         │
         ▼
Movie m = (Movie) o;
```

The second argument is null, assuming that your program calls notifyObservers without an argument. If your program supplies an argument to notifyObservers, then that argument is handed over to update as well, as the second argument.

740 The attachObservers method has the responsibility of connecting and disconnecting Movie instances, the models, to the MeterCanvas instance, the view. Disconnecting occurs only if the movie variable has a Movie instance value, rather than the initial null value, as shown in the following definition of the MeterCanvas class:

```java
import java.util.*;
import java.awt.*;
public class MeterCanvas extends Canvas implements Observer{
 Movie movie;
 String title = "Title to be Supplied";
 int minValue = 0, maxValue = 30, value = 15;
 // Set the title:
 public void setTitle(String s) {title = s; repaint();}
 // Set the current value:
 public void setValue(int v) {value = v; repaint();}
 public void attachObservable (Movie m) {
  if (m != movie) {
   if (movie != null) {movie.deleteObserver(this);}
   movie = m;
   movie.addObserver(this);
   movie.changed();
  }
 }
 public void update (Observable o, Object x) {
  Movie m = (Movie) o;
  setTitle(m.getTitle());
  setValue(m.rating());
 }
 public void paint(Graphics g) {
  // Obtain Dimension instance and draw:
  Dimension d = size();
  int meterWidth = d.width * 3 / 4;
  int dialPosition = meterWidth * (value - minValue)
                     / (maxValue - minValue);
  int xOrigin = (d.width - meterWidth) / 2;
  int yOrigin = d.height / 2;
  g.drawLine(xOrigin, yOrigin, xOrigin + meterWidth, yOrigin);
  g.drawLine(xOrigin + dialPosition, yOrigin,
            xOrigin + dialPosition, yOrigin - 10);
  // Write title:
  g.setFont(new Font("Helvetica", Font.BOLD, 12));
  FontMetrics f = g.getFontMetrics();
  int height = f.getHeight();
  int descent = f.getDescent();
  int stringWidth = f.stringWidth(title);
  xOrigin = (d.width - stringWidth) / 2;
  yOrigin = d.height * 3 / 4;
  g.drawString(title, xOrigin, yOrigin);
 }
 public Dimension minimumSize() {return new Dimension(150, 100);}
 public Dimension preferredSize() {return new Dimension(150, 100);}
}
```

The attachObservers method also calls the changed method when a movie is assigned to the movie variable. Nothing inside the assigned movie is changed at this point, of course, but the changed method is called nevertheless, so that the chain of events that leads to repainting the display via update is initiated.

741　Now, all that remains is to define a MovieApplet class, which builds on the MeterApplet class defined in Segment 692.

In the MovieApplet definition, you see a wired-in Movie instance based on On to Java!, the forthcoming movie version of this book. The MovieApplet definition also defines and calls attachObservers, which, in turn, calls attachObservable, with the MeterCanvas instance as the target and the movie as the argument.

```
import java.applet.*;
import java.awt.*;
public class MovieApplet extends Applet {
  MeterCanvas meterCanvas = new MeterCanvas();
  public void init () {
    setLayout(new BorderLayout());
    add("Center", meterCanvas);
    attachObservers(new Movie(10, 10, 10, "On To Java!"));
  }
  public void attachObservers (Movie m) {
    meterCanvas.attachObservable(m);
  }
}
```

742　There are two reasons that the init method calls attachObservers, rather than calling
SIDE TRIP attachObservable directly. First, a movie-revision method, defined in Section 41, needs to call attachObservable via the movie applet. Second, other observables will be added in Section 42 and in Section 44.

743　Now suppose that you run the applet by using a web browser on the following HTML file:

```
<TITLE>Welcome to the Model--Viewer Demonstration</TITLE>
<BODY>
<HR>
<APPLET CODE="MovieApplet.class" width=300 height=200></APPLET>
<HR>
</BODY>
```

Nothing happens, other than the appearance of a window with default meter values displayed, until the attachObservers method is called. Then, many methods are called, as shown in the following diagram, in which the location of each method's definition is indicated by the column heading:

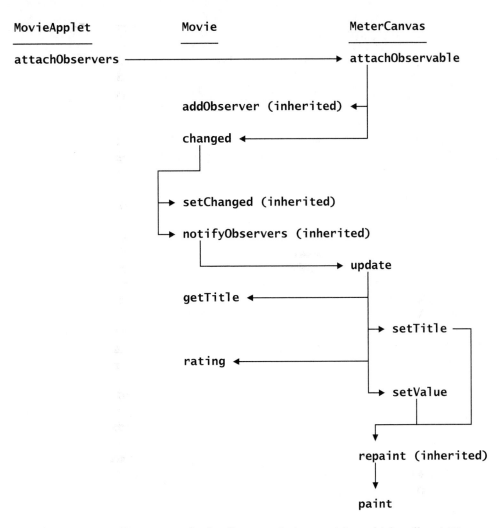

1. The attachObservers method calls attachObservable, which calls addObserver, which attaches the Movie instance, a model, to the MeterCanvas instance, a view.

2. The attachObservable method calls the changed method defined in the Movie class, which in turn calls setChanged and notifyObservers.

3. The notifyObservers method tells Java to call the update method defined in the attached MeterCanvas class, with the Movie instance as the argument.

4. The update method calls the getTitle and rating methods defined in the Movie class. Then update uses the values returned as arguments for the setTitle and setValue methods defined in the MeterCanvas class.

5. The setTitle and setValue methods call repaint with the MeterCanvas instance as the target.

6. The repaint method calls the paint method, updating your display.

744 Thus, a call to the `attachObservers` method launches a long sequence of calls that leads ultimately to the appropriate change in the display. Using the `MeterCanvas` class defined in Appendix B, rather than the simpler version defined in Segment 740, you see the following:

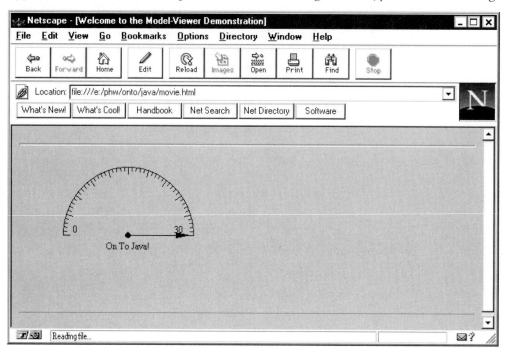

The sequence of calls may seem convoluted at first, but practice has demonstrated that great virtue is to be found in the separation of responsibilities reflected by the sequence of calls that the model–view approach produces:

- Classes that extend the `Observable` class contain methods that establish and announce changes.

- Classes that implement the `Observer` interface contain methods that determine what to do with the display after changes are established and announced.

745   Modify the `Thermometer` class you were asked to define in Segment 685 so that it imple-
PRACTICE   ments the `Observer` interface. Use the definition of the `MeterCanvas` class in Segment 740 as a guide.

Then, modify the definition of `MovieApplet` shown in Segment 741 such that the applet displays not only a meter but also a thermometer.

746
HIGHLIGHTS

- **If you want to build a GUI, then** adopt the model–view approach.

- **If you want to link a model with a view, then**

  - Arrange for the model class to extend the `Observable` class, and for the viewer class to implement the `Observer` interface.

- Insert calls to `setChanged` and `notifyObservers` in the setters of the model.

- Define an `update` method in the view.

- Have the `update` method handle all display changes.

41 HOW TO USE CHOICE LISTS TO SELECT INSTANCES

747 The principle defect of the program shown in Segment 738 is that the program works with but a single, wired-in movie. Accordingly, you need to learn to prepare a vector of movies and to display the movies in that vector as selectable choices.

748 A **list** is an instance of the `List` class. Such instances produce graphical displays of choices from which you can select.

The following creates a new list:

```
List l = new List();
```

749 Once you have a list, you can use the `addItem` method to add strings to be displayed. To add a movie title from a movie in the movie vector, at the location identified by the `counter` variable, you evaluate the following expression. As usual, the class of a vector element is the `Object` class, so you must cast the element to the `Movie` class before you attempt to extract the title:

```
           ┌─ List                     ┌─ An object
           │                           │   ─────────────────────
           ▼
choices.addItem(((Movie)(movies.elementAt(counter))).getTitle());
                ─────────────────────────────────────────
                         ▲
                         └─ A movie
```

750 In the following `ListPanel` definition, you see movies added to the list in the `ListPanel` constructor, in which you also see the list attached to the panel via the border layout manager.

```java
import java.awt.*;
import java.util.*;
public class ListPanel extends Panel {
 Vector movies;
 List choices = new List();
 public ListPanel (Vector v) {
  movies = v;
  int counter, limit = movies.size();
  for (counter = 0; counter < limit; ++counter) {
   choices.addItem(((Movie)(movies.elementAt(counter))).getTitle());
  }
  setLayout(new BorderLayout());
  add("Center", choices);
 }
// ... rest of definition ...
}
```

751 You can determine which item has been selected from a list using the `getSelectedIndex` method. If that method returns, say, 3, then the selected item was the fourth one that you placed on the list, inasmuch as the indexing is zero based. The following illustrates:

```
         ┌─ List
         │
         ↓
choices.getSelectedIndex()  ◄─ Returns location of selected item
```

752 If you have added elements to the list in the same order that they appear in a vector, then you can determine which element in the vector is selected by using the result returned by the `getSelectedItem` as an index into the vector.

753 To detect when a list item is selected by a mouse click, you define a `handleEvent` method in the panel that contains the list. Then, you test the event's `id` instance variable to see whether it has the same value as the `LIST_SELECT` class variable of the `Event` class:

```
public boolean handleEvent (Event e) {
  if (e.id == Event.LIST_SELECT) {
    ...
    return true;
  } else {return false;}
}
```

754 Responding to an item selection seems complex until you take apart the response. First, you use a getter to obtain the item's index; then, you obtain the corresponding element from the movie vector; finally, you cast that element into a `Movie` instance:

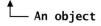

```
                                        ┌─ An index
                                        │
                                        ↓
                    _____
Movie m = (Movie)(movies.elementAt(choices.getSelectedIndex()));
                    _____
                         ↑
                         └─ An object
```

755 You call the `attachObservers` method defined in the `MovieApplet` class using the newly obtained movie as the argument. However, the target is not an instance of the `ListPanel` class, but rather is the `MovieApplet` instance to which the `ListPanel` instance is attached. Fortunately, you can get at the parent applet using the `getParent` method and a cast:

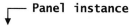

```
              ┌─ Panel instance
              │
              ↓
    ____
((MovieApplet)(this.getParent())).attachObservers(m);
    ____
      ↑
      └─ Parent, viewed as an Object instance
```

756   Now, you can construct a definition for the `ListPanel` class that includes a complete definition for `handleEvent`:

```
import java.awt.*;
import java.util.*;
public class ListPanel extends Panel {
 Vector movies;
 List choices = new List();
 // ... constructor goes here ...
 public boolean handleEvent (Event e) {
  if (e.id == Event.LIST_SELECT) {
   Movie m = (Movie)(movies.elementAt(choices.getSelectedIndex()));
   ((MovieApplet)(this.getParent())).attachObservers(m);
   return true;
  } else {return false;}
 }
 public Dimension minimumSize() {return new Dimension(200, 100);}
 public Dimension preferredSize() {return new Dimension(200, 100);}
}
```

757   Next, you create a modified version of the program shown in Segment 738 in which the list panel is embedded, along with a statement that creates a movie vector from a file. Of course, the reader must be `readMovieURL`, shown Segment 716, because it is to read a file identified by a URL:

```
import java.applet.*;
import java.awt.*;
import java.util.*;
public class MovieApplet extends Applet {
 MeterCanvas meterCanvas = new MeterCanvas();
 Vector movieVector
  = Auxiliaries.readMovieURL("file:///e:/phw/onto/java/general.movies");
 ListPanel listPanel = new ListPanel(movieVector);
 public void init () {
  setLayout(new BorderLayout());
  add("West", meterCanvas);
  add("East", listPanel);
  attachObservers((Movie) movieVector.firstElement());
 }
 public void attachObservers (Movie m) {
  meterCanvas.attachObservable(m);
 }
}
```

758   In the definition shown in Segment 757, the meter is attached as a viewer of the current movie, but the list is not a viewer.

Accordingly, selecting a movie from the list changes the movie observed by the meter, which leads to changes in the meter display, but setter methods defined in the `Movie` class, which call `notifyObservers`, have no effect on the list display.

759 Now suppose that you run the applet shown in Segment 757 by using a web browser on the following HTML file, which is adapted from the file shown in Segment 706:

```
<TITLE>Welcome to the Movies!</TITLE>
<BODY>
<HR>
In the following display, click on a movie to see its rating.
<HR>
<APPLET CODE="MovieApplet.class" width=400 height=150></APPLET>
<HR>
</BODY>
```

Java greets you with the following display:

760 You can control the number of lines displayed in a list by providing the `List` constructor
SIDE TRIP with two extra arguments. The first fixes the number of lines displayed; the second governs whether or not multiple selections are allowed. For the application developed in this section, the second argument should be `false`.

761 Modify the definition of the `MovieApplet` class in Segment 757 such that two lists of
PRACTICE movies are shown. One list is to be taken from the `general.movies` file; the other list is to be taken from the `horror.movies` file.

252

- If you want to choose from a list of displayed options, **then** instantiate the following pattern:

  ```
  List list variable = new List();
  ```

- If you want to add an element to a list of displayed options, **then** instantiate the following pattern:

  ```
  list variable .addItem( a string );
  ```

- If you want to determine which item is selected from a list of displayed options, **then** instantiate the following pattern:

  ```
  public boolean handleEvent (Event e) {
   if (e.id == Event.LIST_SELECT) {
    ··· list variable .getSelectedIndex() ···
    return true;
   } else {return false;}
  }
  ```

42 HOW TO INCORPORATE IMAGES INTO APPLETS

763   In this section, you learn how to move information from image files into your applets. You also learn that the movement of image files is handled by a separate thread—an arrangement that enables your application to present a snappy look-and-feel, even though the movement of image files may be slow.

764   To display images, you need to define an `ImagePanel` class that, like the `MeterCanvas` class, produces instances that are viewers of `Movie` instances:

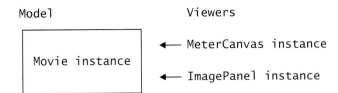

765   Thus, the structure of the `ImagePanel` definition is much like that of the `MeterCanvas` definition shown in Segment 740:

```
import java.awt.*;
class ImagePanel extends Panel implements Observer {
 Movie movie;
 Image image;
 // ... setImage definition ...
 // ... attachObservable definition ...
 // ... update definition ...
 // ... paint definition ...
 // ... minimumSize and preferredSize definition ...
}
```

766   The definition of the `attachObservable` method is exactly the same as the corresponding definition in the `MeterCanvas` class:

```
public void attachObservable (Movie m) {
 if (m != movie) {
  if (movie != null) {movie.deleteObserver(this);}
  movie = m;
  movie.addObserver(this);
  movie.changed();
 }
}
```

The definition of the `update` method differs only in that it calls an `ImagePanel` setter, rather than two `MeterPanel` setters:

```
public void update (Observable o, Object x) {
  Movie m = (Movie) o;
  setImage(m.getPoster());
}
```

767   The value of the instance variable, `image`, is an instance of the `Image` class. That value is changed by `setImage`, a setter method that calls `repaint`, which, in turn, calls the `paint` method that presents the image on your display.

768   The definition of `ImagePanel` is complex only because `setImage` has a good deal of work to do to prepare for image display, and `paint` has a good deal of work to do to present the image in proper proportion.

769   If the current movie has no image file associated with it, the argument handed to the `setImage` method is `null`. Accordingly, the first task of `setImage` is to determine whether its argument is a real file name. If the argument is `null`, then `setImage` sets the instance variable, `image` to `null` as well:

```
public void setImage (String s) {
  if (s == null) {image = null;}
  else {
    // ... respond to image-file argument ...
  }
}
```

770   Image display requires cooperation between a Java program and the operating system under which Java is running, because the procedures that actually spray images on your display belong to the operating system.

Methods associated with an instance of the `Toolkit` class enable the required cooperation between your Java program and the operating system.

You obtain the required `Toolkit` instance, within the `setImage` method, by way of a class method, `getDefaultToolkit`, which returns the appropriate, operating-system–specific toolkit.

```
public void setImage (String s) {
  if (s == null) {image = null;}
  else {
    // Get the image stored in the file:
    Toolkit tools = Toolkit.getDefaultToolkit();
    // ... rest of setImage ...
  }
}
```

771   Then, to create an `Image` instance, you must use the `getImage` method provided by the default toolkit, with a file name:

256

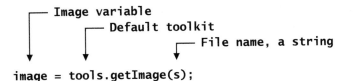

```
image = tools.getImage(s);
```

772 Fortunately, the getImage method is defined both for ordinary strings and for URL instances. In applets, you use the following:

```
image = tools.getImage(new URL(s));
```

773 Because the getImage method engages in input activity, the call to the getImage method must be embedded in a try–catch statement:

```
public void setImage (String s) {
  if (s == null) {image = null;}
  else {
  // Get the image stored in the file:
  Toolkit tools = Toolkit.getDefaultToolkit();
  try{image = tools.getImage(new URL(s));}
  catch (IOException e) {}
  // ... rest of setImage ...
}
```

774 Images are not retrieved from files at the time that the getImage method is called. Instead, images are retrieved by a **media tracker**, which is an instance of the MediaTracker class, and which not only retrieves images, but caches and keeps track of images retrieved, so that repeated use of one image does not require that image to be read from a file repeatedly.

775 Because the MediaTracker instance needs to know the panel or other component to which images are to be attached, that panel is supplied as a constructor argument. Typically, media trackers are created in one of the panel's instance methods, so the panel is available as the value of the this parameter:

```
MediaTracker tracker = new MediaTracker(this);
```

776 Once you have both an Image instance and a MediaTracker instance, you add that image to that media tracker using addImage, an instance method defined in the MediaTracker class:

```
tracker.addImage(image, 0);
```

The second argument is an index, which happens to be 0 in the example. In general, the index provides a way to divide images into groups, with each index corresponding to a group.

777   With the creation of the media tracker, the attachment of the image to the media tracker, and a call to `repaint`, `setImage` is complete:

```
public void setImage (String s) {
  if (s == null) {image = null;}
  else {
    // Get the image stored in the file:
    Toolkit tools = Toolkit.getDefaultToolkit();
    try{image = tools.getImage(new URL(s));}
    catch (IOException e) {}
    // Create a tracker and add the image:
    MediaTracker tracker = new MediaTracker(this);
    tracker.addImage(image, 0);
  }
  repaint();
}
```

778   Once an image has been loaded into the `MediaTracker` instance, you can display the image within a `paint` method using `drawImage`—an instance method of the `Graphics` class.

First, however, you have to determine the appropriate size for the image from the panel in which the image is to be displayed. You determine that size by using the `size` method to obtain a `Dimension` instance, which then provides `width` and `height` instance-variable values:

`Dimension d = size();`

Then, with the `Dimension` instance in hand, you call the `drawImage` method, which takes arguments specifying the image, the origin, and the dimensions. Also, because the `drawImage` method needs to know the panel on which actually to draw the image, that panel is supplied as the final argument:

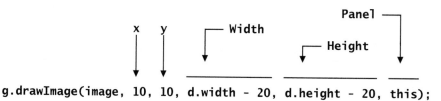

`g.drawImage(image, 10, 10, d.width - 20, d.height - 20, this);`

As illustrated, the image is drawn with a 10-unit border.

779   Thus, `paint` can be defined as follows:

```
public void paint(Graphics g) {
  Dimension d = size();
  if (image != null) {
    g.drawImage(image, x, y, width, height, this);
  }
}
```

780 The definition of paint shown in Segment 779 works, but is likely to distort the image, because the height-to-width ratio of the image will differ from the height-to-width ratio of the panel in which the image is to be displayed.

Accordingly, you might choose to use the getWidth and getHeight methods to obtain the width and height of the image, and might adjust the arguments provided to drawImage accordingly. Both getWidth and getHeight use an Image instance as the targets and the panel on which the image is to be drawn as the argument:

```
         ┌── Image        ┌── Panel
         │                │
         ▼                ▼
image.getWidth(this)
```

781 The scaling computations required to adjust the arguments of drawImage are straightforward, albeit tedious:

```
public void paint(Graphics g) {
 Dimension d = size();
 if (image != null) {
  // Tedium starts here:
  int x, y, width, height, border = 20;
  double imageRatio
   = (float) image.getHeight(this) / image.getWidth(this);
  double windowRatio = (float) d.height / d.width;
  if (imageRatio > windowRatio) {
   height = d.height - border;
   width = (int)((float) image.getWidth(this)
              * (d.height - border) / image.getHeight(this));
  }

  else {
   width = d.width - border;
   height = (int)((float) image.getHeight(this)
              * (d.width - border) / image.getWidth(this));
  }
  x = (d.width - width) / 2;
  y = (d.height -height) / 2;
  // Tedium ends here:
  g.drawImage(image, x, y, width, height, this);
 }
}
```

782 The setImage and paint methods, with suitable definitions for attachObservable, update, minimumSize, and preferredSize, are included in the following definition of the ImagePanel class:

```
import java.net.*;
import java.io.*;
import java.awt.*;
import java.util.*;
class ImagePanel extends Panel implements Observer {
 Image image;
 Movie movie;
 public void attachObservable (Movie m) {
  if (m != movie) {
   if (movie != null) {movie.deleteObserver(this);}
   movie = m;
   movie.addObserver(this);
   movie.changed();
  }
 }
 public void setImage (String s) {
  if (s == null) {image = null;}
  else {
   // Get the image stored in the file:
   Toolkit tools = Toolkit.getDefaultToolkit();
   try{image = tools.getImage(new URL(s));}
   catch (IOException e) {}
   // Create a tracker and add the image:
   MediaTracker tracker = new MediaTracker(this);
   tracker.addImage(image, 0);
  }
  repaint();
 }
 public void update (Observable o, Object x) {
  Movie m = (Movie) o;
  setImage(m.getPoster());
 }
 public void paint(Graphics g) {
  Dimension d = size();
  if (image != null) {
   int x, y, width, height, border = 20;
   // ... scaling statements assign width and height ...
   g.drawImage(image, x, y, width, height, this);
  }
 }
 public Dimension minimumSize() {return new Dimension(200, 300);}
 public Dimension preferredSize() {return new Dimension(200, 300);}
}
```

783   The setImage method defined in Segment 782 does not wait for an image to be added to the media tracker. You see the image emerge incrementally, as its chunks are loaded. Meanwhile, the rest of your display shows the properties of the current movie quickly.

784 Separation of the image loading from the operation of the rest of your program ensures a responsive look and feel. The separation is possible because Java is **multithreaded**. You learn about multithreading in Section 43.

785
SIDE TRIP
If you want your program to pause while an image is loaded, you call the `waitForID` method of the tracker. The first argument specifies the index of the image group for which you are waiting, and the second specifies the time in milliseconds that you are prepared to wait, with 0, strangely, specifying forever:

```
try {
 tracker.waitForID(0, 0);
}
catch (InterruptedException e) {
 image = null;
}
```

Alternatively, you can use the `waitForAll` method, which waits for all images to be loaded. The `waitForAll` method takes a single time argument.

786 The panel defined in Segment 782 is put to use in the following revision of the applet defined previously in Segment 757.

```
import java.applet.*;
import java.awt.*;
import java.util.*;
public class MovieApplet extends Applet {
 MeterCanvas meterCanvas = new MeterCanvas();
 Vector movieVector
  = Auxiliaries.readMovieURL("file:///e:/phw/onto/java/general.movies");
 ListPanel listPanel = new ListPanel(movieVector);
 ImagePanel imagePanel = new ImagePanel();
 public void init () {
  setLayout(new BorderLayout());
  add("West", meterCanvas);
  add("Center", listPanel);
  add("East", imagePanel);
  attachObservers((Movie) movieVector.firstElement());
 }
 public void attachObservers (Movie m) {
  meterCanvas.attachObservable(m);
  imagePanel.attachObservable(m);
 }
}
```

787 Now, suppose that you run the applet defined in Segment 786 by using a web browser. The required following HTML file is the same as the one shown in Segment 759, except for an increase in the width parameter:

261

```
<TITLE>Welcome to the Movies!</TITLE>
<BODY>
<HR>
In the following display, click on a movie to see its rating.
<HR>
<APPLET CODE="MovieApplet.class" width=600 height=150></APPLET>
<HR>
</BODY>
```

Then, Java greets you with the following display:

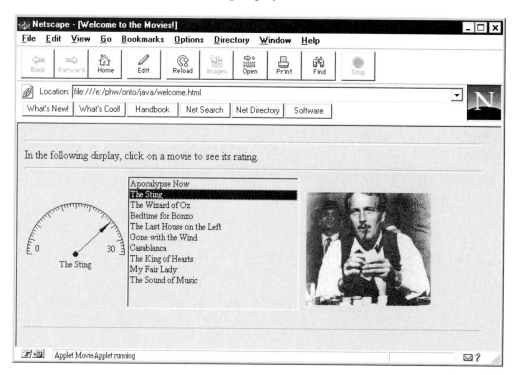

788
788
PRACTICE   Modify the definition of the imagePanel class such that an image is displayed only if the rating of the current movie is 25 or greater.

789
PRACTICE   Modify the definition of the MovieApplet class defined in Segment 786 such that if no image is available for the current movie, the message "No Image" is displayed instead.

790
HIGHLIGHTS

- If you want to prepare to display an image, **then** instantiate the following pattern:

```
MediaTracker tracker variable = new MediaTracker(this);
Toolkit toolkit variable = Toolkit.getDefaultToolkit();
image variable = toolkit variable .getImage(new URL( URL ));}
tracker variable .addImage( image variable , 0);
```

- If you want to display an image, after you have prepared it, then instantiate the following pattern inside the paint method of the panel in which the image is to appear:

```
graphics-context variable .drawImage
   ( image variable , x , y , width , height , this);
```

43 HOW TO USE THREADS TO IMPLEMENT DYNAMIC APPLETS

791 In Segment 783, you learned that you can write a program that appears to be loading an image at the same time that the program is doing other computations. Such apparently simultaneous computations are possible because Java is multithreaded. In this section, you learn about multithreading in the context of a program that moves a message across the bottom of a display as though the message were presented on a theater marquee.

792 A **process** is a running computer program. In a **multiprocessing system,** the operating system maintains a collection of values, called an **execution context,** that keeps track of the each process's state. Execution contexts allow the operating system to interrupt one process, to run another process for a time, and then to resume the first process.

Each process in a multiprocessing system runs in **time slices** that are interdigitated with the time slices of other processes, thus sharing the computer's time. If the time slices are short enough, all processes appear to be running simultaneously, although each process appears to run more slowly than it would were it to have all the computer's time to itself.

793 In an ordinary multiprocessing system, because each process operates in its own private chunk of memory, each program is said to have its own **address space.**

794 A running Java program is like a multiprocessing system, because a running Java program involves multiple processes that share time. However, a running Java program also is unlike a multiprocessing system, because all the processes share a single address space.

A **thread** is a process that shares a single address space with other processes. Each thread works its way through a program independently, sharing time and a single address space with other threads.

Because Java supports threads, Java is said to be **multithreaded.**

795 Creating and running your own thread is a three-step process:

1 You define a subclass of the Thread class. In that definition, you include a definition for a run method.

2 You create an instance of that subclass of the Thread class.

3 You call the start method with the instance as the target, whereupon the run method begins to run independently.

796 To see how threads work, suppose that you decide to define a MarqueeCanvas class such that instances display a message, provided via a constructor, at a position dictated by the values of the position and drop instance variables.

If the value of the ready variable is true, paint displays the message in a large bold font. If the value of the ready variable is false, paint arranges for all instance variables, other than message, to be initialized:

```
import java.awt.*;
public class MarqueeCanvas extends Canvas {
 String message;
 int position, drop, initialPosition, delta, messageWidth;
 Font messageFont = new Font("TimesRoman", Font.BOLD, 24);
 boolean ready = false;
 public MarqueeCanvas (String s) {
  message = s;
 }
 // ... definition of decrement position ...
 public void paint(Graphics g) {
  if (ready) {
   g.setFont(messageFont);
   g.drawString(message, position, drop);
  }
 else {
  // Determine size:
  Dimension d = size();
  // Set initial position to be the width:
  position = initialPosition = d.width;
  // Set the font and determine the message width:
  g.setFont(messageFont);
  FontMetrics f = g.getFontMetrics();
  messageWidth = f.stringWidth(message);
  // Set delta to be equal to the width of the letter e:
  delta = f.stringWidth("e");
  // Set drop so as to center the text vertically:
  drop = (d.height + f.getHeight() + f.getDescent()) / 2;
  ready = true;
 }
// ... definitions for minimumSize and preferredSize ...
}
```

797 You cannot see the message the first time that paint is called, because the message starts
     at the extreme right side of the canvas. Each time that decrementPosition is called,
     however, the position shifts left by the value of delta.

```
public void decrementPosition() {
 if (position + messageWidth < 0) {
  position = initialPosition;
 }
 else {
  position = position - delta;
 }
 repaint();
}
```

266

Eventually, with enough calls, the message shifts entirely to the left of the canvas, at which point decrementPosition resets the position variable.

798   The complete definition of MarqueeCanvas is as follows:

```java
import java.awt.*;
public class MarqueeCanvas extends Canvas {
 String message;
 int position, drop, initialPosition, delta, messageWidth;
 Font messageFont = new Font("TimesRoman", Font.BOLD, 24);
 boolean ready = false;
 public MarqueeCanvas (String s) {
  message = s;
 }
 public void decrementPosition() {
  if (position + messageWidth < 0) {
   position = initialPosition;
  }
  else {
   position = position - delta;
  }
  repaint();
 }
 public void paint(Graphics g) {
  if (ready) {
   g.setFont(messageFont);
   g.drawString(message, position, drop);
  }
  else {
   Dimension d = size();
   position = initialPosition = d.width;
   g.setFont(messageFont);
   FontMetrics f = g.getFontMetrics();
   messageWidth = f.stringWidth(message);
   delta = f.stringWidth("e");
   drop = (d.height + f.getHeight() + f.getDescent()) / 2;
   ready = true;
  }
 }
 public Dimension minimumSize() {return new Dimension(300, 50);}
 public Dimension preferredSize() {return new Dimension(300, 50);}
}
```

799   By arranging to call decrementPosition at regular intervals, you can ensure that the message will scroll from right to left.

Accordingly, you need to define a subclass of the Thread class—say MarqueeThread—that runs independently, and that calls decrementPosition, with the canvas as the target, at regular intervals.

800 So that the run method in the MarqueeThread class has access to the appropriate instance of the MarqueeCanvas class, that instance of the MarqueeCanvas class is provided to the thread via the thread's constructor, and is held by the canvas instance variable. Note that the Tread class is provided by the lang package.

```
import java.lang.*;
public class MarqueeThread extends Thread {
 MarqueeCanvas canvas;
 public MarqueeThread (MarqueeCanvas p) {
   canvas = p;
 }
 // ... definition of run ...
}
```

801 With the MarqueeCanvas instance available as the value of the canvas instance variable, the run method is readily defined so as to call decrementPosition periodically:

```
import java.lang.*;
public class MarqueeThread extends Thread {
 MarqueeCanvas canvas;
 public MarqueeThread (MarqueeCanvas p) {
   canvas = p;
 }
 public void run () {
  while (true) {
   canvas.decrementPosition();
   // ... pause statement ...
  }
 }
}
```

802 You can tell a thread to pause by using the sleep instance method. The argument is the number of milliseconds that you want to the pause to last. Accordingly, if you want, say, 0.2 second to elapse between calls to decrementPosition, you insert the expression sleep(200).

The expression has to be surrounded by a try–catch statement, however, because the sleep method can throw an exception. In the event an exception is thrown, the stop method stops the thread:

```
import java.lang.*;
public class MarqueeThread extends Thread {
 MarqueeCanvas canvas;
 public MarqueeThread (MarqueeCanvas p) {
   canvas = p;
 }
 public void run () {
  while (true) {
   canvas.decrementPosition();
   try{sleep(200);}
   catch (InterruptedException e) {stop();}
  }
 }
}
```

803   At this point, you have definitions for MarqueeThread and MarqueeCanvas. All that remains is to install a canvas and thread in an applet, and to start the thread. The following definition of MovieApplet is an augmentation of the definition in Segment 786.

```
import java.applet.*;
import java.awt.*;
import java.util.*;
public class MovieApplet extends Applet {
 MeterCanvas meterCanvas = new MeterCanvas();
 Vector movieVector
   = Auxiliaries.readMovieURL("file:///e:/phw/onto/java/general.movies");
 ListPanel listPanel = new ListPanel(movieVector);
 ImagePanel imagePanel = new ImagePanel();
 MarqueeCanvas marqueeCanvas = new MarqueeCanvas(
   "Read On to Java, available now at your local bookstore"
 );
 MarqueeThread marqueeThread = new MarqueeThread(marqueeCanvas);
 public void init () {
  setLayout(new BorderLayout());
  add("West", meterCanvas);
  add("Center", listPanel);
  add("East", imagePanel);
  add("South", marqueeCanvas);
  marqueeThread.start();
  attachObservers((Movie) movieVector.firstElement());
 }
 public void attachObservers (Movie m) {
  meterCanvas.attachObservable(m);
  imagePanel.attachObservable(m);
 }
}
```

804   Now, suppose that you run the applet defined in Segment 803 by using a web browser on the following HTML file:

```
<TITLE>Welcome to the Movies!</TITLE>
<BODY>
<HR>
In the following display, click on a movie to see its rating.
<HR>
<APPLET CODE="MovieApplet.class" width=600 height=200></APPLET>
<HR>
</BODY>
```

Then, Java greets you with the following display, in which the message is mostly—but not completely—exposed:

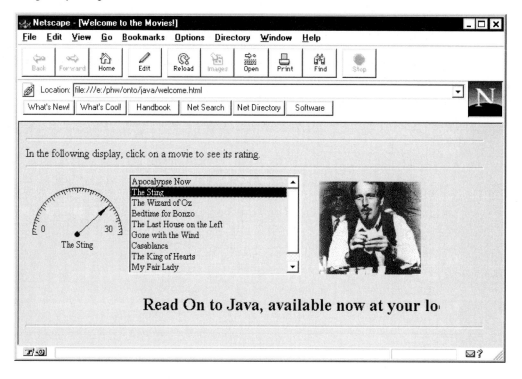

805   All together, there are five important methods that determine whether a thread is running:

- The `start` method starts threads, and the `stop` method stops threads, forever.

- The `suspend` method stops threads temporarily, and the `resume` method restarts suspended threads.

- The `sleep` method suspends and resumes after a prescribed passage of time.

If the `run` method returns, the thread is considered to have stopped, as though the `stop` method were called.

270

806   The program shown in Segment 786 is not likely to produce a flickering image when run on your computer, because the message takes so little time to display. Flicker can be a problem, however, if you display a sequence of complex drawings in a short time. Appendix D explains how to control such flicker.

807
SIDE TRIP
    You can direct a program to wait for a thread to finish its work using the join method, as shown in the following example, in which the thread is the value of the thread variable:

```
thread.join(0);
```

The argument specifies a time interval in milliseconds that your program is to wait. Specifying zero indicates you want your program to wait as long as necessary.

808
SIDE TRIP
    You can use the setPriority method to tell Java about the importance of a particular thread in your application. If the thread assigned to thread is not at all important, you evaluate the following statement:

```
thread.setPriority(Thread.MIN_PRIORITY);
```

On the other hand, if the thread is extremely important, you evaluate the following statement:

```
thread.setPriority(Thread.MAX_PRIORITY);
```

809
SIDE TRIP
    Multithreaded programs may require **synchronization**, which is a way of ensuring that two methods will not run at the same time.

One classic example is that of bank-account deposits and withdrawals. If you have threads called deposit and withdraw methods, there is a chance that both methods will fetch the current balance from an instance variable before either method performs the appropriate addition or subtraction. Thus, a method may work on an out-of-date balance, as illustrated by the following event sequence, producible by two threads running deposit and withdraw methods independently:

```
Deposit thread                          Withdraw thread
──────────────                          ───────────────

Fetch current balance, 100

                                        Fetch current balance, 100

Add 10 to 100,
Write balance, 110

                                        Subtract 10 from 100
                                        Write balance, 90
```

810
SIDE TRIP
    To solve the interference problem illustrated in Segment 809, you need to ensure that the deposit method does not allow the withdraw program to run at the same time, even though both are under the control of independent threads.

As long as both methods are defined in the same class, you need only mark both with the synchronized keyword:

271

```
public synchronized void deposit(int amount) {
  ...
}
public synchronized void withdraw(int amount) {
  ...
}
```

Such synchronized methods cannot run at the same time, because Java has what is called a **locking mechanism**. Conceptually, each class has exactly one **lock**, and any synchronized method must have that lock to start. Once a synchronized method starts, it holds onto the lock until it has completed its work. Thus, no other synchronized method can run during that time.

811
SIDE TRIP The run method shown in Segment 802 uses a while statement:

```
while (true) {
  ...
}
```

A version that uses the isAlive method, instead of true, is viewed by careful programmers as a more robust way of writing the while statement:

```
while(thread.isAlive()) {
  ...
}
```

812
PRACTICE Develop a dynamic logo consisting of a moon revolving around a planet. Have the moon go around the planet once every 10 seconds. Modify the MovieApplet definition shown in Segment 803 to include your dynamic logo.

813
HIGHLIGHTS

- If you want to create a thread that calls a method in another class, the controlled class, **then** instantiate the following pattern:

```
public class class name extends Thread {
  controlled-class name instance variable ;
  public class name ( controlled-class name parameter ) {
    instance variable = parameter ;
  }
  public void run () {
    // ... method calls with instance variable as the target ...
  }
}
```

- If you want a thread to pause, **then** instantiate the following pattern:

```
try{sleep( time, in milliseconds );}
catch (InterruptedException e) {stop();}
```

- If you want to start or stop a thread, then call `start`, `stop`, `suspend`, or `resume`.

44 HOW TO CREATE TEXT FIELDS AND BUTTONS

814   In this section, you learn how to use components that allow data to be typed into text fields, so that you can display and edit a movie's instance variables. You also learn more about the model–view approach to interface design.

815   The key elements in a form are instances of the `Label` class and the `TextField` class.

     Instances of the `Label` class, when added to a panel, display the string provided to the `Label` constructor. Thus, when the following `add` statement appears inside a panel's constructor, the word *Script* appears at a place dictated by the panel's layout manager:

```
add(new Label("Script"));
```

816   The constructor for instances of the `TextField` class specifies an initial string and the number of columns associated with the text field:

```
Textfield scriptField = new TextField("0", 20);
```

     When the following `add` statement appears inside the constructor for a panel, the initial string, `"0"`, is displayed in a text field at a place dictated by the panel's layout manager:

```
add(scriptField);
```

817   To fetch the current string that appears in a text field, possibly after you edit that field, you use the `getText` method:

```
scriptField.getText()
```

818   Often, you want the value of an integer that a string represents, so you have to convert the string into an integer using the `parseInt` class method found in the `Integer` class. Thus, the following produces the integer 5 from the string `"5"`:

```
Integer.parseInt("5")
```

819   Later on, if you want a program to change what appears in a text field, the `setText` method does the work. The following, for example, makes 5 appear:

```
scriptField.setText("5")
```

820   Often, you want the value of a number to appear in a text field. First, you have to convert the arithmetic value into a string using the `valueOf` class method found in the `String` class. Thus, the following produces the string `"5"` from the number 5:

```
String.valueOf(5)
```

821   To display forms, you need to define a `FormPanel` class that, like the `MeterCanvas` class and the `ImagePanel` class, produces instances that are viewers of `Movie` instances:

MeterCanvas instance
ImagePanel instance
FormPanel instance

822 Thus, the structure of the FormPanel definition is much like that of the MeterCanvas and
     ImagePanel definitions shown in Segment 740 and Segment 782:

```
import java.awt.*;
class FormPanel extends Panel implements Observer{
 Movie movie;
 // ... other instance variables ...
 // ... setImage definition ...
 // ... attachObservable definition ...
 // ... update definition ...
 // ... paint definition ...
}
```

823 The definition of the attachObservable method is exactly the same as the corresponding
     definition in the MeterCanvas class:

```
public void attachObservable (Movie m) {
 if (m != movie) {
  if (movie != null) {movie.deleteObserver(this);}
  movie = m;
  movie.addObserver(this);
  movie.changed();
 }
}
```

The definition of the update method differs only in that it calls FormPanel setters:

```
public void update (Observable o, Object x) {
 Movie m = (Movie) o;
 scriptField.setText(String.valueOf(m.script));
 actingField.setText(String.valueOf(m.acting));
 directingField.setText(String.valueOf(m.directing));
}
```

824 You arrange labels and text fields in a panel using an instance of the GridLayout layout
     manager. The GridLayout constructor takes four arguments: the number of rows, the
     number of columns, spacing between rows, and spacing between columns. Because there
     are three instance variables of interest in the Movie class, the form is laid out in three rows
     and two columns, with each row containing a Label instance, which provides the name
     of a Movie instance variable, and a TextField instance, which is part of the apparatus
     that makes it possible to change the variable's value.

As you add labels and fields, you fill in the rows and columns row by row. For example, if you use the grid layout manager in the constructor of the FormPanel class, as defined next, you end up with a column of labels and a column of text fields:

```java
import java.awt.*;
import java.util.*;
class FormPanel extends Panel implements Observer {
 Movie movie = null;
 TextField scriptField = new TextField("0", 20);
 TextField actingField = new TextField("0", 20);
 TextField directingField = new TextField("0", 20);
 public FormPanel () {
  setLayout(new GridLayout(3, 2, 3, 3));
  add(new Label("Script"));      add(scriptField);
  add(new Label("Acting"));      add(actingField);
  add(new Label("Directing")); add(directingField);
 }
 // ... definition of attachObservable ...
 // ... definition of update ...
 // ... definition of action ...
}
```

825   The only complex addition to the FormPanel class is the action method.

In reaction to certain events, such as a press of the Enter key, the handleEvent method—the one inherited via the Panel class—calls the action method.

Accordingly, when you want to deal with the Enter key, you define an action method that shadows the do-nothing action method inherited via the Panel class.

826   Note that the handleEvent method and the action method are inherited *via* the Panel
SIDE TRIP   class, rather than *from* the Panel class. Both methods are actually defined at a higher level, in the Component class, which makes both of them widely available.

827   Instead of defining an action method, you could define a handleEvent method. In the
SIDE TRIP   definition of that method, you would test for events for which the id instance variable is equal to Event.ACTION.

It is better to define action, rather than to define handleEvent, because the definition of handleEvent would have to include a call to the shadowed handleEvent method, as described in Segment 642. Thus, the handleEvent method would be more complex.

828   The action method receives two arguments from the handleEvent method. The first argument is an Event instance that brings along an instance variable, target, which is equal to the TextField instance that was current when the Enter key was pressed. The second argument is a string, masquerading as an Object instance, that provides the text in the text field that was current when the Enter key was pressed.

Once that TextField instance is identified, the action method converts the string to an integer, and calls the appropriate setter defined in the Movie class:

```
import java.awt.*;
import java.util.*;
class FormPanel extends Panel implements Observer {
 Movie movie = null;
 TextField scriptField = new TextField("0", 20);
 TextField actingField = new TextField("0", 20);
 TextField directingField = new TextField("0", 20);
 // ... definition of constructor ...
 // ... definition of attachObservable ...
 // ... definition of update ...
 public boolean action(Event e, Object o) {
  if (movie == null) {return false;}
  if (e.target == scriptField) {
   movie.setScript(Integer.parseInt((String) o)); return true;
  }
  else if (e.target == actingField) {
   movie.setActing(Integer.parseInt((String) o)); return true;
  }
  else if (e.target == directingField) {
   movie.setDirecting(Integer.parseInt((String) o)); return true;
  }
  else {return false;}
 }
}
```

829   The string in the text field is obtained from the second argument to the `action` method by casting:

(String) o;

Alternatively, that same string could have been obtained from the individual text fields:

scriptField.getText();

830   Now, suppose that you incorporate the FormPanel into another revision of the MovieApplet class, previously defined in Segment 803. The revision drops the marqueeCanvas instance and adds a formPanel instance:

```
import java.applet.*;
import java.awt.*;
import java.util.*;
public class MovieApplet extends Applet {
 MeterCanvas meterCanvas = new MeterCanvas();
 Vector movieVector
  = Auxiliaries.readMovieURL("file:///e:/phw/onto/java/general.movies");
 ListPanel listPanel = new ListPanel(movieVector);
 ImagePanel imagePanel = new ImagePanel();
 FormPanel formPanel = new FormPanel();
```

```
public void init () {
  setLayout(new BorderLayout());
  add("West", meterCanvas);
  add("Center", listPanel);
  add("East", imagePanel);
  add("South", formPanel);
  attachObservers((Movie) movieVector.firstElement());
}
public void attachObservers (Movie m) {
  meterCanvas.attachObservable(m);
  imagePanel.attachObservable(m);
  formPanel.attachObservable(m);
}
}
```

831 Nothing happens when the applet runs until the attachObservers method is called. Then, the following sequence of calls occurs. Inherited methods are marked by (i).

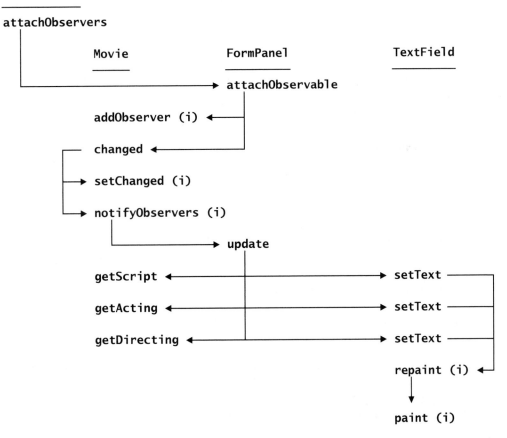

832　A similar sequence of calls also occurs when you press the Enter key, after you have edited, say, the text field holding the value of the `script` instance variable. Inherited methods are marked by (i).

MovieApplet

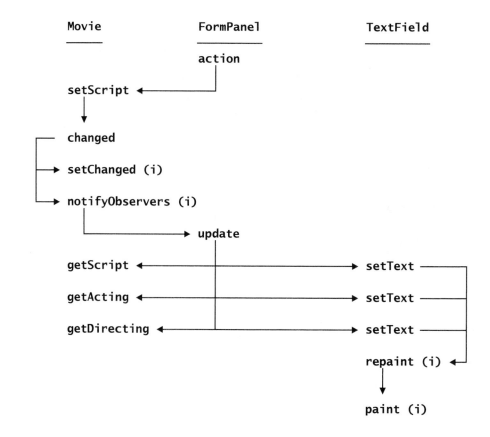

833　Now, suppose that you find it tiresome to edit text fields. You can, if you like, add buttons that increment and decrement values in the adjacent text fields.

834　Buttons are instances of the `Button` class. Declaring a labeled button is much like declaring a text field:

```
TextField scriptField = new TextField("0", 20);   ← Text field
Button scriptPlus = new Button("+");               ← Button
```

Adding a labeled button is much like adding a text field:

```
add(scriptField);   ← Text field
add(scriptPlus);    ← Button
```

835 Arranging to react to a labeled button is much like arranging to react to a text field. You need to have appropriate `if` statements in the `action` method defined in `FormPanel`:

```java
import java.awt.*;
import java.util.*;
class FormPanel extends Panel implements Observer {
 Movie movie = null;
 TextField scriptField = new TextField("0", 20);
 TextField actingField = new TextField("0", 20);
 TextField directingField = new TextField("0", 20);
 Button scriptPlus = new Button("+");
 Button actingPlus = new Button("+");
 Button directingPlus = new Button("+");
 Button scriptMinus = new Button("-");
 Button actingMinus = new Button("-");
 Button directingMinus = new Button("-");
 public FormPanel () {
  setLayout(new GridLayout(3, 4, 3, 3));
  add(new Label("Script"));     add(scriptField);
  add(scriptMinus);             add(scriptPlus);
  add(new Label("Acting"));     add(actingField);
  add(actingMinus);             add(actingPlus);
  add(new Label("Directing")); add(directingField);
  add(directingMinus);          add(directingPlus);
 }
 public void attachObservable (Movie m) {
  if (m != movie) {
   if (movie != null) {movie.deleteObserver(this);}
   movie = m;
   movie.addObserver(this);
   movie.changed();
  }
 }
 public void update (Observable o, Object x) {
  Movie m = (Movie) o;
  scriptField.setText(String.valueOf(m.script));
  actingField.setText(String.valueOf(m.acting));
  directingField.setText(String.valueOf(m.directing));
 }
 public boolean action(Event e, Object o) {
  if (movie == null) {return false;}
  if (e.target == scriptField) {
   movie.setScript(Integer.parseInt((String) o)); return true;
  } else if (e.target == actingField) {
   movie.setActing(Integer.parseInt((String) o)); return true;
  } else if (e.target == directingField) {
   movie.setDirecting(Integer.parseInt((String) o)); return true;
```

```
    } else if (e.target == scriptPlus) {
      movie.setScript(movie.getScript() + 1); return true;
    } else if (e.target == actingPlus) {
      movie.setActing(movie.getActing() + 1); return true;
    } else if (e.target == directingPlus) {
      movie.setDirecting(movie.getDirecting() + 1); return true;
    } else if (e.target == scriptMinus) {
      movie.setScript(movie.getScript() - 1); return true;
    } else if (e.target == actingMinus) {
      movie.setActing(movie.getActing() - 1); return true;
    } else if (e.target == directingMinus) {
      movie.setDirecting(movie.getDirecting() - 1); return true;
    } else {return false;}
  }
  public Dimension minimumSize() {return new Dimension(300, 75);}
  public Dimension preferredSize() {return new Dimension(300, 75);}
}
```

836 Given the definition of the FormPanel class from Segment 835 and the definition of the MovieApplet class from Segment 830, the applet, viewed by a web browser, via the same HTML file defined in Segment 759, produces the following display:

837 Of course, when a text field or button produces a change in the value of an instance variable in a movie, the notifyObservers method called in the Movie class activates not only the

update method defined in the `FormPanel` class, but also the `update` methods defined in the `ImagePanel` class and the `MeterCanvas` class.

Thus, the value shown by the meter changes whenever you change a value via a text field or button, although no method in the `FormPanel` definition calls any of the `MeterCanvas` setters directly. The model–view approach couples the action taken in the form viewer to an appropriate response in the meter viewer via the movie model.

838   At this point, you could easily revise the definition of the `MovieApplet` class to include a method that, when requested, writes the movie information back into a file. Such a revision turns the application into a complete rating editor.

839   You can create a button without a label by using a zero-parameter constructor:
SIDE TRIP

```
Button button = new Button();          ←— Labelfree button
```

840   The implementations of the classes in this section are easy to improve in various ways.
SIDE TRIP For example, you can add instance variables to the `FormPanel` class to keep track of the current values displayed in the text fields. Then, when the `update` method is called, you can arrange to call only the setters that change values, thus reducing calls to the `changed` method.

Such improvements have been suppressed here, so that the already-complex definitions do not grow even more complex.

841   Create a panel with one label and one text field. The purpose of the text field is to allow
PRACTICE you to type the name of an image file.

Then, modify the definition of the `MovieApplet` class in Segment 830 such that your new panel is displayed and such that the contents are connected to the `image` field of the current `Movie` instance.

842
HIGHLIGHTS

- If you want text fields in your application, **then**

  - Insert the following statement in the viewer:

    ```
    setLayout(
     new GridLayout( rows , columns ,
                     row spacing , column spacing )
    );
    ```

  - Use `Label` instances to create labels.

  - Use `TextField` instances to create text fields.

  - Use `getText` to retrieve strings.

  - Use `setText` to insert strings.

- Use `parseInt`, from the `Integer` class, to convert strings to integers.

- Use `valueOf`, from the `String` class, to convert integers to strings.

45 HOW TO DESIGN APPLETS USING LAYOUT MANAGERS

843   In this section, you learn about several layout managers so that you can solve a variety of layout problems and produce more attractive graphical user interfaces.

844   Every **component** fits into a surrounding **container**. In the other direction, every `container` may have one or more `components` embedded in it.

The relative sizes of all the panels are governed by a complex arbitration process, which is managed by a layout manager. Each type of layout manager handles the size-arbitration process in its own way.

845   As they attempt to arbitrate among panels, layout managers work with information provided as follows:

- An HTML file specifies an applet window into which all the applet's panels must fit.

When you include a reference to an applet in an HTML file, you must supply window dimensions, and your applet will have to work itself into those dimensions, however Procrustean they may be.

- If a `resize` method is called in a frame, that method specifies a window into which all panels must fit.

If you do not supply a `resize` method in a frame, Java will work with the operating system to choose a frame-window size.

- Every panel can define a `minimumSize` method and a `preferredSize` method.

If you do not supply `minimumSize` and `preferredSize` methods in your panels, Java works with the operating system to establish a minimum size and a preferred size.

846   If you do not include a call to the `resize` method in your frames, and you do not include definitions for `mimimumSize` and `preferredSize` in your panels, the choices negotiated by Java and your operating system may lead to unintelligible layout results, possibly with some panels not appearing at all.

847   Layout managers often seem to have mysterious minds of their own. Accordingly, you need to see a variety of layout managers in action, in a variety of circumstances, to get a feel for what sorts of layouts are possible.

848   To assist in your experiments with layout managers, you need to define a panel with appropriate `mimimumSize` and `preferredSize` methods defined. One convenient way to define such a panel is to extend the `Button` class, overriding the `minimumSize` and `preferredSize` methods. In the following definition, the width and height are both 30:

```
import java.awt.*;
public class SquarePanel extends Button {
 public SquarePanel (String t) {
  super(t);
 }
 public Dimension minimumSize() {return new Dimension(30, 30);}
 public Dimension preferredSize() {return new Dimension(30, 30);}
}
```

849 Having defined the SquarePanel class, you can use instances of that class to experiment with the border layout manager. The following, for example, defines a test applet using the TestApplet class defined in Segment 693.

```
import java.applet.*;
import java.awt.*;
public class TestApplet extends Applet {
 // The main method is included for testing only:
 public static void main (String args []) {
  AppletTestorFrame f = new AppletTestorFrame("BorderLayout Test");
  TestApplet p = new TestApplet(); p.init();
  f.add("Center", p); f.resize(200, 150);  f.show();
 }
 public void init () {
  setLayout(new BorderLayout());
  add("North", new SquarePanel("N"));
  add("East", new SquarePanel("E"));
  add("South", new SquarePanel("S"));
  add("West", new SquarePanel("W"));
  add("Center", new SquarePanel("C"));
  show();
 }
}
```

850 When you run the program shown in Segment 849, you see the following display:

851   Of course, you do not need to place a panel at any particular position. The following shows the border layout with the south panel omitted. The center panel expands southward to take up the vacated space.

BorderLayout Test _ □ ✕

N

W   C   E

Similarly, the following shows the border layout with the east panel omitted. The center panel expands eastward to take up the vacated space.

BorderLayout Test _ □ ✕

N

W   C

S

Finally, the following shows the border layout with the center panel omitted. A hole appears in the space vacated by the center panel.

BorderLayout Test _ □ ✕

N

W   E

S

852   As you learned in Segment 824, the grid layout manager lays out panels on a regular grid. The following grid layout places panels in two rows and three columns:

```
import java.applet.*;
import java.awt.*;
public class TestApplet extends Applet {
 // ... main method for testing with 200 x 150 window goes here ...
 public void init () {
  setLayout(new GridLayout(2, 3));
  add(new SquarePanel("A")); add(new SquarePanel("B"));
  add(new SquarePanel("C")); add(new SquarePanel("D"));
  add(new SquarePanel("E")); add(new SquarePanel("F"));
  show();
 }
}
```

853 When you use the definition shown in Segment 852, you produce the following display:

854 You can separate the panels by supplying the GridLayout class constructor with row- and column-spacing arguments:

```
setLayout(new GridLayout(2, 3, 15, 10));
```

When you use such spacing, you see the following:

855   You can use the grid layout manager to place panels in a single row or column. All you need to do is to use arguments of 0 and 1. If you use 1 as the first argument, you get a row:

If you use 1 as the second argument, you get a column:

856   The flow layout manager lays out panels from left to right, top to bottom, placing as many panels in a row as the space allows. The following flow layout places five panels in the first row and one in the second:

```
import java.applet.*;
import java.awt.*;
public class TestApplet extends Applet {
  // ... main method for testing with 200 x 150 window goes here ...
  public void init () {
    setLayout(new FlowLayout());
    add(new SquarePanel("A"));
    add(new SquarePanel("B"));
    add(new SquarePanel("C"));
    add(new SquarePanel("D"));
    add(new SquarePanel("E"));
    add(new SquarePanel("F"));
    show();
  }
}
```

857 When you use the definition shown in Segment 856, you produce the following display:

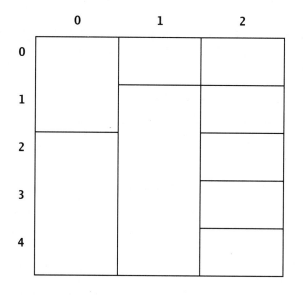

858 Instances of the Panel class use the flow layout manager by default.

859 The most complex layout manager, the gridbag layout manager, provides fine control over panel layout. Conceptually, the gridbag layout manager divides your display into rows and columns, and any panel can span any number of rows and any number of columns.

860 Note that the numbering of rows and columns is zero based, with the origin in the upper-left corner:

The rows do not all need to have the same height, and the columns do not all need to have the same width:

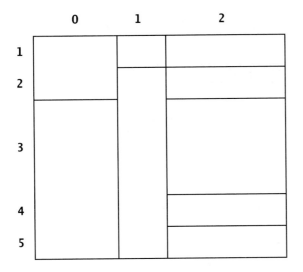

861   To specify a gridbag layout, you create an instance of the `GridBagLayout` class, which you then associate with the surrounding applet using the `setLayout` method:

```
GridBagLayout gbl = new GridBagLayout();
setLayout(gbl);
```

862   The allocation of checkerboard squares into panels is governed by an instance of the `GridBagConstraints` class:

```
GridBagConstraints gbc = new GridBagConstraints();
```

863   Among the many ways that you can condition the instance of `GridBagConstraints`, two deserve special mention. First, you arrange for particular panels to be able to expand by setting either the `weightx` or `weighty` instance variables, or both, of the gridbag constraint:

```
gbc.weightx = 1.0;  ←── Spread out horizontally
gbc.weighty = 1.0;  ←── Spread out vertically
```

Second, you arrange for the expandable panel to fill the available space by setting the `fill` instance variable to the value of the BOTH class variable:

```
gbc.fill = GridBagConstraints.BOTH;  ←── Fill space
```

If you want to fill one way, but not the other, you use the HORIZONTAL or VERTICAL class-variable values, rather than the BOTH class variable value.

864   Once you have set the `weightx`, `weighty`, and `fill` instance variables, you can place individual panels.

First, you condition the placement of the next panel by adjustments to `gridx` and `gridy` instance variables of the `GridBagConstraints` instance:

```
gbc.gridx = 1;  ←— Upper-left corner of panel is in the second row
gbc.gridy = 2;  ←— and third column
```

Second, you specify the number of rows and columns that the panel is to span by adjusting gridwidth and gridheight instance variables:

```
gbc.gridwidth = 2;   ←— Panel spans two columns
gbc.gridheight = 1;  ←— and one row
```

Third, you associate the constraint with a panel using setConstraints, an instance method of the GridBagLayout class:

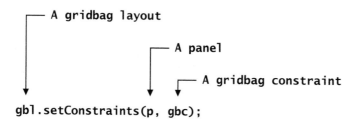

```
gbl.setConstraints(p, gbc);
```

Fourth, and finally, you add the panel to the layout using add:

```
add(p);
```

865   You do not need to create a fresh instance of GridBagConstraints for every panel; you need only one instance, as long as you adjust the instance-variable values that change before each panel placement.

866   Using the gridbag layout, you can produce the following display:

```
┌─ GridBagLayout Test ──────────── _ □ X ┐
│              │       B      │      E       │
│      A       │              ├──────────────┤
│              ├──────────────┤      F       │
├──────────────┤              ├──────────────┤
│              │              │      G       │
│              │      D       ├──────────────┤
│      C       │              │      H       │
│              │              ├──────────────┤
│              │              │      I       │
└──────────────┴──────────────┴──────────────┘
```

867   The display in Segment 866 is produced by the following gridbag layout. All the repetitive part of panel placement is done in the placePanel method, keeping clutter controlled:

292

```
import java.applet.*;
import java.awt.*;
public class TestApplet extends Applet {
// ... main method for testing with 300 x 200 window goes here ...
 public void init () {
  GridBagLayout gbl = new GridBagLayout();
  setLayout(gbl);
  GridBagConstraints gbc = new GridBagConstraints();
  // Fill both ways:
  gbc.fill = GridBagConstraints.BOTH;
  // Allow expansion of all panels:
  gbc.weightx = 1.0;
  gbc.weighty = 1.0;
  // Place panels:
  placePanel(0, 0, 1, 2, "A", gbl, gbc);
  placePanel(1, 0, 1, 1, "B", gbl, gbc);
  placePanel(0, 2, 1, 3, "C", gbl, gbc);
  placePanel(1, 1, 1, 4, "D", gbl, gbc);
  placePanel(2, 0, 1, 1, "E", gbl, gbc);
  placePanel(2, 1, 1, 1, "F", gbl, gbc);
  placePanel(2, 2, 1, 1, "G", gbl, gbc);
  placePanel(2, 3, 1, 1, "H", gbl, gbc);
  placePanel(2, 4, 1, 1, "I", gbl, gbc);
 }
 // Handle placement details:
 public void placePanel
  (int x, int y, int w, int h,
   String s, GridBagLayout l, GridBagConstraints c) {
  c.gridx = x;          c.gridwidth = w;
  c.gridy = y;          c.gridheight = h;
  SquarePanel p = new SquarePanel(s);
  l.setConstraints(p, c);    add(p);
 }
}
```

868 You might think that you would have to worry about the possibility that a user might make your graphical user interface ugly by scaling that interface's window in an odd or extreme way.

In practice, you do not have to worry at all when you are working with applets, because applet size is fixed, once and for all, in the HTML file. And you do not have to worry much, even when you are working with standalone applications, because few users actually change window sizes.

869 You can, of course, arrange complex layouts by embedding component-containing containers in surrounding containers. In the following, for example, border-layout panels are embedded, at all positions, in another border-layout panel:

870
PRACTICE By embedding component-containing containers in surrounding containers, create a display that uses all the layout managers described in this section.

871
HIGHLIGHTS

- **If** you want to place up to five components in a simple, general-purpose layout, **then** use the border layout.

- **If** you want to place components in a checkerboardlike grid, **then** use the grid layout.

- **If** you want components to flow into a space, rearranging themselves to fit, **then** use the flow layout.

- **If** you want a great deal of control over layout, **then** use the gridbag layout.

- **If** you have a truly complex layout problem, **then** embed component-containing containers in surrounding containers.

46 HOW TO DISPLAY MENUS AND FILE DIALOG WINDOWS

872   In this section, you learn to incorporate menus and menu bars in an application. You also learn to use a file-dialog window so that you no longer have to wire a file name into your application. Such features enable your application to present a polished look and feel.

873   You can incorporate menus and file-dialog windows into applets, but applets cannot have a menu bar. Accordingly, this section develops a standalone application based on the applet defined in Segment 830.

874   **Menu bars** exhibit labels, each of which, when clicked, exhibits a **menu**. Each menu, in turn, exhibits **menu items**, some of which may, themselves, be menus.

As the following shows, the standalone application has a menu bar with one menu, File. When clicked, the File menu presents two menu items: Open and Exit. The purpose of the Open menu item is to open a file-dialog window; the purpose of the Exit menu item is to terminate the application.

875   You create menu bars, menus, and menu items as illustrated in the following examples:

```
new MenuBar();
new Menu("File");
new MenuItem("Open");
```

The strings provide labels for menus and menu items. Menu bars have no label.

876   Once you have created menu bars, menus, and menu items, you connect them together using the add method. For example, to add a file menu, assigned to the fileMenu variable, to a menu bar, assigned to the menuBar variable, you execute the following statement.

```
menuBar.add(fileMenu);
```

Similarly, to add a menu item, assigned to the `fileMenuOpen` variable, to a menu, assigned to the `fileMenu` variable, you execute the following statement.

fileMenu.add(fileMenuOpen);

877 You can divide menu items into groups by adding *separators*, using the `addSeparator` method:

fileMenu.addSeparator()

878 Because the `Menu` class extends the `MenuItem` class, you can treat menus as though they are menu items. Thus, you can construct **hierarchical** or **cascading menus**. Judicious use of the hierarchical-menu concept helps you to avoid overly long menus.

879 Once you have created a collection of menu-bar, menu, and menu-item instances, you attach that collection to a `Frame` instance. Typically, you attach the collection to a frame inside a `Frame` constructor, so there is no need for an explicit target for the `setMenuBar` method:

setMenuBar(menuBar);

880 Before you define the `MovieFrame` class, you need to make a change to the `ListPanel` definition shown in Segment 756. The `handleEvent` method calls `attachObservers` on the surrounding container. In Section 41, the surrounding container is an instance of the `MovieApplet` class. In this section, the surrounding container is an instance of the `MovieFrame` class.

The necessary revision to `ListPanel` is as follows:

```
import java.awt.*;
import java.util.*;
public class ListPanelForFrame extends Panel {
 Vector movies;
 List choices = new List();
 public ListPanelForFrame (Vector v) {
  movies = v;
  int counter, limit = movies.size();
  for (counter = 0; counter < limit; ++counter) {
   choices.addItem(((Movie)(movies.elementAt(counter))).getTitle());
  }
  setLayout(new BorderLayout());
  add("Center", choices);
 }
```

```
  public boolean handleEvent (Event e) {
   if (e.id == Event.LIST_SELECT) {
     Movie m = (Movie)(movies.elementAt(choices.getSelectedIndex()));
     ((MovieFrame)(this.getParent())).attachObservers(m);
      return true;
   } else {return false;}
  }
  public Dimension minimumSize() {return new Dimension(200, 100);}
  public Dimension preferredSize() {return new Dimension(200, 100);}
  }
```

881   In the definition of the MovieFrame class, the menu bar, menu, and menu items are all
      assigned to instance variables. All are connected together and to the frame in the construc-
      tor.

```
import java.awt.*;
import java.util.*;
public class MovieFrame extends Frame {
// ... definition of main ...
 MeterCanvas meterCanvas = new MeterCanvas();
 Vector movieVector;
 ListPanelForFrame listPanel;
 ImagePanel imagePanel = new ImagePanel();
 FormPanel formPanel = new FormPanel();
 MenuBar menuBar = new MenuBar();
 Menu fileMenu = new Menu("File");
 MenuItem fileMenuOpen = new MenuItem("Open");
 MenuItem fileMenuExit = new MenuItem("Exit");
 public MovieFrame (String title) {
   super(title);
   resize(600, 275);
   setMenuBar(menuBar);
   menuBar.add(fileMenu);
   fileMenu.add(fileMenuOpen);
   fileMenu.add(fileMenuExit);
   // ... rest of constructor ...
 }
// ... rest of class definition ...
 }
```

882   At this point, the revised application has a menu bar, a menu, and two menu items, but
      clicking on those display elements does nothing. You have a graphical Potemkin village.
      Many software vendors use such villages to sell software projects.

883   To put function behind your menu bar, menu, and menu items, you define an action
      method in the MovieFrame class that determines what has been selected. The action
      method definition is much like the action method definition explained in Segment 828.

Clicking a menu item stimulates the action method, which checks to see which menu item produced the stimulation.

If the menu item is the one with the Exit label, arranging for the proper response is straightforward: Java is to terminate the application:

```
public boolean action (Event e, Object o) {
 if (e.target == fileMenuOpen) {
  // ... read movies from a file ...
 }
 else if (e.target == fileMenuExit) {
  System.exit(0); return true;
 }
 else {return false;} }
```

884   In the event that the menu item is the one with the Open label, arranging for the proper response is less straightforward, because you want to be able to choose a movie file by navigating through the file-system hierarchy.

Fortunately, Java's awt package allows you to create **file-dialog windows** by creating instances of the FileDialog class.

885   Creating an instance of the FileDialog class, assigned to the dialog variable, is straightforward:

```
FileDialog dialog = new FileDialog(this, "Load Attractions");
```

The constructor for a FileDialog specifies both a parent frame and a title. The parent frame is an instance of the MovieFrame class in which the emerging action method is defined; accordingly, you refer to the parent frame using the this parameter.

886   To arrange for a file-dialog window to display only those files that have a particular extension, you restrict display using the setFile method, with a wildcard character, *, as in the following example:

```
dialog.setFile("*.movies");
```

887   When you are ready to display the file-dialog window, you use the show method:

```
dialog.show();
```

The show method defined for FileDialog instances is a **modal** method. Such methods do not return until you act, such as by clicking the Open or Cancel buttons in the file-dialog window.

888   To obtain a selected file, once you click the Open button in the file-dialog window, you use the getFile method, as in the following example, which assigns the file name to the file variable:

```
String file = dialog.getFile();
```

889　If you click the Cancel button, rather than on the Open button, the getFile method returns null.

890　Some of the machinery of file-dialog display is provided by your operating system, rather than by Java. Because that operating system might allocate resources, you need to ensure that allocated resources are released by using the dispose method:

```
dialog.dispose();
```

891　Now, you can assemble what you have just learned into additions to the action method defined in the MovieFrame class:

```
public boolean action (Event e, Object o) {
  if (e.target == fileMenuOpen) {
   FileDialog dialog = new FileDialog(this, "Load Movies");
   dialog.setFile("*.movies");
   dialog.show();
   String file = dialog.getFile();
   if (file != null) {
    // ... respond to the request to look at a new file ...
   }
   dialog.dispose();
   return true;
  } else if (e.target == fileMenuExit) {
   System.exit(0); return true;
  } else {return false;}
}
```

892　To respond properly to a request to look at a new file, you need to define setMovieVector, which is a method that handles many details: it reads a movie file, creates a new instance of the ListPanelForFrame class, attaches that instance to the containing frame, attaches observers to the first movie in the movie file, and calls for display. The setMovieVector also detaches the previous List panel, if any, from the frame using the remove method.

```
public void setMovieVector (String file) {
  movieVector = Auxiliaries.readMovieFile(file);
  if (listPanel !=null) {remove(listPanel);}
  listPanel = new ListPanelForFrame(movieVector);
  add("Center", listPanel);
  attachObservers((Movie) movieVector.firstElement());
  show();
}
```

Because this application is not an applet, files are presumed to be on your computer, accessible via an ordinary file name, rather than via a URL. Accordingly, you need to use the readMovieFile method defined in Segment 563, rather than the readMovieURL defined in Segment 716.

The following definition brings together all the previously described program fragments and adds a main method for starting the program as a standalone application:

```java
import java.awt.*;
import java.util.*;
public class MovieFrame extends Frame {
 // Define main:
 public static void main (String args []) {
  // Create one instance to start the application:
  new MovieFrame("Welcome to the Movies!");
 }
 // Declare and initialize instance variables
 MeterCanvas meterCanvas = new MeterCanvas();
 Vector movieVector;
 ListPanelForFrame listPanel;
 ImagePanel imagePanel = new ImagePanel();
 FormPanel formPanel = new FormPanel();
 MenuBar menuBar = new MenuBar();
 Menu fileMenu = new Menu("File");
 MenuItem fileMenuOpen = new MenuItem("Open");
 MenuItem fileMenuExit = new MenuItem("Exit");
 // Define constructor:
 public MovieFrame (String title) {
  super(title);
  resize(600, 275);
  // Set up menus:
  setMenuBar(menuBar);
  menuBar.add(fileMenu);
  fileMenu.add(fileMenuOpen);
  fileMenu.add(fileMenuExit);
  // Place panels:
  setLayout(new BorderLayout());
  add("West", meterCanvas);
  add("East", imagePanel);
  add("South", formPanel);
  setMovieVector("general.movies");
 }
 // Handle details of vector creation:
 public void setMovieVector (String file) {
  System.out.println("Calling setMovieVector");
  movieVector = Auxiliaries.readMovieFile(file);
  if (listPanel !=null) {remove(listPanel);}
  listPanel = new ListPanelForFrame(movieVector);
  add("Center", listPanel);
  attachObservers((Movie) movieVector.firstElement());
  show();
 }
```

```
// Attach all viewers:
public void attachObservers (Movie m) {
 meterCanvas.attachObservable(m);
 imagePanel.attachObservable(m);
 formPanel.attachObservable(m);
}
// Deal with menu items:
public boolean action (Event e, Object o) {
 if (e.target == fileMenuOpen) {
  FileDialog dialog = new FileDialog(this, "Load Movies");
  dialog.setFile("*.movies");
  dialog.show();
  String file = dialog.getFile();
  System.out.println(file);
  if (file != null) {setMovieVector(file);}
  dialog.dispose();
  return true;
 }
 else if (e.target == fileMenuExit) {
  System.exit(0); return true;
 }
 else {return false;}
}
// Deal with close button:
public boolean handleEvent(Event e) {
 switch (e.id) {
  case Event.WINDOW_DESTROY:
   System.exit(0); return true;
  default: return super.handleEvent(e);
 }
}
}
```

894   Advanced techniques allow you to specify file-dialog displays in which files that have any
SIDE TRIP   of several file extensions are accepted for display.

895   Add a menu item to the file menu that activates a program that writes the current movie
PRACTICE   vector into a file. Obtain a suitable file name to write into using a file-dialog box initialized
with the name of the file that produced the current movie vector.

896

HIGHLIGHTS   • If you want to make use of a menu bar, **then** create instances of the MenuBar,
Menu, and MenuItem classes by instantiating the following patterns:

```
new MenuBar();
new Menu(" label ");
new MenuItem(" label ");
```

- If you want to tie a menu bar to a frame, **then** instantiate the following pattern:

```
setMenuBar( menu bar );
```

- If you want to connect a menu item to a menu, a menu to a menu, or a menu to a menu bar, **then** instantiate the following pattern:

```
menu or menu bar .add(menu or menu item);
```

- If you want to have a program react when a particular menu item has been selected, **then** define an `action` method by instantiating the following pattern:

```
public boolean action (Event e, Object o) {
 if (e.target == menu item ) {
  ...
 }
 else if (e.target == another menu item ) {
  ...
 }
 ...
}
```

- If you want to open a file-dialog window, **then** instantiate the following pattern:

```
FileDialog dialog variable
 = new FileDialog(this, title string );
```

- If you want to limit the files shown in a file-dialog window, **then** instantiate the following pattern:

```
dialog variable .setFile( file-name pattern );
```

- If you want to extract the file name returned by a file-dialog window, **then** instantiate the following pattern:

```
file-dialog variable .getFile();
```

- File-dialog windows return `null` if you select `cancel`.

APPENDIX A:
OPERATOR PRECEDENCE

897   The following table lists Java's precedence and associativity characteristics. Each box contains operators that have equal precedence. The top box contains the highest-precedence operators.

Operator level	Associativity
( ) [ ] .	left to right
! ++ -- + (unary) - (negation) new (data type)	right to left
* / %	left to right
+ -	left to right
< <= > >=	left to right
== !=	left to right
&	left to right
^	left to right
|	left to right
&&	left to right
||	left to right
? :	right to left
= += -= *= /= %= &= ^= |= <<= >>=	right to left

Note that each data type, surrounded by parentheses, is considered an operator—namely, a casting operator. Also, the parentheses following a method name are considered to be the function-call operator.

The & and | operators, as well as the exclusive-or operator, ^, viewed as bitwise operations, rather than Boolean operators, are not described in the body of this text.

898   The following class definition defines the meter used in examples in this book. The definition includes statements that show how to draw elements such as lines, arcs, and triangles.

```java
import java.lang.*;
import java.awt.*;
import java.util.*;
public class MeterCanvas extends Canvas implements Observer {
 Movie movie;
 int minimum, maximum;   // Minimum and maximum values displayed
 int curval;             // The currently displayed value
 String title;           // Title string for the meter
 int xpoints[];          // Coordinates for the arrows endpoints
 int ypoints[];          // Coordinates for the arrows endpoints
 int yoffset;            // Gap at the bottom
 // Zero-parameter constructor calls the three-parameter constructor:
 public MeterCanvas() {this("Title to be Supplied", 0, 30);}
 // Three-parameter constructor takes three arguments specifying the
 // title and the minimum and maximum values that the meter displays:
 public MeterCanvas(String titleString, int minVal, int maxVal) {
  title   = titleString;
  minimum = minVal;   maximum = maxVal;
  // Set the current value to be average:
  curval = (minimum+maximum)/ 2;
  // Create the arrays for holding the arrow end points:
  xpoints = new int[3]; ypoints = new int[3];
 }
 // Title setter:
 public void setTitle(String s) {title = s; repaint();}
 // Value setter:
 public void setValue(int value) {
  // If the value is less than the minimum, set to minimum:
  if (value < minimum) {
   curval = minimum;
  }
  // If the value is greater than the maximum, set to maximum:
  else if (value > maximum) {
   curval = maximum;
  }
  else {
   curval = value;
  }
  repaint();
 }
```

```java
// Value getter:
public int getValue() {
        return curval;
}
// Establishes model-viewer connection:
public void attachObservable (Movie m) {
 if (m != movie) {
  if (movie != null) {movie.deleteObserver(this);}
  movie = m;
  movie.addObserver(this);
  movie.changed();
 }
}

// Honors requirement of observer interface:
public void update (Observable o, Object x) {
 Movie m = (Movie) o;
 setTitle(m.getTitle());
 setValue(m.rating());
}
// Draws the arrow, which consists of a line and a triangle:
public void drawValue(Graphics g, Dimension d, int r) {
 int xoff    = d.width/2;
 int yoff    = d.height/2+10;
 // Compute the angle dictated by the value:
 double angle  = ((double)(curval - minimum)
                  / (double)(maximum - minimum))
                 * Math.PI;
 // The angle increases from left to right:
 angle = Math.PI - angle;
 double cang = Math.cos(angle);
 double sang = Math.sin(angle);
 int x2 = (int)(r * cang);
 int y2 = (int)(r * sang);
 // Draw the line (note that yoff-y2 is computed because the
 // window co-ordinates have y increasing downward):
 g.drawLine(xoff, yoff, x2+xoff, yoff-y2);
 int lArrow = 20;               // Length of the arrow
 int wArrow = 4;                // Half width of the arrow
 // Compute The points on the triangle border:
 xpoints[0] = x2 + xoff;
 ypoints[0] = yoff - y2;
 xpoints[1] = x2 - (int)(lArrow * cang) - (int)(wArrow * sang) + xoff;
 ypoints[1] = yoff - (y2 - (int )(lArrow * sang) + (int)(wArrow * cang));
 xpoints[2] = x2 - (int)(lArrow * cang) + (int)(wArrow * sang) + xoff;
 ypoints[2] = yoff - (y2 - (int)(lArrow * sang) - (int)(wArrow * cang));
 // Draw a filled polygon for the triangle:
 g.fillPolygon(xpoints, ypoints, 3);
}
```

```
// Draws the tick marks associated with the meter:
public int drawTics(Graphics g, Dimension d, FontMetrics f) {
  int i;
  double angInc = Math.PI / 50.0;
  double angle = 0.0;
  int xoff = d.width/2;
  int yoff = d.height/2+10;
  int radius = Math.min(d.height/2-10, d.width/2-4);
  int iradius = radius - (radius / 10);
  int sradius  = radius - (radius / 20);
  // Draw an arc on which to draw the tics:
  g.drawArc(xoff - radius, yoff - radius,
            radius * 2, radius * 2, 0, 180);
  // g.fillArc(xoff - 4, yoff - 4, 8, 8, 0, 180);
  g.fillOval(xoff - 4, yoff - 4, 8, 8);
  // Try to draw about fifty tick marks with about 10 major ticks
  for (i=0; i<=50; i++, angle += angInc) {
    double cang = Math.cos(angle);
    double sang = Math.sin(angle);
    int x1 = (int)(radius * cang) + xoff;
    int y1 = yoff - (int)(radius * sang);
    if (i%5 == 0) {
      int x2 = (int)(iradius * cang) + xoff;
      int y2 = yoff - (int)(iradius * sang);
      g.drawLine(x1, y1, x2, y2);
    }
    else {
      int x2 = (int)(sradius * cang) + xoff;
      int y2 = yoff - (int)(sradius * sang);
      g.drawLine(x1, y1, x2, y2);
    }
  }
  // Now draw the min and max labels:
  int fontHeight = f.getHeight();
  int fontDescent = f.getDescent();
  int stringWidth;
  String sval = String.valueOf(minimum);
  stringWidth = f.stringWidth(sval);
  // Draw the minimum-value string:
  g.drawString(sval, xoff - sradius + 10, yoff - fontDescent);
  sval = String.valueOf(maximum);
  stringWidth = f.stringWidth(sval);
  // Draw the maximum-value string:
  g.drawString(sval,
               xoff + sradius - stringWidth - 10,
               yoff - fontDescent);
  return sradius;
}
```

```java
// Writes the title associated with the meter, centered at bottom:
public void drawTitle(Graphics g, Dimension d, FontMetrics f) {
  int stringWidth = f.stringWidth(title);
  int fontHeight = f.getHeight();
  int fontDescent = f.getDescent();
  g.drawString(title,
               (d.width-stringWidth) / 2,
               d.height / 2 + 10 + fontHeight + fontDescent);
}
// Paint, by calling other methods:
public void paint(Graphics g) {
  Dimension d = size();
  FontMetrics fm = g.getFontMetrics();
  yoffset = (fm.getHeight() * 2);
  int ir = drawTics(g, d, fm);
  drawValue(g, d, ir);
  drawTitle(g, d, fm);
}
// Assist in sizing:
public Dimension minimumSize() {return new Dimension(150, 150);}
public Dimension preferredSize() {return new Dimension(150, 150);}
}
```

APPENDIX C:
APPLET PARAMETERS

899   This appendix explains how you can specify a value for an applet parameter in an HTML file.

900   To create a value for, say, a parameter named `file`, you specify the parameter name and the value, a string, in an HTML file as follows:

```
                    ┌── Name
                    │
                    ▼
          ────
<param name=file value="file:///e:/phw/onto/java/general.movies">
                        ───────────────────────────────────────
                         ▲
                         └── Value
```

Such parameter specifications lie between an <APPLET ···>—</APPLET> pair, as illustrated by the following example:

```
<TITLE>Welcome to the Movies!</TITLE>
<BODY>
<HR>
In the following display, click on a movie to see its rating.
<HR>
<APPLET CODE="MovieApplet.class" width=400 height=150>
<param name=file value="file:///e:/phw/onto/java/general.movies">
</APPLET>
<HR>
</BODY>
```

901   To get the value specified in an HTML file, you use the `getParameter` method defined for the `Applet` class.

```
                      ┌── Parameter name
                      │
                      ▼
            ────
getParameter("file");
```

902   The following definition, adapted from Segment 757, illustrates how you can get at a file name specified in the HTML file. Note that the parameter is not ready to be obtained at the time that the instance variable initializers are evaluated; accordingly, the parameter is obtained in the `init` method.

```
import java.applet.*;
import java.awt.*;
import java.util.*;
public class MovieApplet extends Applet {
 MeterCanvas meterCanvas = new MeterCanvas();
 Vector movieVector;
 ListPanel listPanel;
 public void init () {
  System.out.println(getParameter("file"));
  movieVector = Auxiliaries.readMovieURL(getParameter("file"));
  listPanel = new ListPanel(movieVector);
  setLayout(new BorderLayout());
  add("West", meterCanvas);
  add("East", listPanel);
  attachObservers((Movie) movieVector.firstElement());
 }
 public void attachObservers (Movie m) {
  meterCanvas.attachObservable(m);
 }
}
```

903 Of course, if you use HTML files that hand arguments to applets, you cannot test those
applets using the technique explained in Segment 693.

APPENDIX D:
FIGHTING FLICKER

904 This appendix explains how to reduce the flicker often seen in dynamic applets.

905 Suppose you want to define a logo for your application in which a moon revolves around a planet. The logo, seen with the moon just disappearing behind the planet, looks as follows:

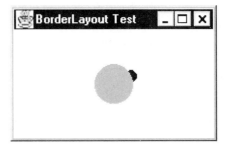

906 You can define the PlanetCanvas class as follows:

```java
import java.awt.*;
public class PlanetCanvas extends Canvas {
 int position = 0;
 public void IncrementPosition() {
  if (position < 100) {++position;}
  else {position = 0;}
  repaint();
 }
 public void paint(Graphics g) {
  Dimension d = size();
  // ... details of drawing computation as in Segment 910 ...
  g.setColor(Color.black);
  if (cosAngle <= 0) {g.fillOval(x0 + dX - sR, y0 + dY - sR, sD, sD);}
  g.setColor(Color.gray);
  g.fillOval(x0 - pR, y0 - pR, pD, pD);
  g.setColor(Color.black);
  if (cosAngle > 0) {g.fillOval(x0 + dX - sR, y0 + dY - sR, sD, sD);}
 }
}
```

When the moon is behind the planet, the moon is drawn first, and then the planet is drawn over the moon, hiding all or part of it. When the moon is in front of the planet, the planet is drawn first, and then the moon is drawn over the planet, hiding all or part of it.

907 Because drawing takes time, the hidden part of the drawing may be seen briefly before the hiding part obscures that hidden part. If so, you perceive flicker.

311

908   One way to fight flicker is to draw on a virtual display first, and then blast the bits in the virtual display onto your real display. There is no flicker because all the hidden parts are fully hidden before any part of the drawing is moved to your display.

909   To draw on a virtual display, you declare a variable of the `Image` class.

```
Image imageBuffer;
```

Then, when you know the dimensions of the window in which the logo is to be displayed, you create an `Image` instance:

```
                          ┌──────────── Value is a Dimension instance
                          ↓         ↓
imageBuffer = createImage(d.width, d.height);
```

From the new `Image` instance, you obtain a graphics context:

```
g = imageBuffer.getGraphics();
```

Then, you draw using the graphics context of the image as if it were the graphics context of your display:

```
                  ┌──────────────────── Previously computed arguments.
                  ↓      ↓     ↓    ↓
g.fillOval(x0 - pR, y0 - pR, pD, pD);
```

Finally, when your drawing is complete, you blast the bits onto your read display using the same `drawImage` method that you see used in Section 42 to draw images obtained from image files:

```
g.drawImage(imageBuffer, 0, 0, this);
```

910   Using the statements explained in Segment 909, you have the following revised definition of the `PlanetCanvas` class:

```
import java.awt.*;
public class PlanetCanvas extends Canvas {
  int position = 0;
  Image imageBuffer;
  public void IncrementPosition() {
    if (position < 100) {++position;}
    else {position = 0;}
    repaint();
  }
```

```
public void prepareImageBuffer(Graphics g) {
  Dimension d = size();
  imageBuffer = createImage(d.width, d.height);
  g = imageBuffer.getGraphics();
  int x0 = d.width / 2;
  int y0 = d.height / 2;
  int pR = x0 / 5, pD = 2 * pR;
  int sR = x0 / 15, sD = 2 * sR;
  int orbitX = x0 / 2, orbitY = y0 / 6;
  double angle = Math.PI * position / 50;
  double sinAngle = Math.sin(angle);
  double cosAngle = Math.cos(angle);
  int dX = (int)(sinAngle * orbitX);
  int dY = (int)(cosAngle * orbitY);
  g.setColor(Color.black);
  if (cosAngle <= 0) {
   g.fillOval(x0 + dX - sR, y0 + dY - sR, sD, sD);
  }
  g.setColor(Color.gray);
  g.fillOval(x0 - pR, y0 - pR, pD, pD);
  g.setColor(Color.black);
  if (cosAngle > 0) {
   g.fillOval(x0 + dX - sR, y0 + dY - sR, sD, sD);
  }
 }
 public void paint(Graphics g) {
  Dimension d = size();
  if (imageBuffer != null) {
   g.drawImage(imageBuffer, 0, 0, this);
  }
  prepareImageBuffer(g);
}}
```

911   To run the `PlanetCanvas` logo, you need to call the `IncrementPosition` method periodically from a thread:

```
import java.lang.*;
import java.awt.*;
public class PlanetThread extends Thread {
 PlanetCanvas canvas;
 public PlanetThread (PlanetCanvas c) {canvas = c;}
 public void run () {
  while(true) {
   canvas.IncrementPosition();
   try {sleep(100);} catch (InterruptedException e) {stop();}
}}}
```

You also need a test applet:

You also need a test applet:

```
import java.applet.*;
import java.awt.*;
import java.util.*;
public class TestApplet extends Applet {
 public static void main (String args []) {
  AppletTestorFrame f = new AppletTestorFrame("BorderLayout Test");
  TestApplet p = new TestApplet(); p.init();
  f.add("Center", p); f.resize(400, 400);  f.show();
 }
 PlanetCanvas planetCanvas = new PlanetCanvas();
 PlanetThread planetThread = new PlanetThread(planetCanvas);
 public void init () {
  setLayout(new BorderLayout());
  add("Center", planetCanvas);
  planetThread.start();
 }
}
```

COLOPHON

The authors produced camera-ready copy for this book using TEX, which is Donald E. Knuth's computer typesetting language.

We transformed source text into PostScript files using the products of Y&Y, of Concord, Massachusetts. PageWorks, of Cambridge, Massachusetts, produced film from the PostScript files.

The text was set primarily in 10-point Sabon Roman. The section headings were set in 14-point Sabon bold. The computer programs were set in 9-point Lucida Sans bold.

We tested all programs using the compiler produced by Sun Microsystems, Inc.

SOFTWARE

The programs in this book are available via the Internet.
To obtain this software, you can use your favorite network viewer with the following URL, provided through
the courtesy of Ascent Technology, Incorporated:

`http://www.ascent.com/books`

INDEX

BOOKS

BOOKS IN THIS SERIES

On To C, by Patrick Henry Winston

On To C++, by Patrick Henry Winston

The *On To* series stands on the idea that the best way to learn a new programming language is to follow an example that answers natural questions in a natural order. Then, once you understand how to express a complete, albeit simple program, you extend your understanding by learning about features that make you more efficient, flexible, and sophisticated.

Thus, you learn a new programming language in much the same way you learned your native tongue—you learn essentials first, then you build on those essentials as situations arise that require you to know more.

OTHER BOOKS BY PATRICK HENRY WINSTON

Artificial Intelligence (Third Edition), by Patrick Henry Winston

Lisp (Third Edition), by Patrick Henry Winston and Berthold Klaus Paul Horn